N. W. ELEVATION:

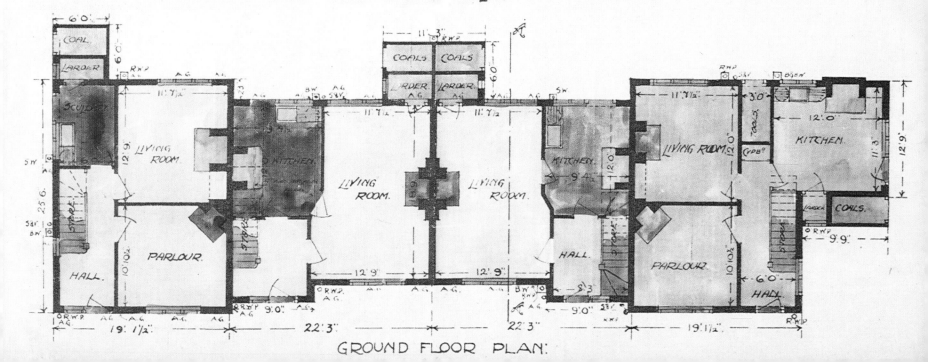

GROUND FLOOR PLAN:

# BRENTHAM

*A history of the pioneer garden suburb*

*1901–2001*

## AILEEN REID

BRENTHAM
HERITAGE SOCIETY

For Doris Palmer (née Marshall)
and tales of Brentham 90 years ago,
and for Barbara Norrice
in memory of her father, Henry Vivian

First published 2000 by the
Brentham Heritage Society
47 Brentham Way, Ealing, London W5 1BE
Registered charity no. 1079724
www.brentham.com

Managing Editor & Picture Researcher: Wendy Sender
Designer & Typesetter: Martin Bristow
Indexer: Isobel McLean

*British Library Cataloguing-in-Publication Data*
A catalogue record for this book is available from the British Library

ISBN 0-9538775-0-7

Printed in Great Britain by BAS Printers Ltd, Over Wallop, Stockbridge, Hampshire

ILLUSTRATIONS
ENDPAPERS: *Designs for 'Four Houses, Nos. 31–37 Holyoake Walk:
for the Ealing Tenants Ltd' by G.L. Sutcliffe, 12 January 1912*
PAGE 1: *Ludlow Road, c. 1910*
PAGE 4: *Porch of 38 Winscombe Crescent*
*Decorative initials taken from* Garden Suburbs, Villages and Homes *(1906)*

# *Foreword by*
# HRH The Prince of Wales

The arts and crafts movement has enjoyed an influence in town planning and architecture that greatly outlasted its heyday in the early years of the last century. At its considerable best it seems to me it has left a legacy that remains extremely relevant to today's concerns for a more humane, elegant and truly sustainable pattern of town planning and design.

I am delighted, therefore, to offer a few words of congratulation to those who have taken the initiative in celebrating the centenary of the Brentham Estate by commissioning this book. Like the better known Hampstead Garden Suburb or Bedford Park, today's flourishing neighbourhood community at Brentham is a testament to the vision of the original pioneers, and proves the lasting value of careful and creative urban planning and architecture. How different from so much of the thoughtless and unloved building that has been thrown up in the years since!

My own efforts to promote a sustainable new community at Poundbury in Dorchester have given me some insight to the challenges and controversies that must have faced those who had the original vision to create the Brentham Garden Suburb. It is astonishing that, a hundred years later, it seems to remain easier to build soulless housing estates than to create places that enhance the surrounding environment and that can help to brighten people's lives.

Perhaps this account of a small, yet inspiring, piece of English town planning will help to encourage others, be they developers, planners or concerned members of the public, to see the lasting benefits of planning at a human scale, of the enduring relevance of building crafts and of the importance of artistry in our architecture, if places of Brentham's quality are to be built again.

The Brentham Society and the Brentham Heritage Society would like to thank the following businesses, charitable trusts and organisations for their generous support.

We would particularly like to thank

for their sponsorship

**Local Heritage** *initiative*

 Heritage Lottery Fund     **Nationwide**     The Countryside Agency

Argent Litho • Arjo UK Merchants
Bradford Property Trust • Brendons
Creative Partnership Marketing
Daily Telegraph Charitable Trust
Grimshaw & Co • John Lewis Park Royal
John Martin Estates • Laing Homes • Marc Fitch Fund
London Borough of Ealing • London Weekend Television
Society of Architectural Historians of Great Britain
(for the award of a Stroud Bursary)
Town and Country Planning Association

# Contents

# Editor's Preface

This book was a mad undertaking. We were a small group of volunteers living in Brentham Garden Suburb, a tiny housing estate in west London. Brentham had made a mark on twentieth-century domestic architecture, town planning and social housing out of all proportion to its size, yet its story had never been fully told. Our aim was to publish a new, comprehensive history. And we had a deadline to meet: the suburb's centenary in 2001. We had plenty of enthusiasm – but we had no funds.

The idea that eventually became *Brentham: a history of the pioneer garden suburb 1901–2001* began as a leap of faith early in 1998. None of us had ever attempted to fundraise on the scale needed to produce a book of the quality we felt Brentham deserved. We would need to raise £25,000 to pay for a specialist writer-researcher and to cover the production costs. The most we had raised before had been £4,000 for a small facsimile booklet in 1990. Undeterred, and under the auspices of the Brentham Society, we formed a project group, conjured up a business plan and crossed our fingers.

Start-up funding from sales of the facsimile and the backing of eight nervous, local guarantors enabled us to commission Aileen Reid to begin research in October of that year. We knew we might have to settle on something no more lavish than a desktop production, though from the start we were aiming for a fully illustrated, printed hardback. Then one member of our group had a brilliant idea. Why not base the fundraising for the book on the share scheme used when Brentham was built at the turn of the century? The Brentham Centenary Book Co-Partnership Share Scheme was born.

'Shareholders' or 'co-partners' bought a share in the venture, and in return were promised a signed copy of the book. Beginning with Brentham residents, the scheme rippled outwards to include former residents, friends and families, local businesses, then individuals and companies further afield. Within just 17 months this scheme had raised a remarkable £15,000. At the same time, we produced a newsletter to keep residents informed of the book's progress and to publicise support given by the local business community. The confidence and interest of shareholders in the project gave us a tremendous boost and ultimately made this book possible.

The task of persuading corporate and charitable organisations was less straightforward. Our applications for funding kept bouncing back. We had established a voluntary group, the Brentham Heritage Society, to take on the book project, but if we were to attract funding from further afield we would need the official recognition of charitable status. After a false start and much labour, this was finally achieved early in 2000, and helped us win a Lottery grant later that year.

The huge amount of local support we were getting meant that we were gaining credibility all the time. Professor Sir Peter Hall, an Ealing resident whose jogging route regularly took him through Brentham, gave invaluable support from the early stages. And our local MP Steve Pound and the Mayor of Ealing,

BELOW: *Professor Sir Peter Hall accepts share number 1 from Brentham resident and* Sky News *presenter, Paula Middlehurst. The Brentham Centenary Book Co-partnership Share Scheme was invented as a way of raising money for this book, and took its inspiration from the co-partnership origins of Brentham.*

ABOVE: *Councillor Philip Portwood, Mayor of Ealing 1999–2000, became shareholder number 200 and Steve Pound, MP for Ealing North (in baseball cap) followed with share number 250. They are seen here with Brentham residents outside the Haven Arms pub in Haven Lane, Ealing on 9 March 2000, before a cycle ride to Brentham where they were presented with their share certificates. It was in this pub, 99 years earlier, that Henry Vivian addressed the Brentham pioneers, and persuaded them that their new estate should be organised as a co-partnership.*

Councillor Philip Portwood, joined forces in publicising our project to a wider audience.

When the manuscript was delivered we were faced with a difficult decision. To keep to our production schedule we would have to decide what sort of book we were going to produce – a highly illustrated and comprehensive history, or a more modest publication with a handful of pictures. Aileen's prodigious research had yielded a book twice as long as originally envisaged; a bigger book would be needed to accommodate this significant piece of work. There was a rich treasure-trove of archive photographs and illustrations to draw upon. By this stage a huge amount of time and energy had gone into the project. We decided to take another leap of faith; we committed to more pages, more illustrations, more colour,

more copies, more expense. The guarantors were hauled back to cover the shortfall between funds raised and our revised target of over £30,000. Even with this figure we would need to save every penny we could. Our local business community donated materials and facilities. Editing, proofreading and all the other pre-production tasks usually undertaken by a phalanx of paid professionals in publishing houses, were executed with extraordinary diligence by a handful of committed volunteers.

Along with the increasing credibility came welcome spin-offs. Some valuable additions were made to the Brentham Archive. Among these were a complete set of house plans, previously believed to have been destroyed, and a collection of marvellous large-format turn-of-the-century photographs, several of which are published for the first time in this book. A further welcome by-product of the project was the renewing of ties with Hampstead, our 'sister' garden suburb, through an exchange programme of walks and illustrated talks.

As the book was due to go to press in the late summer of 2000, we learned that we had been awarded a grant by the Local Heritage Initiative – a partnership between the Heritage Lottery Fund, the Nationwide Building Society and the Countryside Agency – the first urban project to receive support from this new scheme. An endorsement from St James's Palace was a further boost, confirmation that we were producing something of permanent value and interest. It has taken two years of voluntary effort by a large number of people to realise this project. It has been a mad, but ultimately very rewarding undertaking.

WENDY SENDER
Brentham Garden Suburb, London

# Introduction

Brentham represents a neglected, even forgotten, piece of the history of town planning in Britain. And yet it is a very important piece – so much so, that the neglect appears almost inexplicable. The publication of Aileen Reid's book will surely rescue it from that obscurity, and put it in its proper place. No one will have an excuse for ignoring Brentham ever again. There may be a price for its citizens, in the form of busloads of reverent scholars and cultural tourists. They will surely find it a price worth paying.

The story she tells may surprise everyone. As a veteran scholar of town planning and of town planning history, I discovered how much I did not know. The tale of Ebenezer Howard and the garden city movement has of course now become familiar to almost anyone who cares at all for British social history. And everyone who knows it must have a vague sense of Howard's connections with the co-operative movement, founded by the pioneers in Rochdale in 1844. But, until now, the connections have been obscure.

The most important contribution of Aileen Reid's book, then, is to document the history of the Tenants' Co-partnership movement: an offshoot of the co-operative movement, that started in London in the 1880s, and that attracted numbers of influential supporters including Howard himself. She also demonstrates the key role of Henry Vivian, self-made son of a carpenter, who became the driving force behind the movement before becoming a Lib–Lab MP, aged 38, in the famous reforming government of 1906.

It was Vivian who took the critical initiative at a meeting at the Haven Arms pub near Ealing Broadway station in February 1901. He supplied the vision and the drive to encourage his small audience, mainly composed of master builders like himself, that they could build their own suburb.

BELOW: *Brentham Institute and houses in Meadvale Road, seen from the north*, c. 1911

8

Then, as her story goes on to show, the vision began to fade. Within a very few years, by 1907, there was a new national body, Co-partnership Tenants Ltd., which increasingly played a kind of wholesale role to the garden suburbs that by then were springing up across the country. And, in the teeth of opposition from some of the original founder-members, the rules of Ealing Tenants were changed: the central idea, one member one vote, was abandoned, and proxy votes were allowed. This meant that non-members would increasingly control Ealing Tenants, a change that led to bitter disputes in the years that followed. One cannot help being reminded of the very similar disputes that wracked the first garden city at Letchworth, at about the same time, and that effectively meant the abandonment of Howard's co-partnership principle there.

Ironically, at Brentham the change came a few months after the critical development that shaped the suburb we see today: the appointment of Raymond Unwin and Barry Parker as architect-planners to lay out a plan for the estate. As Aileen Reid shows, they designed very few houses themselves; but the two architects to the suburb, Frederic Cavendish Pearson (1907–10) and then George Lister Sutcliffe (1910–15), worked faithfully within their Arts and Crafts tradition, so the entire suburb has a striking architectural unity.

For architectural and planning historians, these chapters will throw a new light on the development not only of Brentham, but of the entire garden-city garden-suburb movement in its critical foundation years before 1914. For them, and for others, Aileen Reid's account will also illuminate another key feature: the social life of the pioneer co-tenants, and in particular the crucial role of the May Day celebration that persists to this day.

This needs to be understood in a more general light: for Patrick Geddes, who emerges as one of the earliest supporters of co-partnership, laid huge stress in his writings on the role of myth and pageant in the lives of urban communities. It was self-consciously an attempt to evoke the traditions of the Middle Ages, which later Lewis Mumford celebrated in his books and which he borrowed with acknowledgement from Geddes, his 'master'.

These are some of the conceptual highlights, but there are many other riches in this book: the extra-ordinary role of George Bernard Shaw, who remained a minority shareholder to his death; the process that led to most tenants buying their homes, in the mid-1930s; the role played by allotment gardens and by the Brentham Club; and much more.

The Brentham Society and its charitable offshoot, the Brentham Heritage Society, deserve warmest congratulations for their initiative in launching this centenary history, and not least for financing it by ingeniously reinventing the co-partnership principle. The book, so richly illustrated, should be acquired not only by every Brenthamite, but by anyone who cares about the history of the British town planning movement.

*Peter Hall*

SIR PETER HALL
Bartlett Professor of Planning
University College London

9

*Some of the many people who helped with the creation of this book, Ludlow–Denison Green, 8 July 2000. Among the 94 people photographed here are 'co-partners',*
*oral history interviewers and interviewees, the descendants of Brentham pioneers, fundraisers, picture researchers, editors, archivists, committee members, photographers,*
*calligraphers and newsletter distributors. Present are Brentham's two longest-serving residents: seated centre at the front (with stick) is Mrs Ramsay Hughes,*
*Ramsay MacDonald's god-daughter, who still lives in the house in Winscombe Crescent that she moved into in 1913, and Frank Turner*
*(right, near the back, in cap), who was born in Brentham in 1912 and has never lived anywhere else.*

# ❧ Co-partners ❧

The Brentham Society and the Brentham Heritage Society are most grateful to the following businesses, organisations, families and individuals – or 'co-partners' – for their kind support of this publishing venture.

## Principal Business Co-partners
Ealing Dance Centre • The Printing Press • Temple Pharmacy • The Travel Studio • Tux "n" Tails • Watson & May Ltd

## Business Co-partners
Aristocat Valet Service • Bobby's News • Brentham Furnishers • Brill's • Busby's Hair & Beauty • T. H. Carr • Colleys • Crescent Arts • Curzon Road Garage • Darlington & Parkinson • The Directors Cut • Hampstead Garden Suburb Archive Trust • Hampstead Garden Suburb Residents Association • Hampstead Garden Suburb Trust • Juniper • Kamps Shoe Repairer and Key Cutting Service • Kin's Chinese Take-away • Knock On Wood • La Jardinière • London Chintz • Margaret Dance Academy • Melton Tailor • Milford Construction Ltd • NatWest • The Pitshanger Bookshop • Pitshanger Dental Practice • Present Company • Ray's Fruit Bowl • Reeves Dry Cleaners • Rodker & Cartlich • Salisbury Cleaners of Ealing • Stepping Out • West Kebab • Corinne Westacott (Licensed Homeopath)

## Family Co-partners
John Aarons, Mo Aarons, Emma Aarons, Annabel McMahon (née Aarons), Olivia Parker (née Aarons), Matthew Aarons • Ian Allkins, Sharon Ellis • John Allport M.A., Harold Allport, Arthur Allport • Mr Ian Anderson, Mrs Mary Anderson, Master James Anderson • Diana Arnott, Sid Arnott • Elizabeth, Simon, Siân and Rachel Atkinson • D. G. Bailey, G. I. Bailey • Mrs Ursula Bale-Heinze, Dr Christian Heinze, Christopher M. S. Bale • Janet Ballard, David Ballard, Lucy Ballard, Neil Ballard • John and Mary Bartlett, Timothy, Christopher, Penny & Robin • Patricia Baxendale, Geoffrey Baxendale, Edward Baxendale, Alice Baxendale • Anna Elizebeth Beattie, John William Beattie, Carol Marion Beattie, Maurice John Beattie • Kirsti Berglund, Paavo Berglund • Peter Best, Susan Best, Samuel Best, Thomas Best • Mr Peter

C. Blauth-Muszkowski, Mrs Izabella Blauth-Muszkowski • Jack Godfrey Boyce, Vera Boyce, John Boyce, Graham Boyce • Barry, Lynne, Diana and Celia Boydell (previously of 4 Woodfield Avenue) • Colin J. Brown, Jessie M. Brown, Susan M. Brown, David A. Brown • Nick, Lisa and James Brown • Paul Bruton, Deborah Jones, Charlotte Bruton, Olivia Bruton • Tim Buckley, Sue Buckley • H. L. & P. D. Burtenshaw • Stuart, Jane, Bruce, Tiffany, Oliver and Charles Campbell • Kathy Cargill, Darryl Godfrey • Philip Cater, Greta Cater • Paul and Susan Cater • Peter Chandler, Sue Chandler, Danielle Chandler, Emma Chandler, Lucy Chandler • Susan Clark, John R. M. Clark, Alexander Clark, Thomas Clark • Mr and Mrs M. Clayton • Pam Collins, Dave Brown • Margaret Jane Conroy, Norman Charles Conroy, Elizabeth Clare Conroy, Rachel Emily Conroy • Cathy, John and Joe Corneille • P. W. Cottam, J. A. Cottam, Kirsten H. Cottam, Anna L. Cottam • Mr Simon Cox, Mrs Penni Cox, Miss Paula Cox, Miss Christie Cox • Tim and Em Cunningham • Ellen V. Cushing, Barry Cushing • Mr D. A. Dabrowski, Mrs K. M. Dabrowska, Mr M. S. E. Bond, Ms A. D. M. Dabrowska • Peter D. Dale, Victoria F. Dale, Christopher Dale, Madeleine Dale, Georgia Dale • Damien Daly, Kate Daly, Emily Daly, James Daly • John Daly, Ana Castellano • Jim, Liz and Josie Day • Javier de Salas, Monica Juanas • David Denscombe, Diane Denscombe, Mark Denscombe, Jamie Denscombe • Nigel Dodd, Catherine Dodd, Emily Dodd, Louisa Dodd • Robert Dodd, Pamela Dodd, Anthony Dodd • Lorna and Robin Duval, Polly Duval, Sophie Duval, Daisy Duval, Matty Duval • Sandra Easton, Graham Easton, Ben Easton, Katie Easton • David Edwins, Marjorie Edwins, Jason David Edwins, Julian Robert Edwins • Sue Elliott and Bevan Jones • Raymond Ellis, Suzette Ellis, George Ellis, Jessie Ellis • Christopher Elwen, Susan Elwen, James Elwen, Caroline Elwen • Bogna Fairbairn, Michael Fairbairn, Alan Fairbairn, Scott Fairbairn • Brian Fallon, Thelma Fallon, Jane Fallon, Nicholas Fallon • Noel Farrey, Jennifer Farrey, Eleanor Joanne Farrey, Alexander James Farrey • Heather Faulkner, Peter Faulkner • Jane Fernley, Peter Gaffikin • Kester Fielding, Jane Hodgson • Paul Fitzmaurice, Elizabeth Fitzmaurice • Margaret Fitzpatrick,

Peter Meikle • Sue and Ernst Floate • Paul Fodrio, Mandy Fodrio, Edward Fodrio • Vanda Foster, Sam Foster, Alice Foster • Graham Fox, Pauline Fox, Elizabeth Fox • Niall Fox, Dorothy Fox, Susan Burbidge (née Fox), David Fox • Jean-Michel Gandon, Anne Gandon, Jean-Louis Gandon • Simeon Gann, Tonia Gann, Brendan Gann, Freya Gann • Mr John H. Gerken, Mrs Sheila M. Gerken, Mr Andrew J. Gerken, Mr Matthew R. Gerken • Colin, Julie, Tom and Toby Gibson • Colin Gilbert, Carol Gilbert, Tamsin Gilbert, Benjamin Gilbert • Alan and Patricia Gillett • Catriona Gordon, Mark Stronge, Caitlin Stronge • Molly Gordon, Lionel and Anna Coleman • David Graves, Diana Graves, Oliver Graves, Nathan Graves • Mark Greenwood, Mandy Greenwood, Sarah Greenwood, Samuel Greenwood • Charles Robert Hall, Deborah May Hall, Samuel Peter Hall, Thomas James Hall • Ruth M. Hall, Keith R. Hall, David F. Hall, James A. Hall • Ian Hamerton, Anne Hamerton, Victoria Hamerton, Bryony Hamerton, Gemma Hamerton, Owen Hamerton • Lawrence, Deborah, Max, Joe and Ted Hamilton • Jean Harper, Derek Pryce, Stefan Harper-Pryce, Sophie Harper-Pryce • Nigel C. Harvey, Patricia Harvey, Claire Harvey • Deevia Healeas, Simon Healeas • John Helliwell, Susan Helliwell, Christopher Helliwell, Rachel Helliwell • Rosanna and Alan Henderson • Clive Hicks, Colleen Hicks • Adam Hill, Wendy Hill, Christopher Hill, Jenny Hill • Simon, Penny, Julia and Charlotte Hoets • Christopher T. Holdsworth, Hiromi S. Holdsworth, Kenji M. S. Holdsworth, Naomi S. S. Holdsworth • Graeme, Cate and Jonathan Horncastle • Gerda Howarth, Noel Howarth • Geraldine A. Howell, Adrian W. Howell, Andrew R. Howell, Joanna-Fleur Howell • Brian Hughes, Sylvia Hughes (née Perry), Alan Hughes, Maureen Hughes • John Hutchinson, Jane Hutchinson, Andrew Hutchinson, Will Hutchinson • Ron Isted, Carolyn Isted, Timothy Vaugon Isted • Anne Jasinski, Stefan Jasinski, Catherine Jasinski, Véronique Jasinski, Lucien Jasinski • Mr Dennis Johnson, Mrs Jean Johnson • Martin Jones, Shirley Lovell • Norman, Lorraine, Nicky and Beverley Jones • Barry, Amoy and Tanya Joyce • Kirsten Kaluzynski, Jan Kaluzynski, Michael Kaluzynski • John Kelly, Sally Kelly, Edward Kelly • Mr and Mrs Russell Knight • Mr David Kohn,

11

Dr Anne Grant • Nancy Labastida, Fernando Labastida • Stephen Francis Lawrence, Christine Lawrence, Thomas Duncan Edward Lawrence • John H. Lawson, Dorothy M. Lawson • David Lefroy, Jessica Lefroy, Naomi Lefroy, Hanna Lefroy • Phillip Lewis, Virginia Lewis, Richard Lewis, Melissa Lewis, David Lewis • Alun J. Lloyd, Alison M. Lloyd • Griff Loydd, Eileen Loydd, Deborah Loydd, Alan Loydd • David Lunts, Hannah Greenwood • John Anthony Mackersie, Krystyna Mackersie, Andrew Mackersie, Jonathan Mackersie • Christopher, Patricia, Iona and Edward Makin • Beryl J. Manley, James F. Manley, Simon J. Manley • Richard Marke, Olive Marke, Siobhan Marke, Vincent Marke • Jayesh, Heather and Kyle Maroo • Paul, Kristin, Heather and Sally Mason • Matthew J. McAllister, Allison M. McAllister, Megan C. I. McAllister, Oliver T. J. McAllister • Carolyn McDermid, Stuart McDermid • Peter McGonigle, Susan Pond, Sam McGonigle • Michael McParland, Sally McParland, Molly McParland, Emily McParland • Simon Middlehurst, Paula Middlehurst, Sophie Middlehurst, Joseph Middlehurst • Margaret Millar, Kenneth Millar • Tony Moore, Bernice Moore, Kane Moore, Sonny Moore, Chelsea Moore • Martin Mortimore, Carolyn Mortimore, Mark Mortimore, Sam Mortimore • James Moss, Jackie Moss, Jasmine Moss, Lucy Moss • Barry, Jane and Matthew Murphy • Tim Murphy, Helen Murphy, James Murphy, Max Murphy, Lauren Murphy • Jurek Narozanski, Alice Narozanska, Marcin Narozanski, Andrzej Narozanski • Janine Neye, Ian Swift, Jake Mac Neye-Swift, Maddi Pippin Neye-Swift • Jim Norris, Jan Norris, Hannah Norris, Elizabeth Norris • Delphine Nunn, Robert Staines • Archibald Jonathan Bowyer Orr-Ewing, Archie Douglas Hugh Orr-Ewing, Hamish Robert Norman Orr-Ewing • Mrs Doris Palmer (née Marshall), Mrs Gillian Howell (née Palmer) • Mr Demetrios Pangalos, Mrs Iasmi Pangalos, Miss Alice Ward, Miss Iasmine Ward • Jason Pearce, Julie Pearce, Thomas Pearce • Jonathan Pearce, Renáta Pearce • Ann E. Perkins, Robert Haydn Perkins, Jeremy M. Haydn Perkins, Sara J. Perkins • Terry Phillimore, Sandra Phillimore, Louise Phillimore, Sophie Phillimore • Mr Tony Pierce-Roberts, Mrs Liz Pierce-Roberts, Miss Gemma Pierce-Roberts • Carol Priestley-Rowbotham, Graham Rowbotham, Giles Rowbotham, Emma Rowbotham • Andrew Rabey, Mary Rabey, James Rabey • David Randell, Elizabeth Randell • Colette Reap, Alan Bellingham • William S. Reid, Eunice S. Reid, Alastair W. J. Reid • Philip Reynolds, Alison Reynolds,

Jack Reynolds, Sophie Reynolds • Christopher Roberts, Jane Roberts, William Roberts, Hannah Roberts • Gordon Roberts, Christine Roberts, Elaine Roberts, Fiona Roberts • John Rolfe, Sue Rolfe, Sarah Rolfe, Joanna Rolfe • Fiona Ann Rudgard, Oliver Guy Rudgard and Dubbin • Jo Salmon, Simon Green • Tony & Mary Scanlan, Matthew Scanlan (Jack-in-the-green 1976–9) Rachel Scanlan (May Queen 1979), Emma Scanlan (May Queen 1984) • Wendy, Peter, Kate and Sam Sender • Tony Sever, Janet Sever • Helen Shaul, Robert Shaul • Clare Smith, Michael Smith, Julian Smith, Fenella Smith • Marion 'Joyce' Smith, Robert 'Bob' Henry Turtill, Jackie Smith • Stephen Smith, Jean Smith, Frederick Smith, Rachel Smith • Christopher, Victoria, Benedict and Lydia Snodin • Dr M. Stella-Sawicki, Mrs T. Stella-Sawicka, Miss J. Stella-Sawicka, Miss D. Stella-Sawicka • Ian Stephen, Jacqueline Stephen, Timothy Stephen, Katy Stephen, Elizabeth Stephen • Miss R. W. R. Stewart, Mrs I. W. R. Maclennan • Walter and Ruth Stokes • Ken and Kathy Stone • Philip Sutcliffe, Melanie Sutcliffe, Charlotte Sutcliffe, Rosie Sutcliffe, Dominic Sutcliffe • Kerry Tasker, John Fillingham • David, Sally, Daniel and Jessica Taylor • Nigel Thompson, Shelley Thompson, Dhara Thompson, Keelan Thompson • E. Tovey, C. F. Tovey, L. A. Tovey-Jacobs, D. J. Jacobs • Dorothea Tsoflias, Carla Tsoflias Zeiner • Mrs D. J. Turner, Mr F. Turner • Mr Colin J. Waters, Mrs Sheila M. Waters, Mr Anthony J. Waters, Mrs Karen Seymour, Miss Linda Waters • David and Pamela Webster and family • Brian and Margaret Wesley • Corinne Westacott, Colin Finnie • Mrs Carolyn Whelan, Mr John Anthony Whelan, Paul Anthony Whelan, Christopher John Whelan • Martin E. Whitaker, Jennie Birkett • John and Lesley White, David and Robbie White • Carolyn Wigmore, Ian Redmond, George Redmond • Andrew Villars, Justine Woodley, Jasper Villars • Mr William Willerton, Mrs Paulette Willerton, Master Spencer Willerton • Tom Woods, Sue Matthews, Florence Woods, Max Woods • Nick Youell, Penny Summerfield, Zack Youell

## Individual Co-partners

Joyce Adefarasin • Marianne Aldridge (née Bruce) • Mr A. J. Allen • Jake Allen • Sam Allen • Keith Ansell • Jennifer Armstrong • Tony Arnell • Diana Barlow (née Hocking) • Elizabeth Anne Barnes • Richard Barras • Nigel A. Beck • Mrs Janet Bell • Iver Benattar • Mr J. Bialynicki-Birula • Betty Black (née Ridley) • Christopher Blackwell • David Andrew

Blackwell • Janet Bloxam • Stella M. Bloxam • Ellen Boon • Mr Edward Bragiel • Mike Brearley • Ian W. Brocklebank • Gillian Burton • Ivor F. Bush • Nicola Cadisch • Patricia R. Cahill • Tracey Callow • Fiona Margaret Clayton • Jessie Coker • Gabriella Costanzo • Eleanor Cowie • Mrs A. Davies • Barbara J. Davies • Jon Davies • Emma Davison • Sasha Davison • Mr Arnold De Souza • Colin Dix • Helen Dixon (May Queen 1991) • Douglas R. Dover • Lawrence Duttson • Mrs Pauline Joan Eaton • Tom Elliott • Gladys May Etheridge • Anthony John Field • Michael Gaunt • Bruce George • Jean George (née Webster) • Michael German • Patricia German • S. J. Gibbons • Mrs Bertha Giblett • A. K. Gilronan • Jan Goodwin • John Michael Greenwood • Judy Gross • Dr Robert Gurd (Ealing Civic Society) • Sheila Haddon • Susan Haisman • Professor Sir Peter Hall • P. Hardiman • Janet Harrison • Keith Hassum • Dr Seamus Hegarty • Yvonne Henwood (née Glasse) • Margaret Hewett • Audrey M. Hider • Dr K. S. Hocking • Robert Holmes • Mrs Barbara Hooton • Mrs Ramsay E. Hughes (née Dudency) • David Humphries • Ellen Jackson • Martin Jiggens • Audrey Jones • Nicholas Jones • Ewa Krygier • Mrs Joan Lucas • John R. Mason • Eileen McAllister • M. Joyce Meldrum • Kelvin Meredith • Mr Jonathan E. Molyneux • M. R. Monaghan • Heather Moore • Alun Moses • Barbara Murray (née Creamer) • Miss Muriel Noppen • Barbara Norrice • Tony Oliver • Mrs Margaret O'Loan • Cllr Diana Pagan • G. F. Parker • Madeleine Parker • Janis Parks • Cllr Phillip Portwood, Mayor of Ealing (1999–2000) • Stephen Pound, MP Ealing North • D. Purkis • Rev. Gerald Reddington • Hilda Richardson • Dr Ruth Richardson • Jane Riches • William P. Roe f.r.i.c.s. • Michael Rowley • Mary C. Rutherford • Peter Ross McAdam Sacks • Dr Selig Sacks • Mrs Hannelore Salzman • Eva Seidner • John Seymour • Tony Shailes • Judy Sharman • Brian N. Sharp • Linda S. Shaw • Mrs Penny Silverman • Norman Silvester • Teresa Skelly • David C. Smith • Janet Smith • John Graham Smith • Fiammetta Solanelli-Tuszynski • Paul M. Spacey • Susan A. Stephenson • Maggie Stevens • Lindsey Strickland • Patricia Winifred Telford • Margaret Tims • Leonard V. F. Tridgell • Miss Pamela A. Turner • Sue van Raat • Mr Brian Vaughan • Josephine Walden • Margaret Warden • Mrs Anthea Ware • Miss S. Warren • Hugh Watkins • Richard Weaver • Sandra West • Anthony B. Westcott • Andrew White • Jennifer White • John Whittaker • Miss Frances M. Whitticase • Mr Bilham Woods

# ❧ Preface ❧

*On a February evening in 1901, a young man named Henry Vivian stood up
in the Haven Arms in Ealing to address a small meeting. It was a time of hope
and confidence. The twentieth century was young, a new Edwardian era had been
ushered in only a few weeks earlier with the death of Queen Victoria, and London,
at the heart of an empire on which the sun never set, was still enjoying the fruits
of the 1890s' building boom.*

*Most of the men gathered in the Haven Arms that night were building workers.
They shared a dream to build houses for themselves, and Henry Vivian had ideas
about how they could realise that dream. Over the next few years those ideas bore
fruit, and by the time the First World War broke out, 600 houses had been built.
Brentham Garden Suburb had become a reality.*

*This book is about how Vivian and his friends in Ealing built their suburb in
west London 100 years ago. It looks at the currents of ideas and events in Britain
at the turn of the century from which Brentham emerged. But mainly it is the story
of a suburb and its people, the story of how they lived through the 'century
of conflict' that we have just left behind.*

AILEEN REID
Holborn, London

Holyoake House

*Brentham
Garden Suburb
Conservation Area*

Brentham Club

St Barnabas Church

ALLOTMENTS legend — Allotments

BRENTHAM FIELDS

RIVER BRENT

SPORTS GROUND

SPORTS GROUND

N

MEADVALE ROAD

NEVILLE ROAD

BRUNSWICK ROAD

BRENTHAM CLUB

BRENTHAM GREEN

HOLYOAKE WALK

DENISON ROAD

LUDLOW ROAD

LUDLOW-DENISON GREEN

RUSKIN GDNS

BRUNNER ROAD

FOWLERS WALK

NORTHVIEW

HOLYOAKE HOUSE

ST BARNABAS CHURCH

War Memorial

HOLYOAKE COURT

PITSHANGER COURT

PITSHANGER LANE

BRENTHAM WAY

WOODFIELD ROAD

WOODFIELD AVENUE

WOODFIELD CRESCENT

WINSCOMBE CRESCENT

WOODFIELD

BRENTHAM WAY

# 'That practical mystic': Henry Vivian and the co-partnership ideal

*Co-partnership is the lifeboat of the working classes, which will one day rescue them from the storms of unregulated, pitiless competition.*

GEORGE JACOB HOLYOAKE, 1904

BELOW: *Henry Vivian, 'guiding light' in the founding of Brentham.*

RENTHAM GARDEN SUBURB was founded, and took on its distinctive physical appearance, because of two movements that are intimately interconnected. One was co-partnership, about which surprisingly little has been written; the other was garden city planning, which has been studied exhaustively in its many aspects. Without garden city planning, Brentham might have looked like any other suburb. But without co-partnership, Brentham would never have been founded at all. It is therefore important to look at what co-partnership was in order to understand how Brentham came into being.

The term 'co-partnership' is rarely heard these days, but in its day, great claims were made for this movement that developed from within the broader co-operative organisation. Co-partnership was a compact between workers and employers. It promised to make strikes a thing of the past, and to guarantee the worker a real financial and organisational stake in the business that employed him. Co-partnership would also prevent world revolution. One reason that co-partnership came about was the narrow way the mainstream co-operative movement had developed, and its perceived failure to deliver a fair share to the workers it employed.

The modern co-operative movement began in Rochdale in the 1840s, when a handful of unemployed weavers set up a shop selling a few staple goods such as sugar and flour. These weavers, who became known as the 'Rochdale pioneers', set out an ambitious programme of five aims and eight principles that made clear the wider aspirations of co-operation. One of their aims was the building of houses; among their principles were the importance of education, and the need to restrict interest payments to investors to five per cent.

In practice, the main difference between co-operative businesses and ordinary commercial firms was that 'co-ops' redistributed surpluses to consumers in the form of a dividend paid in proportion to the amount spent. By the 1880s there was a feeling among many who supported the idea of co-operation that the

LEFT: *Some of the 'Rochdale pioneers',
1865. In 1842 these men founded a
co-operatively run shop in Rochdale,
Lancashire, which grew into the modern
Co-operative movement. Co-partnership,
of which Brentham was the pioneer in
housing, was an offshoot of this.*

PHOTOGRAPH OF THIRTEEN OF THE ORIGINAL MEMBERS
OF THE
ROCHDALE EQUITABLE PIONEERS' SOCIETY.

mainstream movement had moved away from the aims and principles of the Rochdale pioneers. The co-operative movement had grown by this time into a multi-million-pound importing and manufacturing business, with a chain of retail societies. Those wider original aims of house-building, promoting education as a tool for social improvement and, more broadly, community-building, were not central to its activities. Moreover, mainstream co-operation did not deliver a reward to its workers equivalent to the dividend to consumers. Co-op workers were paid a living wage, and were encouraged to protect themselves by joining trades

RIGHT: *Robert Owen (1771–1858). Owen was a mill-owner and a visionary writer who believed that improving social and working conditions would make for better people and a better society.*

BELOW: *Advertisement for Co-operative Tea, c. 1910. By the late nineteenth century the Co-operative movement had grown into a multi-million-pound business involved in both manufacturing and retailing. It had effectively abandoned the wider social aims of Robert Owen that had inspired it initially.*

unions, but they did not share in the profits. It was this specific lack that was the spur to the development of co-partnership as a separate movement.

There were sound economic reasons, rooted in complex economic theory, for co-operatives redistributing surplus to consumers rather than to workers. But not everyone who supported co-operation subscribed to those economic theories. Having failed to persuade the co-operative movement to recognise the contribution of the workers, a group of co-operative enthusiasts led by Edward Owen Greening and Edward Vansittart Neale, set up a new association in 1884. The Labour Association for Promoting Co-operative Production Amongst the Workforce, founded at the Co-operative Congress held in Derby in 1884, aimed to encourage businesses to reward workers as well as consumers, and to foster the wider social aims of the Rochdale pioneers. It was hoped that the new body would 'arouse men, and public opinion generally to the importance of the movement for making workers everywhere partners in workshops, both as regards profits and shares'.

The Labour Association was to be highly successful in its aims. But it was not the first to encourage the involvement of workers in business, nor to stress the wider social possibilities of forms of co-operation. In the early nineteenth century a Welshman named Robert Owen acquired textile mills at New Lanark near Glasgow. Appalled by the typical conditions of mill-workers and by the effects of poverty on the poorest members of society, he tried to do something about it in his own mills. Some of his improvements were entirely practical – eventually reducing hours, and introducing a minimum age of ten for apprentices – but his importance for posterity lies in his grander vision of society.

Owen did not subscribe to the prevailing economic viewpoint of the early nineteenth century that assessed workers only in terms of the value of their labour; he did not see the impersonal mechanism of the market as society's engine. Rather, he believed that environment formed character, and that education, coupled with improvements in social and economic conditions, would make for better citizens, however impoverished their backgrounds. In his *New View of Society* published in 1812–16 he had proposed an Institution for the Formation of Character; and that is what he built at New Lanark. Opened in 1816, the institution provided a school for children from a very young age, as well as evening lectures and concerts for adult workers.

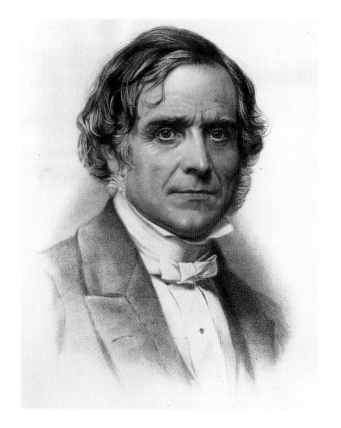

LEFT: *Seven of the most prominent early co-operators and co-partners. This group shows the wide variety of people who supported co-operation and co-partnership: while Hughes (the author of* Tom Brown's Schooldays), *Kingsley (who wrote* The Water Babies) *and Ludlow (after whom Ludlow Road is named) were Christian Socialists, Owen and Holyoake were atheists – Holyoake (in spite of his name) militantly so. Neale was a founder of the Labour Association, which was to play such an important role in the early years of Brentham. E.T. Craig ran a short-lived Owenite colony in Ireland before becoming head-master of Lady Byron's progressive school in Ealing.*

FAR LEFT: *Frederick Denison Maurice (1805–72). Maurice was a leading Christian Socialist, a group who believed that 'a true socialism is the necessary result of a sound Christianity'. Denison Road in Brentham is named after him.*

RIGHT: *A quadrille dancing class at New Lanark, from an engraving by G. Hunt, 1825. Robert Owen put his beliefs into practice at his mills near Glasgow by setting up a school for the children of his employees. This was just one way in which Owen's example was followed in Brentham in the early years, when educational activities for both adults and children were organised.*

Owen was a pioneer, therefore, of both nursery and adult education, and his example was not forgotten by Henry Vivian and the society of Ealing Tenants that built Brentham a century later.

Owen went on to propose a co-operative community built round a quadrangle, with three-room flats, a dormitory for children under three, schools, a dining room and (in spite of his own secularist beliefs) a chapel. In keeping with the idea of mixing the social classes, which the garden city movement was to advocate a

century later, he proposed reserving a section in his quadrangle for professional men. In time he hoped to see 'neat and convenient dwellings . . . with gardens attached . . . surrounded and sheltered by plantations'. The workers would pay a subscription and thus eventually buy their houses. The idea was, as Johnston Birchall has put it, that these '"villages of co-operation" would solve the problem of poverty by allowing working-class people to opt out of capitalist society into a "New Moral World" in which they would grow their

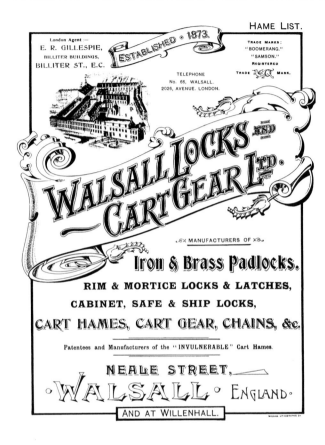

of the retail societies, had been to see society transformed on an entirely co-operative basis.

On a smaller and more practical scale, there had been other experiments in founding co-partnership workshops in the nineteenth century, most notably by the Christian Socialists, who believed that 'a true socialism is the necessary result of a sound Christianity'. Among them were F. Denison Maurice and J.M. Ludlow, both of whom believed that workers should be given a share in the profits and responsibilities of a business. They argued that working men would then be less likely to seek redress for their grievances in revolution – which Ludlow had witnessed at first hand when he lived in France in 1848 – or by violent direct action, which the Chartists had advocated.

These workshops failed largely because of poor organisation, but by the early 1880s a further 15 such co-partnerships, producing goods including textiles, locks and hosiery, had been founded with a similar underlying political agenda. By 1901, with the encouragement of the Labour Association, more than a hundred co-partnership societies had been founded. Their turnover approached £3 million, while a dividend on wages of more than £20,000 was paid from profits of £145,000. Some of these businesses were run as true self-governing workshops where the shareholders all worked for the company; others were run as ordinary commercial companies with some form of profit-sharing scheme for their employees.

The Labour Association's success in promoting these co-partnership ventures was due in no small part to its secretary from 1890, Henry Vivian, who eleven years later was to provide the impetus for the founding of Brentham. Most of the men and women who promoted

LEFT: *Advertisement for Walsall Locks and Cart Gear Ltd, c. 1900. While all the self-governing workshops set up in the 1840s and 1850s by Ludlow, Maurice and their supporters failed after a few years, a second wave of 'co-partnerships' began in the late 1860s, of which the Walsall company was one.*

own food, make their own clothes and eventually . . . become self-governing.' Although schemes were set up on Owenite lines at Orbiston in Scotland and New Harmony in Indiana, they failed in the long run, mainly because of problems of finance. But Owen's vision of a New Moral World resonated down through the nineteenth century, right to the founding of Brentham and beyond. The original final goal of the co-operative movement, although it was soon forgotten in the growth

RIGHT: *Cornwood, Devon, c. 1905.*
*Cornwood was the birthplace in 1868*
*of Henry Vivian. Like his father, who*
*trained him, Vivian was a carpenter,*
*but by the time he was 18 he had moved*
*to London. There he became heavily*
*involved both in trade unionism and,*
*as secretary of the propagandist Labour*
*Association, in promoting the idea of*
*co-partnership.*

co-partnership did so as affluent middle-class social reformers, and Henry Vivian might seem to fall into this category as well: he was, after all, a Member of Parliament in later years.

But Vivian's beginnings were far from bourgeois. He was a Devon man, born at Cornwood on Dartmoor in 1868, where his father, William, was a carpenter on the estate of Lord Blatchford. After leaving school Henry worked for a while in his father's workshop, and when he was 16 he moved on to an apprenticeship in Plymouth. It seems that he was always ambitious. His daughter, Barbara, who was only a small child when he died, returned to Cornwood in the 1950s to see if she could find out more about him. There she met a very

## THE TRUE CO-PARTNER SPIRIT.

1st and 2nd Co-partner (simultaneously): "Good morning; lovely morning, isn't it?"

old man, a contemporary of her father's, who knew him as a youth: 'He wasn't going to stay around here working for his father. He went off to Plymouth. I don't know what happened to him after that . . .'

What happened was that Vivian moved to London in 1886 to practise his trade as a carpenter, and it was there that he became involved in trade union activity as a member of the Amalgamated Society of Carpenters and Joiners. Within a year of joining the union he had

become president of its Pimlico branch, and he was to remain a member of the union for the rest of his life. In 1890 Vivian became secretary of the Labour Association. He was still only 22.

Vivian's role as the Association's secretary was far from honorary. He gave up to a hundred lectures a year, in which he promoted the idea of co-partnership to industrial and education centres around the country. He also found time to organise and attend industrial and co-operative conferences. Vivian advised workmen intending to set up co-partnerships, as well as employers interested in introducing co-partnership schemes to existing firms. Another way in which he helped others was to organise trips to such places as Godin's 'Familistère' at Guise, near Paris, an Owenite iron foundry and colony whose owner had achieved the co-partnership goal of transferring ownership of the company to his workers. Vivian was also the founding editor in 1894 of the journal *Labour Copartnership*. Although no one alive today remembers him speaking, he was clearly an impassioned and articulate orator. Photographs show him standing foursquare to the crowd, leaning forward like a fire-and-brimstone preacher, delivering the co-partnership gospel to the gathered masses.

No doubt it was this skill that saw Vivian chosen in 1893, when he was still only 25, to give evidence to the Royal Commission on Labour. Here he defined the Labour Association simply as 'the representative of that party in the co-operative movement which seeks to establish workshops in which the workers share in profits and participate in the management'.

Given this stress on 'the workers' and the links between mainstream co-operation and the Labour Party,

LEFT: *'The true co-partner spirit', a cartoon of 1911. This image of two co-partners meeting in a typical London 'pea-souper' fog suggests the sunny optimism of the movement's followers. It appeared in* Co-partnership*, the Labour Association's journal founded in 1894 by Henry Vivian (then called* Labour Copartnership*).*

RIGHT: *George Jacob Holyoake (1817–1906). Holyoake, a campaigning Liberal journalist steeped in the ideas of Robert Owen, deplored the mainstream co-operative movement's reluctance to share its profits with its employees. From the 1880s he became a supporter of the Labour Association and co-partnership, and later one of Brentham's most distinguished supporters and shareholders. His name is commemorated in Brentham in Holyoake Walk, Holyoake House and Holyoake Court.*

it might be inferred that co-partnership was a socialist movement. This was clearly not the case, in the sense of socialism meaning the public ownership of the means of production. The Association's position came to be defined, rather, in opposition both to the notion of state socialism and to the violent revolutionary means that were seen as a likely step to achieving it. As the Association's annual report of 1885–6 put it: 'The rise of violent modern State–Socialism has also contributed to add importance to our peaceful and practical programme.' In seeking to stress their anti-revolutionary credentials, the leading lights of the Labour Association also made clear their unwillingness to rock the capitalist boat. George Jacob Holyoake, the secularist Owenite journalist, grand old man of co-operation and future supporter of Brentham, said in a speech which was recorded in the Labour Association's annual report of 1887–8: 'We make no war on property [*hear, hear and cheers*] – we envy no man his riches [*hear, hear*]'.

Until the 1880s the co-partnership societies that had been set up were all craft workshops or industrial producers of various kinds. But with the success of these the question arose as to whether the co-partnership system could be extended to housing. One of the principal aims of the Rochdale pioneers had been the co-operative building of houses, and although some houses had been built by the 1860s, house-building had never evolved into a principal activity of co-operative societies. Among those societies that did build, such as the Royal Arsenal Society which created the substantial Bostal estate at Woolwich, many of the houses were sold off, often with the aid of loans from the Co-operative Building Society. There was clearly room for an experiment in which co-partnership could be applied to housing.

The idea of a tenants' co-partnership was first mooted by Edward Owen Greening in 1881. Greening pointed out that London workers were unlikely ever to be able to afford to buy a house, a difficulty that was compounded by the need for frequent moves to take up work. This problem was addressed by Benjamin Jones, London manager of the Co-operative Wholesale Society, who proposed a series of 50 estates around London. Tenant members of the society would be able to move from one to the other without too much difficulty or expense, and to retain their say and financial stake in the company. In 1888 Tenant Co-operators Limited was registered, and over the following twelve years five small estates (some consisting of only a few houses) were built at Penge and Camberwell in South London, West Ham and Upton Park in East London, and Epsom in Surrey. Prospective tenants had to take up a minimum shareholding of £1, and once other expenses had been met, they would receive a dividend on their rent as well as one on their shares.

A start was made on these estates to give the tenants some sense of community, in keeping with the Owenite notion of the creation of a co-operative commonwealth. At both Lucas Road, Penge (1888–90), and Neale Terrace, Epsom (1900–1), garden competitions were held, with the Epsom tenants winning Surrey county awards for their efforts. But this was about as far as social life evolved on the estates of Tenant Co-operators Ltd. One problem that was to be a feature of later co-partnership estates, including Ealing Tenants' at Brentham, was that to maintain their commercial viability, all the estates had to a greater or lesser extent to admit tenants who were not members of the society. This was compounded by the fact that each Tenant Co-operators' estate was too small to sustain much collective activity, and the estates were too spread out over the metropolitan area for a sense of community to develop among the estates. This fragmented character also affected the tenants' involvement in the running of the society, as most found it too time-consuming to travel to central London for meetings. This apparent apathy was also due in part to the low level of tenant investment – to

become members, would-be tenants had only to buy a £1 shareholding, not enough to give them much sense of financial commitment to the society. The result was that Tenant Co-operators had to be run largely on the lines of a philanthropic trust.

Two of the Tenant Co-operators' estates also demonstrated the limitations of co-partnership in tackling the housing of poor, unskilled labourers. While the houses in Penge and Epsom were aimed at

ABOVE: *Neale Terrace, Hook Road, Epsom, 1906. Neale Terrace (1900–1) was one of five small estates around London built by Tenant Co-operators Ltd. It was the first attempt to apply to housing the co-partnership principles that had been developed in craft workshops.*

RIGHT: *A group of unemployed men march for the right to work, 1908. It was hoped that co-partnership, by offering a financial stake to the workers, would subvert the threat of riot – even revolution – made explicit in these banners (although one wonders if the lettering on the banner in this photograph has been improved).*

DEMANDING THE RIGHT TO WORK —OR RIOT

the skilled artisan (as Ealing Tenants' houses at Brentham were to be), the property on the Plashet estate at West Ham consisted of 'tenement houses inhabited by the casual labourer'. Here the combination of a shifting population, along with the need to keep the rent low enough to be affordable to the casual labouring class at whom it was aimed, meant it was not a commercial success, and the losses incurred reduced the tenants' dividend in the society as a whole. The same problems occurred to a lesser extent at Burton Houses, the block of 14 flats without bathrooms built in Brief Street, Camberwell, in 1893.

The experience of Tenant Co-operators had an important impact on later co-partnership estates, and the types of houses they decided to build. As Sybella Gurney of the Labour Association put it a few years later during a talk on 'co-operative housing', 'with this class . . . it would seem there is scope for municipal housing, the losses on which . . . should be considered as a tax on the community, while the buildings, though sanitary, should not be such as to attract a better class'. State socialism had its uses.

The example of Tenant Co-operators was crucial to Henry Vivian later when he came to help set up Ealing Tenants Ltd at Brentham, but it may have had an impact much earlier when he was first made secretary of the Labour Association. Vivian's duties as union activist and Labour Association secretary, extensive though they undoubtedly were, did not stop him becoming involved in the practical application of the co-partnership ideals he was promoting. In 1891 he set up his own co-partnership building firm, General Builders.

A number of Vivian's obituaries state that it was the builders' strike of 1891 that led him to set up a co-partnership building firm. In fact, although the strike no doubt focused the minds of those involved, the firm was already in formation by the time the strike was called. Vivian stated that the twin objects of the society were 'to provide employment for its members connected with the building trade on a co-operative basis', and 'to take contracts, and provide

LEFT: *Burton Houses, Camberwell, 1906. This block of flats was the third 'estate' (1893) built by Tenant Co-operators Ltd. Such small flats proved to be uneconomical for Tenant Co-operators Ltd as the rents had to be kept very low to suit casual labourers. The block survives in Brief Street, London SE5.*

houses to suit the requirements of its members'. Its aims therefore encompassed and extended those of Tenant Co-operators – the idea was to build houses on a co-operative basis, but for themselves. Capital was to be raised in the same way, with £1 shares. 'Thus whilst gradually extending the self-employment of its members, it provides the market for the property it builds, and brings the tenant and builder into one society, making their interest

RIGHT: *Three leading co-partners, photographed in 1911. From left, Aneurin Williams (1859–1924), Edward Owen Greening (1836–1923) and Fred Maddison (1856–1937). Williams was one of many affluent middle-class supporters of co-partnership. An active member of the Labour Association, he became Chairman of First Garden City Ltd at Letchworth and was an early investor in Ealing Tenants Ltd, the co-partnership society that built Brentham. Greening was the key figure in the founding of the Labour Association in 1884. Maddison, one of Vivian's closest friends, was a Liberal MP, journalist, republican and seeker after world peace.*

identical'. The proposal was very neat – it contrived to be both a producer and consumer society. And implicit in 'taking contracts' was the idea that other building work could be undertaken. This would generate the surplus needed over and above the capital raised by the £1 shares, to enable them to start building for themselves, and in this way dispense with the need for outside capital.

Vivian's Co-operative Building Society, as it was initially called, got off to a slow start. By the spring of 1892 the joiners' strike of the previous year had 'necessarily checked' the initial development of the society, but much work had been done to ensure that it would conduct its business fairly for the benefit of the workers. There was to be a general council, and a special feature was that it would be a federal organisation, with district branches, each of which would elect a representative to the general council. This federal approach was felt necessary because of London's vast scale, and it was not thought that branches would 'injuriously compete with each other'.

By the following year its name had changed to the General Builders Co-operative Society, perhaps to distinguish it from a 'building society', a term that was coming to have its modern meaning of a permanent, money-lending building society. By the spring of 1896 it was reported that General Builders Ltd, as they were now called, had finally started 'building houses suitable for the members', as had been promised five years earlier. The hope was further expressed 'that on the basis of their strong trades union the London Builders may set an example to the provinces of a great movement in Co-operative Production and of utilising their savings for furthering self-employment rather than

fighting employers'. And so it proved, as co-partnership building firms were set up in Brighton, Lincoln, Exeter, Leicester and Cambridge, although none was involved in house-building for its own members.

By 1897 General Builders had grown greatly, with 800 members in 16 London branches. However, the original aim of building houses for themselves was already running into difficulties. Two houses had been completed in Napier Road, south Tottenham, and although 'No difficulty is experienced in letting . . . they will be glad to find a purchaser and thereby turn over their capital more quickly'. The firm was finding that £1 shares were insufficient to raise capital to run the business. Nor could the shares give the members a stake in the business that would either make them feel part of it or yield much in the way of profit. Without the wealthy backers of Tenant Co-operators, the problem of capital became pressing. The following year the houses were sold 'or let at a remunerative rent', and that was the end, apart from the notable exception of Ealing Tenants in 1901, of General Builders' efforts at co-partnership housing. They continued to do a good trade in general building work, supplying joinery to the London School Board, and building a telephone exchange in Ealing and new stores (and a bakehouse) for the Wood Green Co-operative Society. By 1901 they had established 18 branches around London.

Their efforts at co-partnership housing may have come to nothing, but General Builders demonstrated in other ways that they were more than just a federation of building firms who paid their workers a bonus and involved them in running the business. The Owenite belief in the importance of education was alive and well at their works in Wharf Road, Notting Hill. Although many of the talks and discussions they held were, as might be expected, on co-operative subjects, their ambitions extended beyond learning to be good co-operators. In 1901 James Bonar, the eminent political economist, led a series of discussions. One of these was a talk by Fred Maddison on Giuseppe Mazzini, the hero of Italian independence and author of *The Duties of Man*, a book that was key to Vivian's thinking.

The Labour Association, and those who joined, never lost sight of Robert Owen's grander vision. Members included workers and peers, dreamers and doers. The membership lists also featured many names, apart from Vivian's, that were to be crucial to Ealing Tenants Ltd and Brentham: Ralph Neville, Aneurin Williams, J.M. Ludlow. G.J. Holyoake, Sybella Gurney, J.H. Greenhalgh, Fred Maddison, were all there. And there were other names with a wider resonance. There, in 1888, is Patrick Geddes, the father of regional planning, paying his five-shilling subscription fee. And there, in 1885, is plain 'Albert Grey', the future Earl Grey, who as Governor General of Canada was to invite Vivian across the Atlantic to spread the co-partnership housing gospel to the Empire.

Another name that pops up is Ebenezer Howard. Howard had been inspired by the propaganda work of the Labour Association in 1885, when he was working in London as a stenographer. That year, at the Co-operative Congress, he acquired a pamphlet published by the Association on 'Ethics of Co-operative Manufacturing', which gave him the idea of setting up a printing firm along co-partnership lines. Only the economic downturn of 1886–9 put a stop to his plans. Howard did not join the Labour Association until 1901, but the Association was already aware of him. In 1898 it had acquired for its library a small book he had written; the book's lack of commercial appeal meant that Howard had had to subsidise its publication. Its title was *Tomorrow: A Peaceful Path to Real Reform*. The book made little impact then, even if the Labour Association managed to acquire one of the few copies in general circulation. However, the book went into a second edition, and under its new title was to send out ripples that were felt around the world throughout the new century: its title was *Garden Cities of Tomorrow*.

ABOVE: *Giuseppe Mazzini (1805–72). Best remembered with Garibaldi for his efforts to achieve Italian unification, Mazzini was as well known in Britain for his book* The Duties of Man. *Its emphasis on personal responsibility and self-help as corollaries to rights and freedoms appealed to many late-nineteenth-century Liberals, including Vivian and Maddison, and this may explain why 'Mazzini Road' appears on an early plan for Brentham.*

# 2

# From dystopia to utopia: Ebenezer Howard and the early garden city movement

*A map of the world that does not contain utopia is not worth glancing at.*

OSCAR WILDE, 1891

BELOW: *Ebenezer Howard, founder of the garden city movement.*

 T IS NOT HARD TO SEE WHY the Labour Association should have taken to the small book Ebenezer Howard brought out in 1898. *Tomorrow: A Peaceful Path to Real Reform* was as grand in its ambitions as it was modest in scale. What Howard proposed was an entirely new type of city, laid out on what we now call green-belt land, planned and administered in an entirely new way. It had an Owenite grandness of ambition, and because it involved all the inhabitants, it must have appealed to the proponents of co-partnership. This latter feature was to be of the greatest importance in the shaping of Brentham in the years before the First World War.

But for all its grand ambitions, the book did not attract much attention to start with. One reason was no doubt the relative obscurity of the author. Ebenezer Howard was neither well-connected nor especially prominent in radical circles, and, like Henry Vivian, he came from a modest background. Born in the City of London in 1850, the son of a baker and confectioner, Howard had had a varied career by the time his book

was published. On leaving school he had worked as a clerk for a stockbrokers' firm, and the laborious business of copying longhand in quill pen no doubt spurred him to learn the newly developed Pitman's shorthand. This led to a job as private secretary to Dr Joseph Parker, a non-conformist minister with an interest in progressive causes, and it is said that Howard perfected his shorthand by transcribing Parker's sermons as they were delivered.

But the sedentary life palled, and in 1871 Howard set off with two friends to the United States to try his hand at homestead farming in Nebraska. Howard built a shack and tried to raise a crop, but his life as a secretary had hardly prepared him for the frontier, and he met with little success. In 1872 he moved to Chicago where he resumed his career as a stenographer. Chicago must have been an invigorating experience for the young Howard. Only a few months before he arrived, the city centre had been swept by a devastating fire, which had left a buzz of building activity in its wake. One part of Chicago that had escaped the fire was the belt of parks that surrounded it. This had earned the city its nickname: 'the Garden City'.

While he was in Chicago Howard started a lifelong quest for self-improvement. He began with a course of reading that included Darwin's *The Descent of Man* and Thomas Paine's *The Age of Reason*. This provoked a religious crisis in Howard, but he soon found consolation for his loss of faith in the doctrine of the 'New Dispensation' espoused by Cora Richmond, a 'trance medium' who combined the occult with progressive utopian beliefs. These included the equality of the sexes, universal education and the brotherhood of man, and from Richmond Howard derived a belief in cosmic forces that were willing humanity towards altruism. He maintained his commitment to 'modern spiritualism' for the rest of his life.

By this time Howard was also reading works with a more direct bearing on humanity's physical well-being. One of these was *Hygiea: A City of Health*, a pamphlet of a talk given in London in 1875 by an Englishman, Benjamin Ward Richardson. The pamphlet described an ideal community in which every family occupied a house of stipulated minimum size; each house was to have a garden, and the streets were to be wide and tree-lined. One of Richardson's other recommendations was that houses should not have basement kitchens, and that all living accommodation should be at ground level or above. Richardson's book had an immediate effect in London: it was as a result of reading it that Jonathan Carr decide to build the 'prototype garden suburb', Bedford Park in Chiswick.

The impact on Howard took many years to find practical application, but he later recorded that reading *Hygiea* had caused him to imagine a 'defined conception of an intelligently arranged town, a sort of marriage between town and country, whereby the workers would be assured the advantage of fresh air and recreation and nearness to their work'.

In 1876, soon after reading *Hygiea*, Howard returned to London. There he took up a position as an official reporter in the Houses of Parliament, and began devoting considerable time to improving the space bar on the typewriter, in an unsuccessful attempt to provide for his growing brood of children. At the same time he pursued his interests in social reform and spiritualism. Cora Richmond had developed a following in London, where *Medium and Daybreak*, a journal dedicated to the New Dispensation's aims, was published. The journal's offices soon became a gathering place for her most enthusiastic followers, including Howard. The address of those offices – 15 Southampton Row, Bloomsbury – is of interest to the history of Brentham, because it was also the address of the Labour Association, whose secretary was, of course, Henry Vivian. Howard also pursued his social interests in the less arcane environs of the Zetetical Society, a discussion group whose members included the Fabians George Bernard Shaw and Sidney Webb, and which, with typically bushy-tailed late-Victorian hubris, made it its business to address 'all matters affecting the human race'.

Howard continued his programme of reading, and one book that had a profound effect on him was Edward Bellamy's *Looking Backward*, published in Britain in 1889. In it Bellamy described Boston as he imagined it in the year 2000. His social vision was of a highly centralised socialist state that guaranteed its citizens employment, early retirement and considerable leisure time. The city's form was also novel, with

ABOVE: *Firemen fight the blaze that destroyed Chicago in 1871. Ebenezer Howard arrived here only a few months later: the sight of Chicago (known sometimes as 'the Garden City') being rebuilt from the ashes must have impressed him with the possibilities of building a city anew.*

RIGHT: *Bedford Park, Chiswick, west London, after a drawing by Maurice B. Adams. Bedford Park, begun in 1875, is sometimes seen as the 'prototype garden suburb' because it shares certain features – such as some curving streets, small-pane windows, ample street and garden trees and an organised social life – with Brentham and Hampstead Garden Suburbs. It was, in reality, only a more imaginatively designed than usual speculative development that attracted middle-class progressive and artistic residents who furthered their interests at clubs and lectures.*

open squares, small houses fitted with labour-saving devices, broad tree-lined boulevards, and a high-speed transportation system. Public laundries and central dining rooms encouraged communal life.

Bellamy's vision, as well as the grand ambitions of the Zetetical Society, is reflected in Howard's book *Tomorrow: A Peaceful Path to Real Reform*. It is important to realise that *Tomorrow*, for all that Brentham would probably look very different today if it had never been written, said nothing about garden suburbs. In fact, it aimed to call a halt to urban expansion by building an entirely new community in the countryside. All the major British cities were afflicted by squalor and overcrowding, as high urban land values meant that the poor, however large their families, could only afford to rent one or two rooms in a house. Attempts to relieve these problems, such as the flats built by the Peabody Trust, were never on a scale large enough to be successful. Howard's solution was more radical and, because it went to the heart of the problem, more practical: what he proposed fulfilled the Owenite dream of a new type of community, but it also recognised that to build affordable housing, cheap land was needed.

Howard had thought through many aspects of the problem. To build a 'garden city', as he termed it, it would be necessary to acquire an estate of 6,000 acres at cheap agricultural land prices; 1,000 acres would be used to build the city itself, which would sustain a population of 30,000. The rest of the land would be retained as an enclosing agricultural belt, where a further 2,000 people would be employed to supply the city with food and raw materials. Although it was a major catalyst to the garden city and town planning movement, the book said very little about planning.

The key to Howard's idea of a garden city was his notion of 'town–country', which he represented in a diagram illustrating the three magnets of 'town', 'country' and 'town–country', each pulling on 'the people' at the centre. Town–country would combine all the advantages of town and country and avoid all the disadvantages. While acknowledging that modern cities were overcrowded and unhealthy, Howard nevertheless believed that cities offered many social and economic opportunities for people. By the same token, the countryside might offer all the advantages of a natural environment, but many rural districts lacked proper sanitation as well as opportunities for employment, following the agricultural depression that began in the 1870s. Depopulation had also eroded the possibilities for a well-developed community life in many

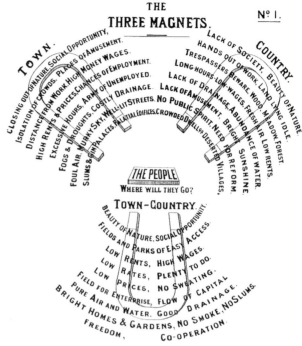

LEFT: *A slum alleyway in Glasgow, c. 1865. One of Howard's aims in devising a 'garden city' was to make dark cramped conditions a thing of the past.*

ABOVE: *Slum children, London, 1910.*

ABOVE RIGHT: *'The Three Magnets' diagram from Howard's book* Garden Cities of Tomorrow. *In building a new garden city in the countryside, Howard hoped to combine the best features of urban and rural life.*

rural areas. In his diagram Howard listed all the advantages of town–country, including Beauty of Nature/Social Opportunity, Low Rents/High Wages and Low Rates/Plenty to Do.

The suggested plan of the city was circular, with straight, radiating boulevards and concentric rings of 'avenues' (page 35). Around the outside was a railway that would link in with the existing system. The city was arranged within this formal network, with gardens at the centre surrounded by public buildings, a further park beyond that, and a 'crystal palace' or glass-covered shopping arcade. Next came another wide band of greenery, called the 'Grand Avenue', where schools

and churches were located. Beyond this were residential districts, an industrial belt, a ring of allotments and, finally, the railway.

This garden city was only the start of Howard's scheme. In time a ring of garden cities would be established around a larger 'centre city', each joined by the railway, but separated from one another by the green belt. This conurbation, with a population of around a quarter of a million, is what he called the 'social city'.

The physical form of the garden city and its progeny takes up only a small proportion of Howard's book, and it was not this that particularly appealed to the Labour Association. The culmination of his town–country magnet was the pairing Freedom/Co-operation. Throughout his book, Howard stressed the importance of co-operation. His garden city was to be collectively owned, with some groups of houses sharing communal gardens and kitchens. A development company would buy the land at cheap, agricultural prices, and raise capital to develop the city. As this company belonged to the citizens, profits would return to them once interest had been paid into a sinking fund and on the borrowed capital.

Crucially, any increase in the value of the land would also return to the citizens. At the time it was usual for such an increase to go to the owner of the land as 'unearned increment', rather than to the people who lived on the land or were responsible for developing it. As Howard put it on another occasion, they would have an 'honest landlord, namely ourselves'. Co-operatives would build some of the houses with some help from capitalists, who would play a major part in developing the garden city, by building houses, running businesses, and providing finance to the development company.

For Howard, co-operation went beyond collective ownership of the land and the co-operative building of houses. As the land increased in value and loans were paid off, surplus funds would be used to found a welfare state, including the provision of old-age pensions (this, nearly a decade before the state provided them). However, his garden city was never going to be run on state socialist lines: it was more anarchistic than communistic. Co-operation would arise from a spirit of self-help and brotherly love: 'those who have the welfare of society at heart will, in the free air of the city, be always able to experiment on their own responsibility, and thus quicken the public conscience and enlarge the public understanding'. Howard's vision was in the tradition of

Robert Owen's utopian schemes of more than half a century earlier. But Howard also believed that the pursuit of a common goal would serve to defuse class conflict, a belief that echoed the co-partnership ideals held by Henry Vivian and the Labour Association.

Howard's book was, therefore, far more concerned with notions of community and of social and land reform than with planning, which it dealt with briefly and diagrammatically. It was this strong element of co-operation that no doubt accounts for its favourable reception by the Labour Association, whose journal *Labour Copartnership* was one of the few publications to give the first edition of the book a welcoming review. *The Times* considered the idea of a garden city 'ingenious', but concluded 'the only problem is to create it; but that is a small matter to utopians', while the *Fabian News* observed that 'proposals for building new [cities] are about as useful as arrangements for protection against visits from [H.G.] Wells' Martians'.

One thing that is striking about Howard's notion of a garden city, and must help explain the initial cool reception of the book, is how little his vision of geometric streets, crystal-palace malls and high-speed transport resembles what we think of as the 'garden city' or 'garden suburb' look. Where are the rustic cottages? Where are the winding roads and hedges? They are not there, because garden cities and suburbs as we know them, Brentham included, owe as much to those who took up Howard's ideas, as they do to Howard himself. Although Howard's book struck a chord with certain groups of people, the diagrams he used were not immediately appealing, even to sympathetic readers. George Bernard Shaw, who became a lifelong friend of Howard, reported that on

ABOVE: *George Peabody (1795–1869). This American philanthropist worked tirelessly in the nineteenth century to improve London's housing conditions by building blocks of flats described as 'model dwellings'. Such piecemeal initiatives, useful though they were, barely scratched the surface of the problem as cities continued to grow, and poverty became more widespread.*

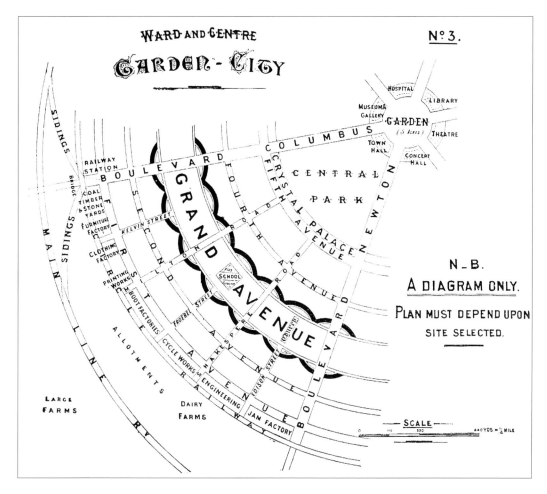

*ABOVE: Part of the plan for a 'garden city', from Howard's* Garden Cities of Tomorrow. *In this second edition of the book, the plan was labelled 'a diagram only', perhaps because its rigid formality was perceived as alienating.*

being sent a review copy of *Tomorrow*, he had 'glanced at the maps and put the book down with the thought, "the same old vision" ' – another vague, utopian plan.

This impression of impracticality derived largely from the alien forms Howard suggested for the city, especially the rigid, geometrical plan. That the details

of Howard's scheme should have had a 'foreign' quality was not unexpected, given that he had drawn much of his inspiration from the works of American writers, including Edward Bellamy. But while Bellamy's vision of a totally organised, technologically advanced environment appealed to Howard, it was an impediment to a British readership trying to envisage his scheme on the ground in the English countryside.

It was natural that such readers should draw on sources closer to home in trying to imagine Howard's garden city. One such source was another writer concerned with society's ills, someone who had also read and been inspired by Bellamy's *Looking Backward*. That man was William Morris. Morris was much more open than Howard to the socialist message of *Looking Backward*, but he found Bellamy's vision of its realisation distasteful. Instead, for nearly 40 years Morris had looked to the pre-industrial guild system of the Middle Ages for a model for the reform of society. He believed that medieval daily life was organised on much more natural lines, and communities were pervaded by collective values. Partly as a response to *Looking Backward*, Morris published *News from Nowhere* in 1890. Here he depicted, as an alternative to Bellamy's mechanistic Boston, a future London remade as a collection of villages separated by woods and streams, its communities organised into farming and craft guilds, all infused with a deep spirit of brotherhood. Morris's name is also associated with the Arts and Crafts movement in architecture that grew up at the end of the nineteenth century. This promoted the revival of traditional methods of building, using locally produced and hand-crafted building materials, as against mass-produced and machine-finished products. In practice, this had a greater effect on architectural taste than on the revival of handcraft, and led to a proliferation of features such as tile-hanging, roughcast, casement windows, and a general enthusiasm for a cottage aesthetic.

All this appealed more readily to a nineteenth-century British public that had absorbed the idea of 'Merrie England' – a belief in a mythic past of village life, with stout yeomen, plentiful harvest, and sturdy children dancing round a maypole on the village green. The notion appealed almost as much, it should be added, to the radical critics of industrialised Britain, as it did to conservatives. Indeed, by the time Howard's book appeared, this marrying of progressive views on social issues with a built environment that sought to mimic the form of a 'typical old English village', was already being put into practice at the industrial villages of Bournville, near Birmingham, and Port Sunlight, near Liverpool. Both of these villages had received wide coverage in newspapers and periodicals in the decade before *Tomorrow* was published.

Such villages were not, in the 1890s, a complete novelty. Since the eighteenth century at least, landowners had built 'model cottages' for their tenants. Industrialists had also, on occasion, built housing for their workers. By the middle of the nineteenth century the idea had evolved of industrial villages as self-contained communities in which housing was provided, along with facilities such as schools, churches, laundries and parks. Akroyden, near Halifax, begun in 1849, and Saltaire, near Bradford, begun in 1853, are the largest and best-known of these. Sir Titus Salt, who built Saltaire in the 1850s and 1860s to house the workers at his alpaca woollen mills, was motivated by a fairly straightforward desire. He aimed to make his mark by

leaving a lasting memorial of his care for his workers, which, in keeping the workers happy, would have the more immediate benefit of ensuring the continuing success of his business.

Bournville and Port Sunlight grew out of this tradition, but developed it in two ways that are relevant to Howard and to the way the garden city idea was put into practice. George Cadbury, who built Bournville, had a more complex mission in mind. He had inherited a chocolate and cocoa business that was in poor shape, but had, from the 1860s, turned its fortunes around by concentrating on the perfection of consistently high-quality products. The key to the

LEFT: *William Morris (1834–96), c. 1875. Although best remembered today for the textiles and wallpaper he designed, Morris was well known to his contemporaries for his radical writings. His book* News from Nowhere *(1890), in which he described a future London remade as a collection of villages separated by woods and streams, its communities organised into farming and craft guilds, was especially influential on those who put Howard's vision of a garden city into practice.*

ABOVE: *George Cadbury (1839–1922). Cadbury was a successful chocolate manufacturer, who built Bournville, an industrial village beside his works near Birmingham. Inspired by his Quaker faith that there is 'that of God in everyone', that every life is valuable and to be cultivated, Cadbury provided many social, educational and sporting facilities at Bournville. These benefited the tenants and, consequently, as Cadbury saw it, society as a whole.*

RIGHT: *An early plan of Bournville, notable for the recreational facilities and open spaces available to the tenants.*

way he ran his business, and ultimately Bournville, was his Quaker faith that stressed the 'inner light' in every soul, which meant that every life was valuable and should be cultivated; even before he founded Bournville in 1895, Cadbury introduced educational and health benefits and a pension plan for his workers. He also subscribed to the view that underpinned the Labour Association, that the interests of employer and employee were essentially the same, and that class antagonism and industrial unrest could be avoided by individual members of each class acknowledging their respective 'duties and rights' – a direct echo of the words of Henry Vivian's hero Giuseppe Mazzini.

The village that Cadbury founded reflected his belief in his duties as a citizen as well as an employer. Bournville was not intended just for his employees, and the running of it was handed over to a trust. This meant that no individual, including Cadbury himself, could profit excessively from increases in land value. To start with, houses were built for sale, but when the purchasers began selling them on at a handsome profit, Cadbury changed his mind, and subsequently houses were only built for rent.

The form that Bournville took reflected Cadbury's tastes and had a self-consciously rural appearance, replete with both public and private gardens. Cadbury had a conviction that the cultivation of a garden was both morally and physically invigorating. At Bournville, private gardens were pre-planted before tenants moved in; everyone received a generous provision of eight apple and pear trees, twelve gooseberry bushes, a Victoria plum tree and creepers to adorn the house. Like Morris, Cadbury had a general distaste for modern urban life and, as a corollary, he had a faith in rural and village

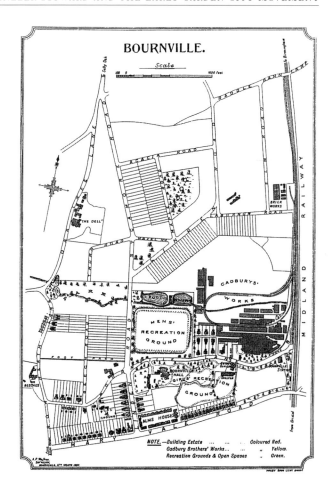

life. This is expressed in Bournville, for although its plan was formal, it was abundantly supplied with trees along the streets.

The houses, designed by W.A. Harvey, are notably rustic in style, with varied materials of brick and rough-cast, and incorporating quaint Arts and Crafts features, such as inglenooks. Brentham residents of houses designed by F.C. Pearson may feel a sense of recognition at the judgment of one contemporary architectural critic: 'There are perhaps, too many features . . . The effect is sometimes a little short of restful'.

William Hesketh Lever was an altogether more abrasive character than Cadbury, but he shared with him a strong belief in the benefits of hard work, and a belief that society as a whole, not just the employer, would benefit from improving the social, living and educational conditions of the workers. Lever's background, although it was Congregational, not Quaker, was similar to Cadbury's. He too had transformed a moderately successful family firm into a hugely profitable enterprise by the development of a product that was of notably higher quality than his competitors'. In Lever's case this was soap, the Sunlight soap that gave its name to his village.

Lever made no bones about the fact that he saw treating his workers well as a way of ensuring the profitability of his business; indeed he took a perverse pleasure in stressing how he was motivated by self-interest. But alongside this he campaigned for radical causes, such as old-age pensions and the extension of the franchise to women, and he looked forward to the day when working men – and presumably women – would be in the majority in parliament. For all his espousal of progressive causes, Lever, like Cadbury, had a nostalgic attachment to a mythical rural past, where, he believed, a 'close family brotherhood' had existed between employer and employee in a village environment. Moving his factory out to a new site gave Lever the opportunity to recreate this relationship, and in 1888 Port Sunlight was founded; unlike Bournville, it was for the sole use of the company's employees.

Port Sunlight, like Bournville, had many communal facilities, including schools, a village institute and shops. Architecturally it was more diverse, reflecting Lever's eclectic architectural tastes. A half-timbered Elizabethan style predominates, but there were houses in assorted Queen Anne, Stuart, Jacobean and Flemish styles. Lever believed, with Cadbury, that gardening was an agent of social tranquillity, so that large gardens were provided with the houses, as well as allotments. The general appearance of the estate was closely controlled, however. The company planted and maintained all the front gardens, in order to guarantee uniformity in, for example, hedge-trimming. All in all, Port Sunlight expressed Lever's nostalgic vision of England's past, and was a self-conscious attempt to recreate a peaceable but hierarchical village society, with Lever as the squire.

For all their espousal of respectively 'brotherhood' and progressive politics, Cadbury and Lever ran Bournville and Port Sunlight according to what they thought was best for their tenants. While they might have shared Morris's belief in what Lever called the 'good old days of hand labour', they had no truck with socialism. Their schemes were not at heart different from the paternalistic ventures of Akroyden and Saltaire half a century earlier. And although Cadbury and Lever shared many interests and aims with Howard, Howard's garden city aimed at a democratic organisation that was essentially alien to the top-down controls of Bournville and Port Sunlight.

However, the two principal ways in which Cadbury and Lever developed the earlier idea of industrial villages – their belief that providing health facilities, education, and so on, would make workers 'better people' and thereby contribute to the progress of society

RIGHT: *Women workers at Port Sunlight cheer the King and Queen on their visit to the Sunlight soapworks, Cheshire, March 1914. Port Sunlight was an industrial village built by another successful businessman with a social conscience, W.H. Lever. Port Sunlight and Bournville, designed on village lines, with cottages and much greenery, helped shape the way Howard's book on creating a garden city was put into practice.*

as a whole; and their preference for architecture and planning in which greenery was much in evidence – naturally led people to associate Howard's garden city with Bournville and Port Sunlight.

This perceived link between Howard's ideas and these modern garden villages was evident almost from the time *Tomorrow: A Peaceful Path to Real Reform* was published. Despite the cool response from some reviewers, the book appealed to a significant number of people, and, by 1899, a Garden City Association (GCA) had been formed with a view to putting the book's ideas into practice. By 1900 it had more than 300 members, but its core support still came from enthusiastic marginal groups such as the Land Nationalisation Society, or the Brotherhood Trust, which in the 1890s had promoted the idea of co-operative colonies. Funds were very slow in coming in. The breakthrough came in March 1901, and once again the Labour Association played a central role. In that month's issue of the journal *Labour Copartnership*, the Association's former chairman Ralph Neville wrote an article praising the idea of a garden city. A delighted Howard wrote to Neville asking him to be the GCA's chairman, and he accepted.

Neville was a former Liberal MP and a highly successful barrister. He is usually thought of as the hard-headed practical man in contrast to the dreamer Howard, and while this may be true, the reason that his appointment made all the difference to the GCA's fortunes must have had as much to do with his social standing and contacts, in contrast to Howard's. By 1901 the GCA was holding its conference at Bournville, with Earl Grey, Governor General of Canada and long-time supporter of co-partnership, in the chair. The following year the conference was held at Port Sunlight, and George Cadbury and W.H. Lever both joined a long list of bishops, peers and MPs who served as GCA vice-presidents.

With Howard as managing director a company was set up to get a garden city going: the new city was still referred to, simply, as 'Garden City'. The company, First Garden City Ltd, needed £300,000 capital, and although nothing like this had been raised, by 1903 a site had been found. The site, near Hitchin in Hertfordshire, 30 miles north of London, was only 3,800 acres in size, as against the 6,000 suggested in *Garden Cities of Tomorrow* (as Howard's book had been known

since its re-issue in 1902). But, as Howard pointed out, even with careful negotiation, the price of the land meant that 6,000 acres was unfeasibly expensive.

This was only the first of many compromises. Neville tangled with Howard over the latter's suggestion that investors should not expect a profit for some years, and might even tolerate a loss, in order to see Garden City grow. Neville pointed out that large-scale investment would never be forthcoming so long as Howard presented the scheme in this way, and Howard was removed as managing director. Neville and his associates at First Garden City Ltd would forever be walking a tightrope, trying to remain faithful to their and Howard's ideals, yet trying to make Garden City attractive to investors.

The purchase of the site meant that a plan was needed, as Howard's circular plans were evidently not considered practical. Howard acknowledged this in the new 1902 edition of his book, in which the plans had been labelled 'A diagram only'. In 1903–4 a competition was held among three invited architectural partnerships to find a viable scheme, and the winners were Raymond Unwin and Barry Parker of Buxton in Derbyshire. The choice of Unwin and Parker was not perhaps a great surprise – Unwin had given a talk to the 1901 conference of the Garden City Association entitled 'On the Building of Houses in the Garden City'. It was, however, highly significant, as their work determined not only the way that Letchworth Garden City, as the city was now known, would develop in physical terms, but also the whole of the garden-city and garden-suburb movement, including Brentham.

Raymond Unwin was born in 1863 in the north of England to a middle-class family with progressive

ABOVE: *Ralph Neville (1848–1918). Chairman of the Labour and Garden City Associations, Neville combined practical skills with social contacts. Without Neville, Howard's vision of a garden city might have remained on paper forever.*

RIGHT: *Raymond Unwin (1863–1940; far left, back) and Barry Parker (1867–1947; far right). These two architects, who were cousins, were to play a major role in the planning of Brentham. They are seen here with some of Parker's family, including his sister Ethel (front right), who was married to Unwin, and their son Edward (centre front).*

interests, but moved to Oxford as a boy. When he left school he returned to the North and became an engineering draughtsman, first in Manchester, then in Chesterfield. While he was in Manchester he met William Morris and joined his Socialist League. Like Morris, he believed in beauty as 'a positive necessity of life', and he combined a belief in democratic socialism with a faith in pre-industrial models of society.

Around the same time, Unwin met Edward Carpenter, whose ideas influenced him for the rest of his life. Carpenter was the source of the idea that a better society would be created if its members led a 'simple life', which meant abandoning extravagant ways and convention, in favour of the 'real needs of life'. Carpenter led by example, setting himself up as a market gardener, living with a friend, his wife and their children in a single-storey cottage in a type of mini-commune. He grew oats for his horse, cultivated chickens, wheat, fruit, vegetables and flowers for the human beings, and wore homespun knickerbockers.

While he was in Chesterfield, Unwin had designed some cottages for his employers, and in 1896 he went into partnership in Buxton as an architect with his cousin (and brother-in-law) Barry Parker, who had trained with G.F. Armitage, an Arts and Crafts architect. That training had taught Parker that the design of a house and its interior, including furniture and decoration, were inseparable parts of a whole. Together, in their work and in publications such as *The Art of Building a Home* and *Cottage Plans and Common Sense*, Unwin and Parker put into practice the Arts and Crafts notions that form must follow function, that architectural beauty lies in the honest expression of a building's construction, and that most decoration was pretentious and artificial, concealing rather than revealing construction.

These ideas were not new – their lineage goes back through Morris to A.W. Pugin – but where Parker and Unwin departed from architects such as C.F.A. Voysey and M.H. Baillie Scott, the leading Arts and Crafts architects in the 1890s, was in applying these principles to working-class housing. This was only logical for architects who espoused democratic socialism: if beauty was 'a necessity of life', it was surely not the preserve of middle-class connoisseurs of the 'simple life'.

And yet, in contrast to Howard (and in common, in their various ways, with Morris, Cadbury and Lever), Unwin and Parker had a deep nostalgia for rural life and the social and architectural forms of the mythical 'typical English village'. This extended to an enthusiasm, which seems startling, given Unwin's socialist credentials, for the hierarchical ordering of village life in the pre-industrial past, with the squire, the road-mender, the doctor, the blacksmith all living side by side in their rural idyll, content with their lot, in accommodation that suited their stations in life. The explanation lies in Unwin's belief that the solution to class divisions lay not in the class warfare advocated by the Marxists, but in mutual understanding between individuals, the ideal community deriving from feelings of brotherhood which would be cultivated in the 'natural' environment suggested by Morris.

Another belief that Unwin and Parker had in common with Cadbury, in particular, was that a well-designed home made for a better citizen. In *The Art of Building a Home* and *Cottage Plans and Common Sense*, Parker and Unwin suggested that nature should be the principal determinant in building houses and laying

ABOVE: *C.F.A. Voysey (1857–1941), by J.H. Bacon. The influence of Voysey's distinctive architectural manner, which managed to be both simple (in its use of unornamented forms and indigenous materials) and mannered (chimneys just a little taller, buttresses just a little more splayed, than they needed to be) is detectable at Brentham, particularly in the work of F.C. Pearson. Unwin and Parker were admirers of Voysey's simplicity and thoughtful planning, but true to their socialist ideals, extended these principles to working-class housing.*

RIGHT: *Bedroom of a house designed by Raymond Unwin and Barry Parker. This bedroom features built-in wardrobes, a washstand and a chest of drawers. Such fitted furniture became something of a trademark of Parker and Unwin; it was seen as efficient and clean and, as such, an aid to the 'simple life'.*

out streets. This worked on a number of levels. The site would help determine how the building and streets would be planned. But nature also operated on the aspect – the living room should be placed for maximum exposure to the sun – and on the prospect – the best possible views should be obtained from the windows.

Parker and Unwin also believed that they, as architects, were better placed than the client to know what made for a well-designed home. In the 1890s and early 1900s they designed a number of houses for middle-class clients, mainly in the North. The materials and features varied with the location, but included the

43

Arts and Crafts favourites of roughcast, uncoursed stone, stone-mullioned windows (often with casements), and thatch. Inside, the most striking feature was often a large 'living-hall' (reflecting the belief in the benefits of shared activity among family members). Often a small space for private contemplation or reading was created off this, such as an inglenook fireplace or bay window with seats. Some of these halls, such as that at The Gables in Harrogate, were double-height, with a gallery at first-floor level – a conscious evocation of the medieval hall-house. Many were supplied with furniture designed by Parker and Unwin of simple, 'honest' construction, or with fitted furniture, an aid to efficiency that was essential to the 'simple life'.

It was easy to supply the setting for the Simple Lives of middle-class clients who shared their ideals. However, this alone would not realise Parker and Unwin's vision of breaking down class division in part by improving the living conditions of all. A chance to achieve this came in 1902 when Joseph Rowntree of York, another Quaker chocolate-magnate with a social conscience, approached Parker and Unwin to design a new village at Earswick, north of York. As an industrial village, complete with facilities such as schools and a 'folk hall' for social activities, New Earswick was in a sense a smaller version of Port Sunlight and Bournville. The main difference from an architectural and planning viewpoint was that the design of the buildings and the plan of the estate would both be in the hands of a single architectural firm.

In designing the cottages at New Earswick, Parker and Unwin put into practice the idea that well-made, well-planned houses were not just for the comfortably off. The architectural manner is only a reworking on

a small scale of their larger houses, with roughcast much in evidence. But what constituted a well-planned house? At New Earswick, unlike with the larger houses, the client was not the person who would live in the house. What Unwin and Parker and perhaps Rowntree considered well-planned did not necessarily suit the workers who were to live in the cottages.

An example of this is the thorny issue of parlours. Parker and Unwin, in common with many Arts and Crafts architects, could not see the point in having, in a small house, a room 'kept for best' and rarely used. It went against what Carpenter had said about 'real needs' as opposed to convention; it seemed like a squandering of precious space, and a bourgeois pretence to boot. So, many of the New Earswick cottages were designed without them. But the tenants did not like this. Parker and Unwin failed to understand, although they came in time to accept, that certain features such as parlours – and their accoutrements such as mantelpiece knick-knacks, overstuffed sofas and antimacassars – served a symbolic aspirational function that was at least as important to the tenants as practical considerations and convenience. Another example of space-saving that appealed more to Parker and Unwin than the tenants was the incorporation of stairs into the living space rather than in a separate entrance hall.

Other features that enhanced the practicality and wholesomeness of the houses were less contentious. One of these was the abandonment of the back extension that was a feature of most nineteenth-century terraced houses. Unwin and Parker disparaged these as limiting the amount of air and sunlight that reached the rooms at the back of the house, so the cottages at New Earswick brought the rooms of the house under one

ABOVE: *New Earswick, near York, c. 1905. This industrial village was built by Joseph Rowntree, a chocolate manufacturer, like George Cadbury, with a social conscience. Founded in 1902, New Earswick was the first attempt by Parker and Unwin to put into practice their ideas about cottage- and site-planning on a major scale.*

RIGHT: *Pair of cottages built for Garden City Tenants, 1905. In 1905 a 'Cheap Cottages' exhibition was held in Garden City, Letchworth (later known simply as 'Letchworth'), to see if it was possible to build cottages, with adequate space and sanitation, for £150 – a cost that would make the rent affordable to agricultural labourers. This pair of cottages, which survives at Eastholm Green, Letchworth, was built using the labour of Ealing Tenants Ltd. The design had some influence on the houses built in Brentham in 1907–8 in Brunner Road. In the front row, Unwin is fourth from left, Vivian sixth from right (behind the small boy).*

roof. Although Unwin had advocated these ideas in *Cottage Plans and Common Sense* and had experimented in a few cottages before, New Earswick was the first time he and Parker had put their ideas into practice on a large scale. Their cottages became a general model for the type of housing that was later built for tenants in Letchworth, Brentham, Hampstead Garden Suburb and, indeed, for local-authority cottage estates right up to the outbreak of the Second World War.

New Earswick also provided an opportunity for Parker and Unwin to put into practice for the first time their ideas about site planning. Unwin did not publish his highly influential book *Town Planning in Practice* until 1909, but he had been thinking, writing and lecturing about the subject for most of the previous decade. In his 1901 address on 'Houses in the Garden City', Unwin had advocated site plans 'designed with complete acceptance of natural conditions'. This could mean many things, such as retaining existing trees and hedges, but perhaps the most important aspect was following the natural contours of the land.

At New Earswick, however, the site was very flat, with little in the way of contours to follow. Unwin met the challenge with an informal plan of gently curving streets, which created, in combination with the groups of cottages, what he was to call 'street pictures'. Along the straight main street he arranged shops, the school and the folk hall. One of the major principles of *Town Planning in Practice* that Unwin implemented at New Earswick was that the road width did not have to be fixed. Many local authorities, as part of the public health drive to eliminate narrow, airless streets, had adopted a bye-law that fixed the minimum width of a road, usually at 40 feet. Unwin argued that what mattered more was the distance between facing houses, and that lightly used side roads might benefit from having a narrower roadway of perhaps only 18 feet, with a wide grassy strip and trees either side of it.

Planning Letchworth was, of course, a much greater challenge. It had to accommodate areas for industry, different classes of housing and a town centre with shops and public buildings. Unlike the vision in Howard's book, the site was not exactly virgin, bisected as it was by a railway and a major road. Unwin had moved to Letchworth in October 1903, when he and Parker had been invited to compete, and he had spent a lot of time acquainting himself with the site. He had commissioned a detailed site survey with contour lines; his and Parker's plan can be seen as an attempt to achieve a 'complete acceptance of natural conditions', coupled with a more formal treatment appropriate to an urban centre as opposed to a village, perhaps acknowledging the formal aspect of Howard's diagrams. This formal element can be seen in the southwest of the site, which has a town square containing public buildings, with straight avenues radiating from it. Each of these avenues provided views towards the town square of public buildings, or aligned with features in the distance (such as the church in old Letchworth), while others provided more general rural vistas. This creation of axes was to be a feature of Hampstead and, to a lesser extent, Brentham. The industrial area was created away from the centre, to the northeast, and housing was to be provided in discrete 'sub-centres', often grouped around village greens. The existing Norton Common was retained as public open space north of the town centre, and provision was made for amenities such as a recreation ground, a cricket field and small-holdings.

Designing a garden city was one thing, building it quite another. By 1905 only 1,000 people had come to Letchworth, and the First Garden City company did not turn a profit until 1912. By that time, despite the best efforts of Neville and his fellow directors, only 28 businesses had been attracted to Letchworth. These included the Spirella corset firm and several printworks, including W.H. Smith's and J.M. Dent. By 1914 the town's population had grown to 9,000 residents and workers, but the dream of collective ownership was only partly fulfilled: nearly half of the 2,000 houses were built on land let on conventional 99-year leases. One problem with this was that despite Unwin and Parker's best efforts as consulting architects to impose design guidelines, these were not enforced when it was perceived that potential buyers might be put off.

In the event, at least until the First World War, some of the finest houses were those built on these leases,

RIGHT: *The main part of Raymond Unwin and Berry Parker's plan for Letchworth, as it had evolved by 1909. In 1903 Parker and Unwin won a competition to supply the plan for Letchworth. By 1909 considerable building had taken place including (1) Westholm and (2) Eastholm Greens, (3) the houses built for the Cheap Cottages exhibition, (4) Bird's Hill and (5) the beginnings of the Pixmore co-partnership estate, (6) Town Square and (7) Sollershot Circus, the first traffic roundabout in Britain.*

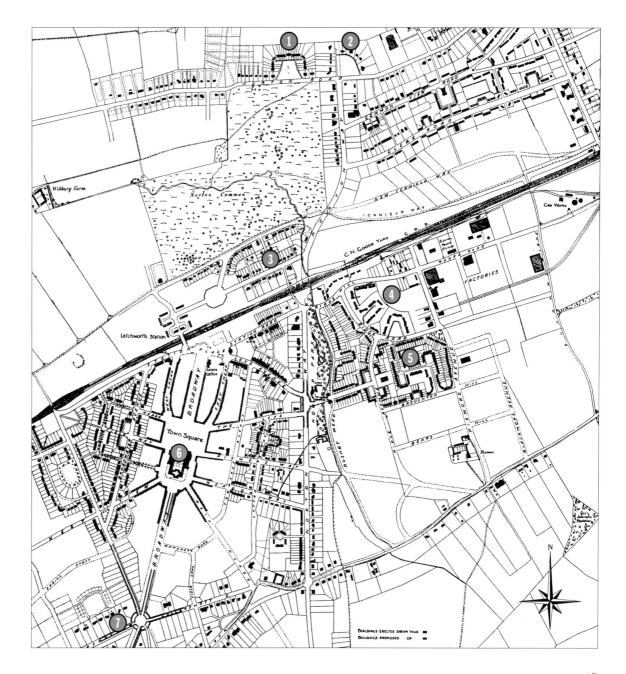

often to designs by Parker and Unwin, for middle-class utopians who shared their social and aesthetic aspirations. Typical of these clients was Edmund Hunter, who moved his handloom weaving firm from Bury St Edmunds to Letchworth in 1908. Unwin and Parker designed a house for him called St Brighids on a fashionable symmetrical 'butterfly' or 'suntrap' plan, a type popular with Arts and Crafts architects because it angled its rooms to receive the maximum of sunlight and it gave a greater variety of garden views than most conventional plans.

This concentration of middle-class housing is symptomatic of one social aspiration of Unwin's that was not achieved at Letchworth. This was his desire for 'as much intermingling of the classes as possible', to promote understanding between the classes. At Letchworth this did not happen – indeed it is notable that none of Unwin's plans even proposed it. The middle classes were concentrated to the south of the city, while the working classes were in discrete 'villages' situated to the north and east.

These working-class estates were, however, important expressions of some of Unwin's other planning ideas. The earliest were Westholm and Eastholm Green, to the north of the centre. These, which consisted simply of informal short terraces of houses grouped around a village green, were derived from one of the illustrations in *The Art of Building a Home*, and provided prototypes for the cul-de-sac in Fowlers Walk in Brentham. The village green arrangement created a sense of enclosure or *place*, as Unwin came to term it, and in Letchworth at least, encouraged a sense of community. The Bird's Hill estate, begun in 1905, was a larger, quadrant-shaped area, again featuring a green

and, for the first time, a cul-de-sac with a narrow access roadway, the prototype for many at Hampstead Garden Suburb. The Pixmore Hill estate, begun in 1910, was larger still, with 280 houses. The layout was more formal in conception, with square greens and allotment areas. One of the most prominent features of this estate was an institute, with a bowling green and tennis courts behind. This was just one of a range of social facilities that, in keeping with Howard's conception of a garden city, was provided at Letchworth.

One particular enthusiasm of Howard's that also found expression at Letchworth was a form of communal living. This had been a feature of most

ABOVE: *Spirella corset factory, Letchworth, 1920s. Spirella was one of only 28 businesses in Letchworth by 1905.*

RIGHT: *'Plan of a hamlet', from* The Art of Building a Home. *Versions of this village green were built at Brentham, Letchworth and Hampstead.*

FAR RIGHT: *A Letchworth cottage, c. 1906. This shows the stairs open to the living room, an arrangement not always popular with tenants.*

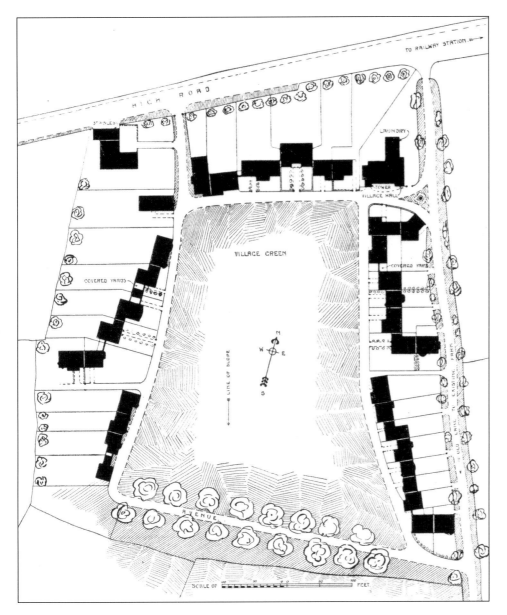

utopian schemes from Robert Owen onwards, and had featured in Unwin's *Cottage Plans and Common Sense*. One illustration showed a quadrangle of cottages grouped around a central green, with communal facilities including common rooms, laundry, kitchens and bathrooms. Such an arrangement, it was felt, was more efficient, and the communal activity would help to foster collective life and brotherhood. This came to fruition, through Howard's efforts, at Letchworth, when 'Homesgarth', a quadrangle of service flats notable for its central kitchen and communal dining room, was opened in 1910.

Howard lived at Homesgarth until he left for Welwyn, the second garden city, in 1920. Clearly there were tensions at Letchworth. Homesgarth may have appealed to Howard, but the working-class tenants were even less attracted to communal living than they were to parlourless cottages, while the businessmen who had to keep Letchworth afloat frowned on it as having marginal appeal, attracting the sort of cranks who might put off businesses from settling in Letchworth.

And although Homesgarth was true in principle to what Howard envisaged for his garden city, even if it had appealed to working-class tenants, the rents, which began at £22 a year, would have been too high for them. This was a continuing problem at Letchworth. It transpired that some of the workers drawn there to take up jobs could not afford the rents of the houses, and were living in the sort of cramped conditions in Hitchin or the surrounding villages that Letchworth was supposed to have made a thing of the past.

This was just one way in which Howard's vision of a garden city was compromised in its realisation in Letchworth. The need of the businessmen who controlled it to make it financially viable meant that the wider social aims were always secondary. There was no Cadbury, Lever or Rowntree figure underwriting the enterprise. This helps to account for the segregation of the classes, the inability to provide affordable housing for the poorest classes, and the fact that control of the city resided not with the people who lived there, but with the company.

What was effectively a top-down control, on the lines of Port Sunlight and Bournville, extended to the social life in Letchworth, which was determined to a great extent by middle-class enthusiasts for Howard's ideas who had settled in Letchworth in its early days. Although Howard had been open to the idea of a properly controlled licensed pub, the only establishment available to the residents was the Skittles Inn, which offered non-alcoholic beverages and a range of facilities including a skittle alley, billiard tables and a reading

room. The wider social activities on offer were extremely varied. By 1910 there were 90 clubs and societies, and although they encompassed mainstream interests such as the Letchworth Football Club and a Residents' Union, they were dominated by the progressive and improving concerns of the middle-class settlers. At Howard Hall, discussions and lectures took place on the 'liquor question', 'the unemployed', 'anti-vivisection', and 'science and civilisation', while the dramatic society put on plays

ABOVE: *'A co-operative quadrangle', from Raymond Unwin's* Cottage Plans and Common Sense, *1902. Unwin believed that such quadrangles encouraged a sense of community, as did activities such as communal cooking and eating. Holyoake House in Brentham is modelled on this idea, although the communal aims were more modest.*

RIGHT: *The Skittles Inn (building on right), Letchworth, 1912. The Skittles Inn offered non-alcoholic drinks, a skittle alley, billiard table and a reading room.*

BELOW: *In this 1930s' cartoon Osbert Lancaster mocks the 'rows and rows of quaint and whimsey little cottages . . . in the . . . suburbs of London . . . which their builders considered themselves justified (by the presence of two sunflowers and a box hedge) in calling Garden cities. . . . From surroundings such as these did the New Woman emerge to bicycle off to a . . . meeting of the Fabian Society'.*

by Tolstoy, Shakespeare and Goldsmith. A campaign to build a music hall came to nothing – music halls, like pubs, were perceived as bad for the workers.

But what happened to Howard's vision of a garden city as the first of a ring of such cities, building up to the 'social city'? Before the First World War, 'very little' is the answer. Welwyn, the second garden city, was not established until 1920, by which time the idea of solving the housing problem by the state, a movement in which Raymond Unwin was a key figure, was beginning to eclipse the way Howard's ideas were put into practice. Before this another development had taken place, under the inspiration of Howard's book, in a form that he had clearly not anticipated when he first thought up his garden city idea, and once again Raymond Unwin was a leading player. This was the notion of the garden suburb, and its realisation in north London as Hampstead Garden Suburb.

Hampstead Garden Suburb owed its foundation to a happy mix of self-interest and paternalistic do-gooding. Henrietta Barnett, its guiding light, was, with her husband Canon Samuel Barnett, a proponent of 'practicable socialism', similar in intent to the philosophy of rights and duties, progress and self-help that inspired Henry Vivian. From the 1880s the Barnetts had worked at Toynbee Hall, a settlement in the East End of London that promoted the mixing of the social classes, by encouraging Oxford graduates to come down to teach adult education classes aimed at the poor of Whitechapel. At weekends the wealthy Barnetts escaped to a house on the edge of Hampstead Heath.

It was the threat to views from their house, by a proposal to extend the Underground northwards, that prompted Henrietta Barnett to wage a campaign to save the Heath from the development that would inevitably follow the Tube. In the end she realised that housing would help finance the purchase of what became known as the Heath extension, from its own-ers Eton College, and by 1903 Barnett was negotiating to buy a further 243 acres to build a 'garden suburb' that would be both architecturally improving and socially diverse. With her enthusiasm for social reform and a familiarity with Howard's book, it was natural that Raymond Unwin should be the choice of architect to build what Barnett called her 'green golden schemes'.

Unwin's plan for the suburb, first produced in 1905 and revised in 1907, develops many of the ideas he had been working out at New Earswick and Letchworth. The long narrow site, which ran either side of the Heath extension, rose northwest from it before falling sharply away to the 'Artisans' Quarter'. Unwin designed a curving street plan that followed the contours of the

site, and provided far wider possibilities for 'street pictures' and views, than either New Earswick or Letchworth. The original plan included an informal central square with the character of a village green, shops, a school and groups of houses arranged infor-mally and linked by paths. When the plan was partly revised by Edwin Lutyens this was lost. The present rather chilly, monumental arrangement was adopted, with the two great churches St Jude's and the Free Church, surrounded by formal blocks of houses in North and South Squares.

The scheme proved popular, and by 1912 more than 1,000 houses and flats had been built in Hampstead Garden Suburb. While the Artisans' Quarter followed

ABOVE: *The fifth anniversary of the cutting of the first sod at Hampstead Garden Suburb, May 1912. Brentham's early benefactor, John H. Greenhalgh, presents a spade to Henrietta Barnett, while Henry Vivian looks on.*

RIGHT: *A suburban street, c. 1904. Henrietta Barnett used this photograph at lectures to illustrate what Hampstead Garden Suburb would* not *be like. With it she was suggesting that the Suburb was not intended principally as a solution to poverty (the houses shown were not slums), but as a place that would be interesting architecturally, avoiding the monotony and lack of greenery evident in the photograph.*

New Earswick and Letchworth in its general appearance, with short terraces of Arts and Crafts cottages, the architectural vocabulary of the estate as a whole was more varied than Letchworth and New Earswick. But the suburb throughout was characterised by trees, hedges, ample gardens and open spaces.

All this contributed to a visual unity. But what of Henrietta Barnett's avowed aim to build a suburb of social unity where classes intermingled for their mutual benefit, thereby defusing class conflict? A mix of classes was certainly reflected in Unwin's laying out of the suburb: there is an Artisans' Quarter on the lower land to the northwest, an area 'for clerks' to the east, while the higher ground around North and South Squares, which has the best views, and the land around the Heath extension, was designated by Barnett for 'richer' houses. The very designation of these separate areas meant that from the start the possibilities for social intermingling were restricted. This was perhaps inevitable. Wealthy residents, even those sympathetic to Barnett's ideas, were less enthusiastic about living cheek-by-jowl with the workers; even Unwin, who had moved to

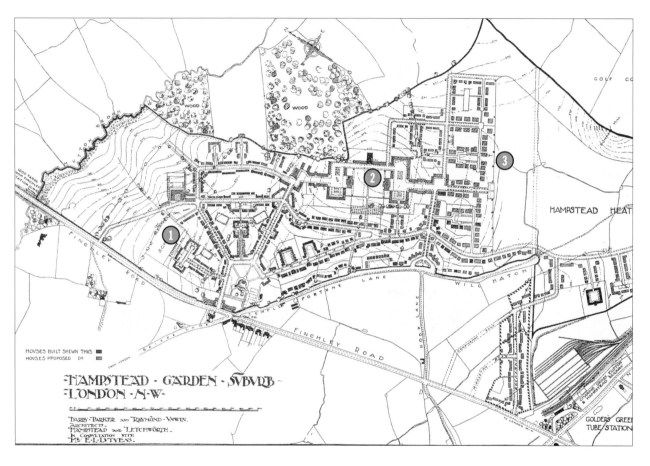

LEFT: *The principal part of Raymond Unwin and Barry Parker's plan for Hampstead Garden Suburb, from the first edition of Unwin's book* Town Planning in Practice, *1909. Unwin and Parker produced their first plan for the Suburb in May 1905. The plan illustrated incorporates changes suggested by the architect Edwin Lutyens, including the more formal design of Central Square (2), which was conceived originally by Unwin more as a type of village green. The plan also shows the segregation of the working-class Artisans' Quarter (1) from the 'rich' houses overlooking the Hampstead Heath extension (3).*

Hampstead in 1906, lived at the opposite end of the suburb from the Artisans' Quarter.

And these divisions ran through all aspects of the suburb's social life. The middle-class residents of the high ground and around the Heath extension attended improving progressive lectures, classes and clubs at the Institute in Central Square, the residents of the Artisans' Quarter went to the Clubhouse on Willifield Green;

the middle-class residents' children were privately educated, which meant that they were in effect segregated from the children who attended the state-funded elementary school.

The suburb, and Unwin's involvement with it, did not enjoy widespread approval with those who had helped form the ideas that had inspired it, notably the Garden City Association. Many of its members,

RIGHT: *One of the Hampstead Tenants cottages in Hampstead Way, 1910. Hampstead Tenants Ltd was one of the co-partnership tenant societies formed after the model of Ealing Tenants in Brentham.*

including Ralph Neville, considered garden suburbs at best a distraction from, at worst counterproductive to, the main purpose of building new garden cities, and staunching suburban sprawl. But this did not stop Hampstead Garden Suburb from being hugely influential. In the years before the First World War, Unwin's ideas about planning, and the example of the suburb saw, first, the acceptance of the notion of town planning: the first university department dedicated to the discipline was founded at Liverpool in 1907. Then, all over the country garden suburbs sprang up, many of which merely mimicked a few of the physical aspects of Hampstead, such as informal street layout and street trees.

What this shift in emphasis away from the wider social ambitions of the suburb and from Ebenezer secretary of the Labour Association. More than half of the houses at Letchworth – all those at Westholm and Eastholm Green, Bird's Hill and Pixmore Hill – and more than three-quarters of those at Hampstead built before the First World War, were built by co-partnership housing societies. And these societies looked for their inspiration, and took as their model, the pioneer co-partnership tenants' society, the subject of this book, Brentham Garden Suburb in Ealing.

Howard's book helped to do was to submerge a fundamental feature of both Letchworth and Hampstead Garden Suburb. That wider ambition, one that was central to Howard's book, was the collective ownership of houses and land. This had been achieved only partially at Letchworth and Hampstead, but insofar as it had been realised, it had not been because of the efforts of Howard, Neville or Henrietta Barnett, but because of Henry Vivian,

LEFT: *Report on the cutting of the first sod at Hampstead Garden Suburb, from the* Ealing Gazette, *4 May 1907. The Ealing paper proudly points out that Brentham's example was the inspiration for the Hampstead Tenants society.*

# 3

# Ealing Tenants and the building of Brentham, 1901–1915

*There is no social experiment the development of which I shall watch with greater interest
than this co-operative scheme of Mr Vivian's. It seems to me that it is along such lines
that the progress to a happier state of society is to be secured.*

Henry Demarest Lloyd, on Ealing Tenants Ltd, 1901

*FACING PAGE, RIGHT: The Clubhouse,
Willifield Green, Hampstead Garden
Suburb, 1910. This building, designed
by Charles Paget Wade, was built for
the Hampstead Tenants co-partnership
societies. It clearly had some influence
on the design of the Brentham Institute,
which opened the following year, but it
had to be demolished following bomb
damage in September 1940.*

*RIGHT: Postcard of Ealing Broadway
station, postmark 1907. The station for
the Great Western Railway line, the first
in Ealing, opened in 1838. When the
District line station (visible in the
distance) opened in 1879 commuting
became easier and cheaper, and a surge
in building activity in Ealing followed.*

HE YEAR THAT Henry Vivian arrived at the Haven Arms to talk about co-partnership housing was a significant one for the area, for it was in the summer of 1901 that Ealing was incorporated as a borough, the first municipal borough in Middlesex. Its incorporation is all the more remarkable because it took place less than 50 years after the area had acquired its first local authority, the Ealing Local Board of Health. This body did not even include the land where Brentham was built, because at this time the area was essentially rural in character. Ealing's growth was, therefore, spectacular, even by nineteenth-century London standards.

Ealing has its origins in a medieval settlement around Ealing Green, but although a number of large villas were built in the area in the eighteenth and early nineteenth centuries, including Pitshanger Manor designed by Sir John Soane for himself, sustained development did not occur until the second half of the nineteenth century. Even after the opening in 1838 of the Great Western Railway (GWR) terminus between Haven Green and what is now Ealing Broadway, development was sporadic and largely aimed at the affluent middle classes. The 1860s saw a near doubling of Ealing's population, but real growth and the transformation of

Ealing from a village into a suburb, came only after the introduction, in 1878, of more rail services and cheaper fares on the GWR, and the opening, a year later, of an Underground station close to the GWR terminus. The impact of this can be seen in the huge surge in building activity that took place between 1878 and 1883, especially on the Wood estate north of Haven Green.

Cheaper houses sprang up in south and west Ealing, but one area that remained largely undeveloped was the very north of the borough, the sweep of land that falls gently down to the River Brent from the high ridge stretching between Castlebar Hill in the west and Hanger Hill in the east. There were a number of reasons for this. One was the area's relative isolation from transport, Ealing Broadway's stations being a healthy 20-minute walk away. Another was a tendency for the River Brent to flood periodically, the effects of which were exacerbated by the clay soil of the area. A few large villas, including Winscombe Court and the euphoniously named Porta Westphalia, had appeared on

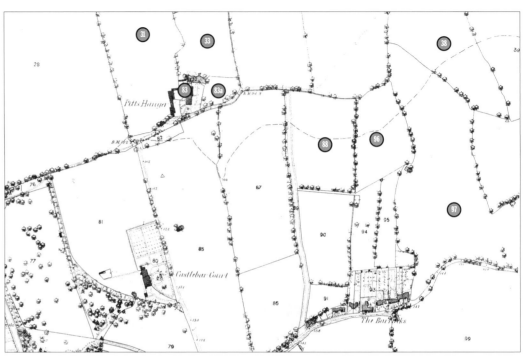

Mount Avenue by the 1880s, but north of these was pastureland belonging to the Pitshanger estate, and the decaying remains of Pitshanger farmhouse.

A mixture of circumstances and pure chance led to Brentham Garden Suburb being built on this site. Over the winter of 1900–1, a group of men held a series of meetings. Some were held in the Haven Arms in Haven Lane, a few hundred yards from Ealing Broadway station; some in the home of one of their number, Hubert Brampton, who lived opposite the pub. By the time the men invited Henry Vivian to outline to them a co-partnership scheme in February 1901, they had already formulated the idea of some kind of building venture.

ABOVE: *Map of north Ealing, 1865. This map shows a number of the fields on which Brentham was built. The first land bought was the Lower Wood Field (88 on this map), and the field to the east (96). The row of trees between the two ran along the backs of the gardens on the east side of Woodfield Avenue. The other fields shown here that were bought later by Ealing Tenants Ltd were 83 and 83a (Pitshanger Farm itself), 31, 33, the two fields east of this, 38 and most of 97.*

RIGHT: *The main committee of Ealing Tenants Ltd, 1906. Ealing Tenants Ltd was set up as a co-partnership in March 1901 to build houses that the members would own collectively and rent themselves, so that every man 'would be his neighbour's landlord'. This group includes three of Brentham's founders or 'pioneers', as they are known – Vivian (seated centre), Harry C. Perry, the works manager (left of and slightly behind Vivian), and Hubert Brampton (front row, right of Vivian). Later arrivals include the deputy chairman, William Hutchings (seated, second from left), Fred Watts, (seated, far right), who was to be one of the victims of the 1944 bomb, Fred Litchfield, the society's fundraiser (standing, far right), and Alfred Frazer (between Vivian and Brampton), a local builder who resigned from the committee and later set up his own small housing co-partnership, Brentham Homes Ltd, which built 50 houses on the streets west of Brentham.*

FAR LEFT: *Pitshanger farmhouse in 1903. All the land on which Brentham is built was originally part of the Pitshanger farm estate, which since 1856 had been owned by the Millard family.*

Most of the men already lived in Ealing, even if they had not been born there, and at least nine of them were craftsmen employed by the Ealing branch of Vivian's co-partnership company, General Builders Ltd. James Mannion, Fred Hellard, and Albert and Hubert Brampton were plasterers; Harry C. Perry and William Pettitt were bricklayers; Albert Paddle was a painter and gilder; Richard White was a carpenter; and Lewis

Reuben Ensor was works manager at General Builders' works in Notting Hill, west London.

But several others appear to have had no building connection, and only one of these seems to have had an Ealing connection: E.W. Roe was an engraver and brass-worker living in Queen's Park, west London; Harold H. Norman was a police constable based in Marylebone, central London; and C. A. Millard was

**GENERAL BUILDERS** LTD.

JOINERY AND MOULDING MANUFACTURERS.

Tel. add.: Squarcetto, London.          Offices and Works :
Tel. No. 583 Western.          WHARF ROAD, NOTTING HILL, W.

Manager : William Grant.          Secretary : Lorenzo Ensor.

WE have specialised and standardised Joinery for Tenants'
Societies, and have supplied large quantities to Societies
given below :—

Garden City
Tenants
Ltd.

Ealing
Tenants
Ltd.

Sevenoaks
Tenants
Ltd.

Hampstead
Tenants
Ltd.

and
numerous
London
and
Provincial
Builders
and
Decorators,
etc., etc.

The
General
Builders'
factory
is a fair
factory,
and works
under
conditions
as accepted
by L.C.C.,
H.M. Office
of Works,
War Office,
G.W.Ry.,
etc., etc.

WE will submit designs free, and quote for Joinery for **COTTAGE** or
for **MANSION**, viz., Doors, Sashes and Frames, Staircases, Dressers,
Fitments, Church and Office Fittings, and Hardwood Wainscoting, Staircases
and Hand Railings, Panelled Ceilings, Mantelpieces and Overmantels, etc.,etc.

**MOULDINGS TO ANY DESIGN IN ANY WOOD.**

STUDY EXCELLENCE, ECONOMY, AND DEAL WITH US.

almost certainly Charles Anthony Millard, the owner (with Edward Millard) of the Pitshanger farm estate, who was to sell to Ealing Tenants most of the land on which Brentham was built. Many of these men remain shadowy figures, about whom we know only that they attended these early meetings or were founding shareholders. But something is known of several of those who were to play the most important roles in the making of Brentham.

Harry Cornelius Perry was a young man of 32 in 1900. Unlike many of the Brentham 'pioneers', as those who attended these early meetings and bought the first shares came to be known, he was a local man, born and bred. His father, Cornelius Perry, was a prominent member of the Liberal Party in Hanwell, Ealing, where Harry, one of five brothers, was born in 1868. When he left school Perry was apprenticed to a builder in Hanwell, and over the years he rose to be a brickwork sub-contractor, organising his own team of bricklayers on building contracts.

Perry had Birmingham connections, which may explain the presence among the pioneers of E.W. Roe, an engraver and brass worker who was born in Coventry in the late 1850s. Ted Roe's grandfather, a silk weaver, had embraced the advent of mechanisation in his trade by building a steam plant to supply the looms of the weaver neighbours in his street. Young Ted became apprenticed to an engraver in Birmingham, the centre of the metalworking trade in Britain at the time.

In 1890 Roe moved to London with his increasing brood of children. There, in Dane Street, central London, he established an engraving and brass-working business. According to his son-in-law, the experience of moving from one set of poor lodgings to another inspired him to think of a house-building scheme. Roe was an autodidact, with a 'a keen intellect which he stimulated by courses of study'. But it is doubtful whether he was the principal driving force, described by his son-in-law, without whom '[the movement] would not . . . have survived the first few months of life'.

LEFT: *Advertisement for General Builders Ltd, 1906. Many of the Brentham pioneers were employed by this co-partnership firm, which was run by Vivian. By 1906 the company had all but given up general building work and was specialising in joinery. It later became Woodworkers Ltd, relocated to Letchworth, and supplied joinery to many of the co-partnership estates.*

BELOW: *Mr and Mrs Edmund W. Roe. Roe was the pioneer who most fiercely defended the principle that Brentham should be built to house working-class tenants. He was one of the first tenants on the estate, where he lived for many years at 75 Woodfield Road.*

ABOVE: *Ealing's first council houses, at North and South Roads, South Ealing, 1903. The builders of Brentham believed that while it was desirable for the municipal authorities to take care of the needs of the poorest, skilled artisans such as themselves should be able to find solutions to their own housing problems – the principle of self-help was held very dear by many of them.*

If anyone, apart from Vivian or Perry, had that role, it was Hubert Brampton, President of the Ealing branch of General Builders Ltd. Born in Marylebone in 1856, Brampton moved to Ealing when he was ten. He lived with his family in Oak Street, just off the High Street, in an area known then as Ealing New Town. Brampton's father Teddy Brampton, a champion skittles player, was landlord of the Haven Arms.

The founding of Brentham was far from being Hubert Brampton's first foray into collective work. Like Vivian, Brampton was an active trades unionist, as secretary of the Haven Arms branch of the plasterers' union. He was also politically active, a Liberal member of the Urban District Council (UDC), the local authority that replaced the Local Board of Health in

the 1890s, and, after 1901, of Ealing Borough Council. In this role he was able to forward his fellow-workers' cause and, in 1899, to learn something about the development of an estate of houses: that year the UDC built the borough's first council houses, on North and South Roads in South Ealing. In 1900 Brampton was able to secure the UDC's commitment to pay union rates for building workers.

By this time Brampton, who was now living opposite the Haven Arms at 44 Haven Lane, was also involved in a more directly co-operative venture, as secretary of the Haven slate club. Slate clubs were societies for working men; members paid a weekly or monthly sum to a fund (in the Haven's case, augmented by fund-raising concerts where Brampton himself sometimes performed), on which they could draw in times of illness, or which could be used to secure hospital beds. By 1901 the Haven slate club had three beds in a convalescent home in Clacton.

Although we do not know the details of what the founders of Brentham discussed when they met, it appears that one of them, E.W. Roe, favoured building houses that they would own outright. At the turn of the century only ten per cent of houses were privately owned (although it was much higher in Roe's native Midlands), but it was a reasonable aspiration for skilled artisans, such as the Brentham pioneers, to build their own houses. Curiously, private ownership was slightly more prevalent among the lower-middle classes than their immediate social 'superiors'. One reason for this may be that building societies, the means for financing house purchase, had evolved among the working classes. These societies had originated in Birmingham in the 1770s, initially as temporary clubs. Members paid subscriptions that were invested at compound interest. When sufficient funds had accrued, houses could be built; each one allocated to the members by a ballot; and once all the houses had been completed, the society would be wound up – hence the name 'terminating building societies'.

By the middle of the nineteenth century bricks and mortar had come to be seen as a sound investment for savers, and a new type of building society had evolved which offered mortgages. Once a fixed number of houses had been built these societies were not wound up – hence the term 'permanent building society'. One that might have had particular appeal to the Brentham pioneers, as members of the General Builders co-partnership, was the Co-operative Building Society. It was never, therefore, a foregone conclusion that Brentham would be built as a co-partnership. There were other options, and Vivian knew that he would have to sell the idea of a co-partnership tenants' society.

It was later said by W. Henry Brown, the co-operative historian and Brentham shareholder, that Vivian had been looking for a chance to put his ideas into practice ever since coming to London: 'he often wandered about the outskirts of the city and marvelled at the displacement of nature that was going on; and when he was invited to help in starting a society to enable a few men to acquire some plots of land, the opportunity to build around, rather than upon, nature, seemed to lure him to an enthusiastic support of the proposal'. It seems unlikely from the tone of early letters and reports, however, that Vivian spoke in quite such transcendental tones to the special meeting of the Ealing branch of General Builders Ltd that was held in the Haven Arms just north of Ealing Broadway on 16 February 1901.

IT IS IN YOUR HANDS—

whether you pay rent or purchase your house. People do not realise that after paying rent for a house for many years they have for all practical purposes paid for it and yet it is not theirs. Why not take advantage of our **REDUCED** rates and become your own landlord ? Write for our booklets.

The **TEMPERANCE PERMANENT BUILDING SOCIETY**, 4-6-8, LUDGATE HILL, E.C.4. (Two doors from St. Paul's Cathedral).

The scheme he proposed that night was based on the estates built by the Tenant Co-operators in the 1890s, but with some crucial differences that sought to address the problems that that society had encountered. In describing the scheme, Vivian pointed out the advantage of 'building wholesale'. Costs such as buying land, survey fees, legal fees, interest on borrowed money and price of materials would all be reduced per unit (that is, per house) compared to one person doing this by himself. He reckoned the saving to be around 20 per cent. To become a member of the society he suggested a person had to buy a £10 share, with interest fixed at

ABOVE: *Advertisement for the Temperance Permanent Building Society, 1923. It seems likely that the Brentham pioneers considered individual home ownership for the Brentham houses, but were persuaded by Vivian's arguments that co-partnership housing, that is collective ownership, was better as it allowed flexibility if tenants wished to move house, and encouraged collective responsibility and a feeling of community.*

5 per cent. There would be a minimum deposit of £5; in time investors would build up a minimum of £50 in shares, which was the value of the plot on which one house could be built. Shareholding was to be limited to £200 per investor.

The land would be bought with shares subscribed by the tenants, and building would be funded from loan stock at a fixed interest rate of 4 per cent, thereby upholding one of the Co-operative principles of limited interest. Once money had been paid to the reserve fund and interest had been paid on shares, loan stock and any other loans, tenants would receive a share of profit in the form of further shares. The cost of repairs to each tenant's house would be deducted from his individual share capital.

Through dividends in his account, a tenant could, in theory, accumulate share capital to the value of his house, after which he would receive his dividends in cash. Although the interest on shares and loan stock would yield only a limited return for an investor, the society could offer in lieu of high interest the security of the houses. It would be in the interest of tenant members to maintain the property in good order. In the fullness of time, it was hoped that the ownership of the society would be transferred from outside investors to the tenant shareholders.

Despite the co-operative nature of the proposition, Vivian did not underestimate the value of self-interest. Indeed he saw it as a healthy phenomenon. Council housing, it could be argued, offered the advantages of wholesale building, and also relieved the workman of individual risk. However, it was this very lack of risk that Vivian feared. He felt that it was unreasonable for skilled artisans earning a decent wage to expect the local authorities to house them, when the needs of the poorest were so pressing. And he believed this lack of risk ignored the 'very important and good part that individual interest – using the term in its best sense – plays in the management and use of house property, and the value to the individual and the community of enlisting the same'. Ever the master of the sound bite, he went on to add that 'what we want is *wholesale economy and retail responsibility*'.

**To the Ealing Tenants Limited.**

Registered Office and Works: WOODFIELD ROAD, EALING, W.
London Office: 22, RED LION SQUARE, LONDON, W.C.

**APPLICATION FOR SHARES.**

I, the undersigned, hereby apply for..................ordinary Shares of **£10** each in the above-named Society, in respect of which I agree to make the payments required by, or by virtue of, the rules of the Society, and otherwise to be bound thereby, and I enclose **1s. 6d.** as Entrance Fee.

Signature....................

Address....................

Occupation....................

Dated the............of............19......

Cheques and P.O. to be made payable to Ealing Tenants Limited, and crossed London and South Western Bank.

**To the Ealing Tenants Limited.**

Registered Office and Works: WOODFIELD ROAD, EALING, W.
London Office: 22, RED LION SQUARE, LONDON, W.C.

**APPLICATION FOR LOAN STOCK.**

I, the undersigned, hereby apply for **£**............Loan Stock in the above-named Society at **4** per cent. per annum interest.

Signature....................

Address....................

Occupation....................

Dated the............of............19......

Cheques and P.O. to be made payable to Ealing Tenants Limited, and crossed London and South Western Bank.

63

For Vivian, this healthy self-interest had to be balanced by a commitment to collective ideals. As he put it in April 1901, what they were looking for in tenant members was 'a type that would not stoop to rob their fellows, but would work with the intelligence of partners in a great co-operative commonwealth, where every individual must do something'. The ideal, as he repeated many times, was that the tenant should say not 'This house is mine' but 'This estate is ours'.

It was this talk of Vivian's that lit the blue touch paper of Brentham Garden Suburb. Less than three weeks later, on 6 March, another meeting was held. Ealing Tenants Ltd was voted into existence on the model suggested by Vivian, and the first twelve share applications were received. Henry Vivian was chairman, and the committee members included four of the original 12 shareholders – Brampton, Mannion, Roe and Perry. Richard White was elected as acting secretary, with his home at 1 Manor Road, West Ealing adopted as the society's address. The society had also bought its first land in Woodfield Road, on what had been the Lower Wood Field of Pitshanger Farm. The fact that this land had been under consideration by L.R. Ensor of General Builders at the meeting on 6 March, suggests that the Ealing men not only knew about the land but had proposed it as a suitable site, which would explain the presence of Charles A. Millard at the meeting.

The Millard family had been owners of the Pitshanger farm estate since 1856, when C.P. Millard (C.A. Millard's father) had bought 420 acres in the area. The name Pitshanger recalls the Saxon word *hangra*, or wooded slope, and early photographs and maps of the site of Brentham show a considerable number of ancient trees dotted around the site, often running along field boundaries. The Millards had clearly been seeking to develop the site. By the time Ealing Tenants bought their plots, Woodfield Road, Woodfield Avenue and the short stretch of Woodfield Crescent between them had already been laid out, complete with kerbs and (as yet, not functioning) lampposts; the posts of some of these survive.

Building in the area had, in fact, already begun: in 1900 two houses on Woodfield Crescent – now numbers 5 and 6 – had been completed as a speculation by a builder called Frederick Hill, and these, as they are within the conservation area, are in effect the first houses in Brentham. At the time, these houses stood in splendid isolation; the rest of the estate was still all pasture and the plots consequently cheap, and this was no doubt one of its principal attractions. After all, it was a central argument of Ebenezer Howard's book that a garden city should be built on farmland that was cheap to buy, compared to sites in areas that were already under development. Ealing Tenants bought nine plots in Woodfield Road for £441, with an option to buy others in Woodfield Avenue.

Ealing Tenants was a local initiative, for the first members were local men seeking to build for themselves under the guidance of their employer, co-partnership evangelist Henry Vivian. Vivian had been at pains to point out in February that the central organisation of General Builders 'did not desire to push the object but would co-operate and give all possible assistance' to Ealing Tenants. This was perhaps a further indication that the pioneers had seriously considered building for individual ownership. However, it became very clear early on that the initiative could have application on a national and even an international scale; the

ABOVE: *Hubert Brampton (1856–1946), one of the Brentham pioneers, photographed in old age. Brampton was a plasterer who became chairman of the Ealing branch of General Builders. Like Vivian, he was a Liberal with a keen interest in trade union and co-operative activities. He is seen here at 71 Woodfield Road, his home for more than 40 years.*

RIGHT: *Woodfield Avenue, looking south towards Woodfield Crescent, 1904. The two houses visible in the distance, 5 and 6 Woodfield Crescent, were begun in 1900. Built as a speculation by a private builder, they are earlier than any of the Ealing Tenants Ltd houses, so qualify as the 'first houses in Brentham'.*

opportunity for exploiting this in the drive to publicise co-partnership was not one Vivian was likely to pass up. On 20 April 1901 Vivian organised the cutting of the first sod in Woodfield Road, followed by the first public meeting of Ealing Tenants Ltd in Ealing Town Hall. The idea was no doubt to make known to the wider Ealing public what was going on in the rural north of the borough.

The *Ealing Gazette and West Middlesex Observer* reported the event, but only on page 5. The reporter noted Vivian's 'most able and lucid address . . . [that]

quite succeeded in drawing his hearers into the scheme'. It noted too, almost as an afterthought, the presence at the town hall of Mr J.M. Ludlow, Mr H.D. Lloyd 'of U.S.A.' and 'Mr Greenhall'. The 80-year-old Ludlow, one of the grand old men of co-operation, had helped draft the 1852 Industrial and Provident Societies Act that made such ventures as Ealing Tenants possible, and his presence gave the proceedings a certain gravitas.

But nothing underscores more emphatically the high hopes that Vivian had for the society, and the wider significance of Ealing Tenants, than the presence of

Henry Demarest Lloyd. America's best-known and most prominent radical commentator of the late nineteenth century, Lloyd was forever on the lookout for a general theory that could serve as the catalyst for his vision of social justice, and in co-partnership he thought he had found it. In 1897 he had met Vivian at the International Co-operative Festival in Delft. Inspired by what he had heard, he had changed his plans and spent six weeks with Vivian touring the co-partnership workshops of Britain. The result was his book *Labor Copartnership*, published in 1898, in which he praised the 'applied brotherhood' of co-partnership and attacked the tendency of Fabians such as Beatrice Webb to underplay the significance of Robert Owen.

On an extended visit to Europe in 1901, Lloyd stopped off briefly in England to see Vivian and attend the public meeting to launch Ealing Tenants. He also gave an interview to the distinguished radical journalist W.T. Stead, then editor of *The Review of Reviews*, in which he made clear that he saw Ealing Tenants as much more than a few working men self-building: 'There is no social experiment the development of which I shall watch with greater interest than this co-operative scheme of Mr Vivian's. It seems to me that it is along such lines that the progress to a happier state of society is to be secured.'

One cannot help feeling that similar utopian sentiments inspired 'Mr Greenhall' in his support of Ealing Tenants. He was, in fact, John Herbert Greenhalgh, a retired barrister living in Bloomsbury. Greenhalgh was a member of the Labour Co-partnership Association, and it was he who loaned to Ealing Tenants on 3 May the £441 they needed to complete the purchase of the first plots in Woodfield Road.

LEFT: *Henry Demarest Lloyd (1847–1903). Lloyd was a celebrated radical commentator and journalist in the United States in the late nineteenth century. A chance meeting with Henry Vivian in 1897 had alerted him to the possibilities of co-partnership, and this became the subject of a best-selling book he published the following year. In April 1901 he made a special trip to London to give his support at the first public meeting of Ealing Tenants Ltd in the Town Hall.*

Greenhalgh's loan was a much-needed boost to the fledgling society, because although more than 90 shares had been applied for by that time, only part had been paid up. The early shareholders were predominantly, like the first twelve, men involved in the building trade, the great majority from west London, but with a few from as far afield as Slough and East Ham. There were a few oddities – a valet, a coach-body builder, a schoolmaster. And then there were ideological members, most of whom had no intention of becoming tenants. They included Ludlow and Greenhalgh, but also another wealthy supporter of co-partnership, Aneurin Williams. The son of an ironfounder, Williams had, like Ludlow and Greenhalgh, trained as a barrister, but he had never practised, preferring to devote his time to promoting co-partnership and co-operation. A staunch supporter of the Labour Association, he was an early editor of *Labour Copartnership* and a founder of the International Co-operative Alliance.

Building work began following the cutting of the first sod on 20 April 1901, with General Builders contracting to build the first nine houses (Vivian Terrace, now 71–87 Woodfield Road) at prime cost plus 12½ per cent. This arrangement soon ran into difficulties however, because General Builders had other commitments. Complaints were aired at Ealing Tenants' meetings about the slowness of progress and the failure to take advantage of the good weather. Vivian was in an awkward position as both chairman of Ealing Tenants and head of General Builders; he did his best to excuse the General Builders' actions. The last straw was reached when L.R. Ensor, the works manager on Woodfield Road, pulled out the bricklayers' foreman, George Denton, to use him on another job. Irritated at this lack of commitment, Ealing Tenants appointed Harry Perry in Denton's place, which prompted the General Builders' bricklayers to go on strike.

This was an ignominious twist. Here were two co-partnership enterprises, one working for the other, at loggerheads in a way that was not supposed to happen in the brave new world of co-partnership. The irony

was not lost on Ealing Tenants, who wrote to General Builders complaining about 'an action so contrary to the spirit of co-partnership'; but the stalemate remained. The solution was hardly a model of compromise: General Builders were dismissed as contractors. Ealing Tenants made the most of an uncomfortable situation. Many of them were builders, after all. Why not build for themselves by direct labour? That was surely more in the spirit of the enterprise anyway. And that is what they did. Early in 1902 Perry was appointed manager on a permanent basis, and it was a post he would hold for more than 20 years.

By the time Perry took over, the first houses were nearly ready. But even then, matters had not proceeded quite as anticipated. At the earliest meeting a figure of £26 per annum had been fixed as the maximum rent that should be asked for the first houses. Moreover, it was decided that the ballot for tenancies should be restricted to those who had bought shares before the first plots had been bought. Neither of these aims was met. By February 1902 a figure of £35 per annum – a 35 per cent increase from the previous year – had been fixed. Since this was higher than many members could afford, it was reluctantly decided to offer the first tenancies on the open market.

Despite the higher rents, three members – Edmund Roe, Hubert Brampton and Richard Williams – accepted tenancies. Williams, a carpenter, who had recently been elected to the committee, became the estate's first resident when he moved into 4 Vivian Terrace (77 Woodfield Road) on 12 April 1902.

Meanwhile, work had started on Woodfield Avenue. Although Vivian had relieved the society's financial state to some extent by taking out a mortgage on Vivian Terrace, there was little spare capital with which to buy large areas of land. Ealing Tenants had paid a deposit to Charles and Edward Millard for 46 more plots (the whole of Woodfield Avenue) in July 1901, but they completed the purchase only as they were ready to build each block of houses, so that all the land in Woodfield Avenue was only bought outright in 1905. Photographs taken throughout the period show just how piecemeal

the building was. It might have been expected that they would build up one side and then down the other, but they proceeded in apparently random manner, starting with a block of five on the northwest side of the Avenue (31–9), followed by the rest on that side of the street, then both corner houses on that side, and 'Armorel' on the southern corner of the other side.

This method of operating was partly due to the shortness of the money supply. Vivian might have been giving lectures and interviews in which he presented the scheme's development as one of stately and unruffled progress, but the truth was a lot more turbulent. As Perry put it many years later, 'capital was so difficult to procure that I did not know at the beginning of the week whether the wages would be forthcoming at the end of it. I particularly remember one interview with the bank manager of that period . . .' Land had to be bought in small parcels, and Ealing Tenants could only afford to build a few houses at a time. Only when a block was completed could it be mortgaged. The first block in Woodfield Road was mortgaged privately via Charles Millard as an investment; subsequent mortgages came from the Amalgamated Society of Railway Servants, for whom Vivian's friend Fred Maddison worked – an example of mutual assistance by one society of working men for another. But the order of building was also partly a result of supply and demand. The reason that Armorel was built on its own was that a new member, Howard Lycett, wanted a larger corner house, built to his specification, for which he was prepared to pay a higher rent. This involvement of members in the planning of their houses continued to be a particular feature of the estate, and marks it out further from speculative ventures.

ABOVE: *Fred Maddison (1856–1937), 1906. A member of the Labour Association for more than 40 years, president of the TUC and a Liberal MP, Maddison was one of Vivian's closest friends, and shared many of his attributes as a self-made working-class man. Maddison moved to 34 Brentham Way in 1915 where he stayed until 1930.*

RIGHT: *Vivian Terrace, Woodfield Road, under construction, 1901–2. Vivian Terrace is now 71–87 Woodfield Road. From 1901 to 1906 the centre house (73) was used as the office of Ealing Tenants Ltd, and in the evenings as Brentham's first institute. Because the wooden scaffolding still sports an advertisement for General Builders (the lettering has been 'improved' on the photograph), this picture can be dated to before 3 March 1902, the date when Ealing Tenants Ltd dismissed General Builders as contractors, and took over the building work themselves.*

Money continued to be a problem throughout 1902. Arguments continued with General Builders over their bill for the first houses, and design changes were suggested for new houses to keep the costs down. The secretary, Richard White, sought quotes from all over the country for the various kinds of bricks – London stocks (the standard light brown London brick) for the side and rear walls, cheap pink Flettons for internal walls, and red facing bricks for the fronts – and bought supplies from as far away as the Norman Cross brick company in Peterborough. Red facing bricks were more expensive, but there was a point beyond which it was felt that savings would compromise the chances of letting the houses. And even when employing their own members, troubles could arise. Richard Murray, a plasterer, one-time member of the committee and one of those

LEFT: *Armorel, Woodfield Avenue, 1904. The building of Brentham, especially in the early years, proceeded in a somewhat haphazard manner. While it might have seemed more logical to build this terrace on the east side of Woodfield Avenue beginning at one end and ending at the other, Ealing Tenants Ltd were responsive to the wishes of prospective tenants, and when one wanted a larger four-bedroomed house in Woodfield Avenue and was willing to pay a good rent for it, they were happy to go ahead and build it. This accounts for the slightly bizarre, isolated appearance of Armorel in this photograph: from the neat lace curtains it appears that the tenant, Mr Lycett, is keen to ignore the fact that he is, in fact, living in the middle of a building site.*

who had met in the Haven Arms in the winter of 1900, tried to raise his price. When this was refused he 'used very insulting and abusive language, threatening the committee with exposure of sweating [i.e. employing sweated labour]'.

One of the greatest bones of contention continued to be the types of houses that were to be built. Among the pioneers, Edmund Roe was particularly concerned that the society should not lose sight of the reason for which it had been founded – to provide homes for working men. While Roe argued that the houses on the east side of Woodfield Avenue should have a lower rent than those on the west, Richard White was in favour of

slightly fewer and slightly larger houses. Roe also took issue with Harry Perry's argument that if there was a demand for four-bedroom houses, more should be built.

There may have been some justification for Roe's criticisms. By March 1904 there were a number of tenants who were not members of the society: the committee was blasé about this, stating that non-member tenants 'could be got rid of in the usual way' if a member wanted a tenancy; but the situation was contrary to the spirit of co-partnership.

Roe's reservations about the types of houses were partly met by the building of 17–32 Woodfield Crescent in late 1904 and early 1905. These were smaller houses, letting at ten shillings and sixpence a week, but the issue was a wider one than merely the size of the houses. There was clearly a suspicion among some members that their interests might gradually cease to be paramount, particularly if there was an appreciable number of non-member tenants, a subject that was raised regularly by members at meetings. Feelings of discontent about the running of the society may have been behind Edmund Roe's announcement in June 1905 that he was 'unable to complete his shareholding'; although he remained a tenant on the estate for another 30 years, he was clearly unhappy at the way the society was developing, as were others. Rumblings of discontent erupted two months later with the publication of a circular critical of the committee: its exact contents were evidently too defamatory to be recorded in the minutes, but it was felt to 'bring the society into discredit', and the three perpetrators were expelled.

Vivian was well aware of the feeling among some of the original building-craftsmen members that the society should be limited to this one type of member. But he had no time for this tendency which he considered a 'bar to progress': 'The man that makes up ledgers is as truly at work as a man that makes window frames or furniture, and so is the man that educates them all'. By February 1906 the tenant membership had spread beyond its base of carpenters, bricklayers, plasterers and painters, to include two clergymen, six schoolmasters, and several civil servants, insurance agents and chemists. It might well have included Vivian himself. In April 1904 the committee were considering 'plans for Mr Vivian's house', but he apparently had a change of heart, as no further mention was made of it, and he remained in his house in Crouch End till his death in 1930.

Vivian was also aware that some members felt the committee were not always responsive to members' wishes, but again he was dismissive, quoting Mazzini's words that democracy means 'the progress of all through all under the leadership of the best and wisest'. Just what this drift of power to the 'best and wisest' meant for Brentham we shall see, but at the time Vivian was writing in April 1905, the need for guidance 'from the top' was especially pertinent in the case of land purchase and the expansion of building operations.

The issue of land purchase was a knotty one. Brentham Garden Suburb today consists of a little over 60 acres, and just over 600 houses and around 70 flats. All but about 70 of these houses and flats were built by 1915, yet until the early part of 1904 Ealing Tenants had no such grand ambitions. All the land purchases had been made from a single chevron-shaped field that, fully developed, would accommodate around a hundred houses. From the tone of everything said and written up to 1904 it seems likely that this was the limit of the ambition of most of the pioneers back in 1901.

A number of factors helped first Vivian, then most of the committee including Perry and White, change their minds. The first was the success of the venture after the rocky first year. In March 1903 the society was secure enough to make a further issue of loan stock at 4½ per cent, the lower interest (shares attracted 5 per cent) justified by the fact that the loan stock would have the first call on the assets of the society. By the summer of 1904 the society had property worth £20,000 yielding £1,000 per annum in rental; it had more than £8,000 in share and loan capital; and it employed around 40 workmen.

Another factor was the possibility that the cost of land might increase beyond Ealing Tenants' budget. As Vivian pointed out, societies such as Ealing Tenants could be the victims of their own success: their

development could push up the price of adjoining land. The danger of this was illustrated by developments nearby. Commercial builders had built on the plots (41–69 Woodfield Road) adjoining Vivian Terrace and Woodfield Crescent (1–7), and on some plots on the north side of Pitshanger Lane. Charles and Edward Millard, owners of the Pitshanger farm estate, were already planning to sell off for development what became known as the Pitshanger and Woodbury Park estate (starting with Lindfield and Barnfield Roads), northwest of the Ealing Tenants houses. But this was only at the planning stage in 1904, and the Millards were still prepared to sell Ealing Tenants more land at £400 per acre, provided they bought at least 15 acres.

Not all the members shared Vivian's enthusiasm for expansion. The land question was first raised in April 1904, when the committee declared Millard's offer of land to be of 'exceptional value to the society', but a decision to buy was not made until October 1905. The delay was due partly to the problem of drainage in the area. But resistance among certain of the membership was also significant. Hubert Brampton was one prominent figure who expressed 'unease' at the size of the projected land purchase, which was so much 'more than originally projected for the estate'.

But other pioneers, most volubly Richard White, supported Vivian's position that it 'was not in the society's interest not to buy', and Vivian evidently did not take the objection raised too seriously. By December 1904 he was already in consultation with a local architectural firm about laying out the estate, even though only a small deposit had been paid on it. In the event, the drainage problems delayed completion of the purchase of the first 15 acres of Millard's land (the eastern

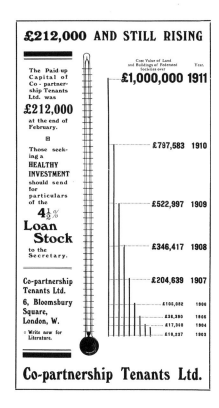

ABOVE: *Advertisement for Co-partnership Tenants Ltd, 1912. The foundation of Co-partnership Tenants Ltd in 1907 was the beginning of the end for Ealing Tenants Ltd as an independent housing co-partnership. Tenants came to have less and less power as shares became concentrated in this central body. Soon new tenants were offered loan stock instead of shares, and in time were actively discouraged from buying shares.*

RIGHT: *Advertisement for Ealing Tenants Ltd and Garden City Tenants Ltd, 1906. By 1906, several other housing co-partnerships had been formed, following Ealing Tenants' example at Brentham. Garden City Tenants at Letchworth, the third society (after Brentham and Sevenoaks), took over many of the houses of the Cheap Cottages exhibition and went on to build the Bird's Hill and Pixmore estates at Letchworth. The prospect of more tenants' societies led in 1905 to the founding of the Co-partnership Tenants Housing Council, as a central advisory body, and then to the founding of Co-partnership Tenants Ltd in 1907.*

part of Brentham, known as the Fowler's Hill estate) until 1906, and the other 16 acres, known as the Pitshanger estate (the north-central part of Brentham), until 1907. That year another small plot on the south side was bought from Frederick Goodenough of Winscombe Court, as well as a tiny piece of land adjoining it belonging to a Mrs Foster.

But there were two other principal reasons for the enthusiasm Vivian and the committee shared for expanding the estate. One was the success of Ealing Tenants' social life. The extent and variety of the social, sporting and educational activities had been achieved partly because the estate was developed on one site, a feature that had been absent from the Tenant Co-operators' estates, whose discreteness prevented that society from developing any coherent identity. This also explains why Ealing Tenants decided against developing an estate of land in South Ealing, following discussions with Ealing Borough Council during the early months of 1904 (the plots were also too small for them to be able to build 'houses to accord with the principles of the society'). It explains too why they declined an offer of land in Hanwell in 1907. But successful though the social side of the estate had been, it had been hampered by the restricted site; what a new estate offered was the possibility of a spacious and permanent recreation ground.

The other reason was the increasing identification, by Vivian in particular, of Ealing Tenants' estate with the ideals of the garden city movement. Ebenezer Howard was at least as much concerned with issues of land tenure and the possibilities of co-operation as he was with the physical planning of a garden city, and this is one reason why the Labour Co-partnership

Association (as the Labour Association had been renamed in 1901) took such a close interest in Howard's ideas and the nascent Garden City Association.

But the planning aspect came, as we shall see, to be a dominant concern of all involved with the Garden City Association, and especially with Letchworth and Hampstead Garden Suburb. The large overlap of membership between the Garden City and Labour Co-partnership Associations meant that Vivian was

conscious of the planning ideas taking shape in the work of Raymond Unwin, in particular. The first parcels of land bought at Brentham were already conventionally laid out with streets and, according to Vivian in 1906, the types of houses were also generally specified in covenants attached to the land. As early as October 1904 he was promoting the purchase of the new estates which held no such restrictions, and

promising that 'something novel in the manner of laying out may be expected'.

But perhaps nothing indicates the impact of Unwin's village aesthetic, already evolved at New Earswick and the early phases of Letchworth, more than the name 'Brentham' itself. Who decided on the name is not clear; it is announced suddenly in the minutes of 26 January 1907, with a positively biblical flourish, 'that the name of the estate shall be called Brentham'. (The appellation Brentham Garden Suburb was in use by 1910.) 'Brentham' means 'town of the River Brent', and recalls several other local names – Brentcot Common field below Perivale church, and Brentford itself, which adjoins the confluence of the Rivers Brent and Thames. The name Brentham is therefore a self-conscious archaism, like many of the names used at Letchworth and Hampstead Garden Suburb (Eastholm, Westholm, Asmuns Hill, for example), and it is in keeping with the garden suburb planning and Arts and Crafts character of the architecture that were about to transform the estate's appearance.

The impetus for the purchase of these extensive new estates, coming from Vivian and committee members Harry Perry, Richard White and William Hutchings, was part of a pattern of change that went far beyond Ealing. The driving force was not the Garden City movement, but the agency of co-partnership. By this date the example of Ealing Tenants had been copied by three other co-partnership tenants' societies, at Leicester (which had yet to start building), Sevenoaks and Garden City, Letchworth.

The connection with Sevenoaks Tenants was particularly close. There were regular visits between the two societies: Ealing Tenants' secretary, Richard White, supplied designs to the Sevenoaks society, and Fred Watts, a tenant who worked on the estate as a bricklayer, went to Sevenoaks to oversee the building. These societies owed their formation, and the nature of their constitutions, to a great extent, to the advice of Henry Vivian. With further societies in the pipeline, it was natural that he should suggest the formation of a standing co-partnership advisory body. This was the

Co-partnership Tenants Housing Council (CTHC), which met for the first time in January 1905. Its secretary was Sybella Gurney, a colleague of Vivian's from the Labour Co-partnership Association, and like that Association, the Housing Council was purely an advisory and propagandist body – to start with, at any rate.

Confirmation that major expansion of Ealing Tenants was inevitable came in October 1905. Frederick Litchfield, formerly of the National Deposit Friendly Society, was taken on as Organising Secretary to raise capital, with his pay linked to the amount of money he

of *Labour Copartnership* and other co-operative magazines. In November 1907 White's share capital was cancelled. It was events like this that saw a tightening of the grip by Vivian and others who kept their eye on the bigger picture of co-partnership.

The foundation of the CTHC was part of a general shift in power away from the tenant members. Symptomatic of this was the prominent position on the main committee of Ealing Tenants held by Alfred Frazer. Frazer was a successful developer who owned land in west Ealing, part of the Woodbury Park estate adjoining Brentham to the west (between Meadvale Road and Pitshanger Lane, west of North View) and in Northolt. The tenant members protested about the presence of a businessman and non-resident on the committee, and Frazer was forced to resign. It is also significant that the committee met increasingly, not in Ealing Tenants' office, but at the offices of the CTHC in central London, or in Vivian's office at the House of Commons: an increasing number of committee members were not resident in Brentham.

Another increasingly prominent committeeman was William Hutchings. Although Hutchings lived on the estate – at 40 Woodfield Avenue – he was a retired civil servant, not a building worker, and was later to become mayor of Ealing. Hutchings' role increased in importance considerably after January 1906, following Vivian's election as MP for Birkenhead. The election of December 1905 swept the Liberals to power under Henry Campbell-Bannerman, and Vivian was one of several dozen MPs classified as 'Lib–Lab', that is Liberal MPs who especially promoted the interests of working men. (It did not signify, as in the 1970s and 1990s, an alliance of the Labour and Liberal Parties.)

LEFT: *William Hutchings (1865–1934), in his role as mayor of Ealing in 1926–7. Hutchings, like Vivian a native of Devon, was a civil servant who moved to Brentham as the first tenant of 40 Woodfield Avenue in 1904. He soon became vice-chairman of Ealing Tenants Ltd and took over when Vivian resigned as chairman in 1911, a post he held till his death. Although apparently well-liked in the suburb, Hutchings presided over some difficult times in Brentham, on several occasions clashing with tenants who felt that their interests had ceased to be the society's main priority.*

raised. Richard White became estate manager, only to be dismissed suddenly the following September for reasons that are not explained in the minutes. White had been a pioneer, so his dismissal cannot have been for trivial reasons. Although it is perhaps fruitless and unfair to speculate, the most likely reason was some form of financial impropriety: employees of co-operative and co-partnership societies were vulnerable to bribery and temptation, a fact often bemoaned in the pages

RIGHT: *The offices of Co-partnership Tenants Ltd at 6 Bloomsbury Square, central London, c. 1907. With the foundation of Co-partnership Tenants Ltd there began a drift of power away from Ealing Tenants Ltd to this central body. The employees on the doorstep include Fred Litchfield, Chalton Hubbard, who remained Ealing Tenants' solicitor into the 1940s, and George Morriss, who lived for many years at 95 Woodfield Road.*

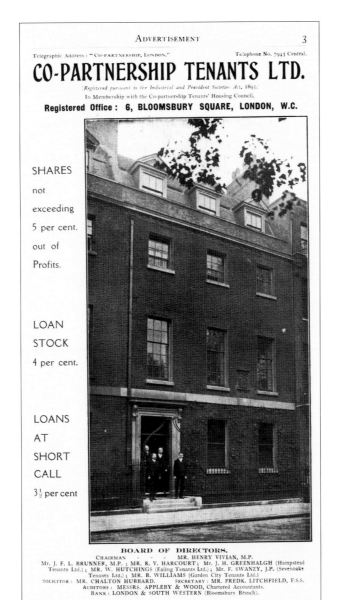

ADVERTISEMENT 3

Telegraphic Address: "CO-PARTNERSHIP, LONDON." Telephone No. 7943 Central.

# CO-PARTNERSHIP TENANTS LTD.

[Registered pursuant to the Industrial and Provident Societies Act, 1893.]

In Membership with the Co-partnership Tenants' Housing Council.

**Registered Office : 6, BLOOMSBURY SQUARE, LONDON, W.C.**

SHARES not exceeding 5 per cent. out of Profits.

LOAN STOCK 4 per cent.

LOANS AT SHORT CALL 3½ per cent

**BOARD OF DIRECTORS.**

CHAIRMAN - - - MR. HENRY VIVIAN, M.P.

Mr. J. F. L. BRUNNER, M.P.; MR. R. V. HARCOURT; Mr. J. H. GREENHALGH (Hampstead Tenants Ltd.); MR. W. HUTCHINGS (Ealing Tenants Ltd.); Mr. F. SWANZY, J.P. (Sevenoaks Tenants Ltd.); MR. B. WILLIAMS (Garden City Tenants Ltd.).

SOLICITOR : MR. CHALTON HUBBARD.     SECRETARY : MR. FREDK. LITCHFIELD, F.S.S.

AUDITORS : MESSRS. APPLEBY & WOOD, Chartered Accountants.

BANK : LONDON & SOUTH WESTERN (Bloomsbury Branch).

But the most significant development was the foundation in 1907 of Co-partnership Tenants Ltd. At first this was mooted merely as a commercial extension of the CTHC; the idea was that with several tenant societies in existence and more likely to be founded, it made sense for these societies to co-operate in matters such as raising capital, and buying materials and services.

As a co-partnership society Co-partnership Tenants Ltd issued its own shares and loan stock. Almost immediately, in August 1907, Ealing Tenants became affiliated, and began transferring its shares and loan stock. At first it was only small amounts – a few shares here, £50 of loan stock there. But one of the earliest acts that signalled a shift in emphasis was the resignation of Frederick Litchfield, the Organising Secretary of Ealing Tenants Ltd, who moved to fulfil a similar fund-raising role for Co-partnership Tenants Ltd.

In December 1907 the suspicion of some tenant members that the foundation of Co-partnership Tenants signalled major changes for Ealing Tenants was confirmed. At a special general meeting in Brentham it was proposed that additional voting powers be given for each batch of ten shares owned, up to a maximum of ten votes. This was a complete reversal of one of the basic principles of co-operation, enshrined by the Rochdale Pioneers in the 1840s, of one member one vote. The move was defeated, but three weeks later, at another special general meeting in Brentham, the proposal was put again. This time a larger turnout of shareholders ensured that the proposal was passed. It is notable that many who supported it, such as Greenhalgh, Vivian, Alfred Frazer, and Lorenzo and Lewis Ensor of General Builders, were not Brentham residents; it was also accepted that proxies could be used at future meetings, which meant that non-resident members could exercise their enhanced voting rights without having to turn up at meetings. The move did not go unchallenged. One tenant-member, R.P. Garrard, stood against both Vivian and another committee member, John Allport, in protest. Under the new voting rules, Garrard was defeated by a huge majority.

What the average Brentham resident felt about this is hard to tell. Much of what we know comes from press reports of public meetings or the tours of the estate that Harry Perry organised. The meetings were carefully orchestrated affairs in which the voices heard were those of people like Vivian and Greenhalgh, and supporters such as Councillor Maurice Hulbert, all of whom colluded in the presentation of a positive image to the outside world. Dissent rarely percolated beyond the minutes of general meetings from which non-members were excluded. A rare exception was Edmund Roe, who 'threw all his weight against' the change in the rules, and when he failed, 'his scheme was dead, killed stone dead, and he had no more concern with it'. This account by Roe's son-in-law Alfred Grosch may be rather melodramatic, but the tone of the meetings suggests Roe's disenchantment was also felt by other tenant members.

The completion of the purchase of the new land signalled a major increase in building activity. One of the first signs of this was the engagement in October 1906 of an assistant to Harry Perry, the manager. This was Frederic Cavendish Pearson, a young, newly qualified architect and surveyor. Pearson was engaged as a draughtsman, but in 1907 he was diverted from this work to take over from Mr Cooke, the secretary appointed temporarily in place of the dismissed Richard White. The following January, Pearson finally took up

his appointment as assistant to Harry Perry, and a Mr Clarke took over as secretary.

Although Pearson was appointed by Ealing Tenants, with Perry responsible for selecting him, the issue of producing a plan for the estate attracted interest and attention far beyond Ealing. Ever since the possibility of buying extensive new land had been mooted in 1904, a local firm, Hall-Jones and Cumming, had been working, on and off, on plans for laying out the streets on the Fowler's Hill estate. This was perhaps a pragmatic move. Frederick Hall-Jones was the son of Charles Jones, the formidable Ealing Borough Surveyor, who had the power, in conjunction with the Borough's Works Committee, to reject designs. Even if Jones did not show favouritism towards his son, Hall-Jones would surely know what his father was likely to approve. But Hall-Jones was hardly at the cutting edge of design. Following the offer of an unnamed member, probably the ever-generous J.H. Greenhalgh, to pay for a new plan, Raymond Unwin and Barry Parker were engaged to lay out the new estates.

The appointment of Unwin and Parker in August 1906 saw a lull in building activity of a month while the new plan was prepared. Until then only about 112 houses had been built in Woodfield Road, Avenue and Crescent, Brunner Road, and Pitshanger Lane, but when work resumed, the pace accelerated greatly, and by this time Ealing Tenants were employing 70 workmen. By the end of 1908, 185 houses had been built, including most of Brunner Road, the extension of Woodfield Crescent east of Brunner Road, 19 terraced and semi-detached houses on the north–south section of Winscombe Crescent, and much of Neville Road. That June the estate had been opened by John Burns,

ABOVE: *John Allport M.A., probably in the 1890s. Allport was a long-term Ealing Tenants committee member and resident of Brentham. In 1935 he presided over the separation of the Ealing Club and Institute from Ealing Tenants Ltd, and became the first licensee of the Club – despite the fact that he was a lifelong abstainer.*

RIGHT: *Sir John Brunner (1842–1919). The industrialist and politician Brunner took an interest in a number of social welfare issues, and in November 1906 made a crucial £7,000 loan to Ealing Tenants. This relieved a temporary financial embarrassment that had caused the society's bank to tell them that 'any more trouble and you can take the account elsewhere'. Brunner Road, originally named Woodfield Crescent East, was renamed in Sir John's honour in May 1907.*

had been appearing regularly in journals and newspapers sympathetic to co-partnership ideals. Among them were socialist, radical and liberal newspapers such as the *Tribune*, *Daily News*, *Morning Leader* and *Labour Review*, plus regular bulletins in the local newspapers, the *Middlesex County Times* and *Ealing Gazette*. As well as *Labour Copartnership* and *The Wheatsheaf*, the co-operators' paper, journals that took an interest included specialist periodicals such as *Railway Review*, *Economic Journal*, *Agricultural Economist* and the *Municipal Journal*.

It is a measure of Vivian's energy and skill as a propagandist that there are so many of these reports, especially before 1906 when his election as an MP curtailed the amount of time he could devote to Ealing. Almost without exception they take a very favourable, even eulogistic, view of the development: the word 'utopia' occurs more than once. A few reservations were, however, expressed. In 1904 the *Morning Leader* suggested that the society's finances did not justify the payment of a 5 per cent dividend on the shares.

A more frequent criticism was that the houses were too expensive for 'working men', and that the society did not therefore address the worst of the housing problem. No doubt this was true, but from the start Vivian had made it clear that these houses were for skilled artisans building for themselves. The Cheap Cottages exhibition at Letchworth in 1905, where an attempt had been made to build houses for £150 that a labourer could afford to rent, and the experience of the Tenant Co-operators' Plashet estate, had together shown that it was simply not possible to build houses below a certain price, as there would have to be a certain minimum rent for the enterprise to be commercially viable. And that

president of the Local Government Board, his presence arranged by his colleague in government, Henry Vivian, who was already making his mark as an MP: by this time Vivian was serving on several Royal and Select Committees, including the Select Committee on Housing and Town Planning.

Burns was not alone in taking an interest in Brentham's expansion. With Vivian's gift for publicity, articles (many of which were written by Vivian himself)

The first survey placing Ealing Tenants within the larger garden city and suburb movement came in 1906 with the publication of a 100-page booklet *Garden Suburbs, Villages and Homes: All About Co-Partnership Houses*, which featured Ealing Tenants' estate, and its new plan by Raymond Unwin, alongside Garden City at Letchworth. This was followed in 1908 by the first publication devoted entirely to Brentham, *The Pioneer Co-partnership Village* by Henry Vivian. This publicity drive was augmented by the regular issue of picture postcards featuring the developing estate. These postcards, which the tenants were actively encouraged to send, were sometimes used for 'mail shots' to members of sympathetic organisations such as the Christian Social Union.

One benefit of this exposure was a greatly increased capital basis from sales of shares and loan stock. The year 1907 saw a particularly large growth in loan stock from £13,935 to £21,525, while the membership grew by only eleven from 171 to 182. This indicates the extent to which the society was becoming dominated by non-resident investors.

This was perhaps an inevitable consequence of the expansion of the society. Although ideally housing co-partnerships sought to fund their building by tenant-owned shares, the amount that the typical tenant could invest was never going to be enough to develop the estate. Hence the issue of loan stock. Investors in 1907 included old friends of Ealing Tenants such as Aneurin Williams and Ralph Neville, as well as Rev. J.F. Cornish, nephew of Thomas Hughes, the Christian Socialist author.

There were also some new names, and one of these was very well known. This was the playwright George

Perivale Church, Near Ealing, W.

**The Pioneer Co-partnership Village.**

EALING TENANTS LIMITED,
BRENTHAM,
EALING,
LONDON,
W.

3<sup>D</sup>..

minimum rent – six shillings and sixpence a week on the Ealing Tenants estate in Brentham – was still more than an unskilled labourer could afford.

*LEFT: The cover of Vivian's booklet* The Pioneer Co-partnership Village *published in 1908. The title and cover image of this publication, the first on Brentham, emphasise its rustic, rather than suburban, qualities. The name Brentham, first used in 1907, is derived from the nearby River 'Brent' and 'ham', an Anglo-Saxon word for a settlement. Probably the original intention was to pronounce the name with a hard 't' in the middle (as in Streatham), but within a few years of the estate being named, 'Brenth-am' was, according to those with the longest memories of Brentham, the favoured pronunciation.*

Bernard Shaw, who on 6 March 1907 bought £2,500 loan stock and 20 shares, which made him the second largest loan-stock holder after Co-partnership Tenants Ltd. Shaw's interest in housing reform dates from at least 1893, when he wrote his first play *Widowers' Houses*, which deals with the subject of slum landlords. But he had also had practical experience of housing as a local councillor from 1897 to 1906 in St Pancras, central London, where he had served on the health committee. In a striking foretaste of Raymond Unwin's credo which he set out in *Town Planning in Practice*, Shaw stated in 1906: 'What we have to do is to sit down and try to settle how many people should be let live on an acre of ground, and then pass a Building Act to enforce our conclusions. What maddens me is to see houses cropping up in such a way as to form the beginnings of slums . . .'

But Shaw's interest in a specifically co-partnership solution to housing problems is slightly puzzling. He was a Fabian socialist, and as such subscribed to Beatrice Webb's view that co-partnership as a system was flawed from an economic viewpoint, and he had outlined, with extraordinary prescience, his reservations to Ralph Neville in a long letter in 1901. Shaw was writing about Howard's vision of the collective ownership of the projected garden city, but what Shaw wrote applied equally well to co-partnership housing. The problem was that if land and housing that was collectively owned rose in value, the collective owners would be tempted to sell and reap a profit; equally the shareholders would be content to accept the 5 per cent dividend only so long as the profits were low. It seems curious, then, that Shaw became an investor not only in Ealing Tenants, but also in Garden City Tenants, Co-partnership Tenants and

Hampstead Tenants, which had come into being in 1906, in anticipation of the building of Hampstead Garden Suburb. A possible explanation for Shaw's involvement is that he perceived that co-partnership societies were vulnerable to commercial investors, who could gradually influence the conduct of the business to the detriment of the tenants. Even if he did not believe that co-partnerships were an answer to society's ills, it made sense, since they did exist, for affluent persons sympathetic to the tenants to invest and provide a possible bulwark against the predatory capitalists.

## Garden Suburb Builders Ltd.

THE WORKMEN ENGAGED ON A CO-PARTNERSHIP ESTATE.

FOR some years the building operations for the Tenants' Societies promoted by Co-partnership Tenants Limited have been carried out by a building staff organised by each separate Society, the staff being dispensed with as the building operations slackened or ceased. To make the continuous and regular employment of a selected staff of operatives possible, and enable a system of Co-partnership or participation by employees in the gains arising from economical building to be adopted with advantage to all concerned, the GARDEN SUBURB BUILDERS LTD. has been registered. It has already entered into a partnership arrangement with the Co-partnership Tenants Ltd. for the construction of a considerable amount of property on the Hampstead Garden Suburb. This promises to provide employment for a large staff of employees for some years to come. In addition, Garden Suburb Builders Ltd. will undertake the work of decorations, alterations, repairs, and upkeep of buildings already built on the Estate.

Applications for £20,000 of Loan Stock are now invited, in multiples of £5, bearing interest at 5 per cent. per annum, payable on July 1st and January 1st. The Loan Stock has priority over Shares.

Send for particulars of this investment to the London Office of the GARDEN SUBURB BUILDERS LTD., 6, BLOOMSBURY SQUARE, W.C.

Another explanation is that Shaw was looking for a reasonably 'ethical' way to invest his income, which had spiralled upwards from less than £1,500 a year in 1905 to more than £13,000 in 1907. Whatever the explanation, consistency is hardly to be expected from someone who expressed support at different times for both Hitler and Stalin, and although Shaw at no time seems to have involved himself in any of the society's controversies, he nevertheless proved to be one of the most tenacious investors in co-partnership.

Loan stock, which was issued at this time at 4½ per cent, was vital to the development of Brentham, but there were cheaper sources of capital. In securing this,

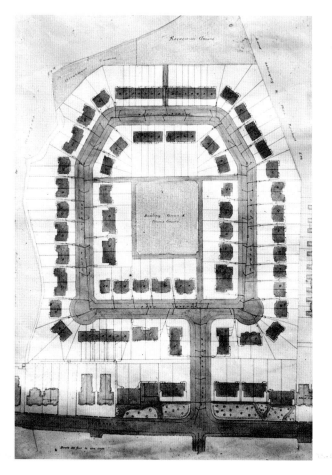

FAR LEFT: *Advertisement for Garden Suburb Builders Ltd, 1912. This firm was one of the results of centralisation of services in Co-partnership Tenants Ltd. Whereas before, all the co-partnership estates had organised their own teams of builders, now a central firm, its offices the same as Co-partnership Tenants, was responsible for all the work. The firm followed Co-partnership Tenants to Hampstead, and later contracted its name to Garsubil. The caption 'workers engaged on a co-partnership estate' reflects the extent to which Brentham was being subsumed into the wider world of co-partnership housing; the picture is, in fact, of Ealing Tenants' own building workers (page 88).*

LEFT: *Plan of the Manchester Tenants estate, 1906. This estate, later known as Burnage Garden Suburb, was unusual in that it was built by the local Co-operative society. The plan owes a lot to Unwin's village-green design (page 47), which was also used in various ways at Letchworth, Hampstead and Brentham. A bowling green and tennis courts were created in the centre of the 'green', with further recreation grounds behind the houses. Burnage, which extends far beyond these first few streets, remained a co-partnership into the 1990s.*

ABOVE: *Brentham Way, looking north, c. 1909. Although lamp standards and pavements are already in place, it would be two years before building would begin on the main section of Brentham Way. Discernible on the right (between the hut and the tree) is a large puddle or stream, evidence of the poor drainage caused by the London Clay soil of this area. This was one reason that Brentham was developed later than other parts of Ealing.*

Vivian's presence in Parliament had a direct benefit for the co-partnership societies. Since 1890 a body called the Public Works Loan Board had been empowered to make loans of up to one half of the cost of housing for the working classes, at rates more favourable than could be obtained on the open market. Ealing Tenants had already borrowed, by the end of 1907, more than £54,000 from the Board, at 3½ per cent over 30 years. The 1909 Housing and Town Planning Act, in the drafting of which Vivian was involved, increased the amount that could be borrowed to two-thirds, and this enabled Ealing Tenants in March 1911 to consolidate a number of different loans into one large one of £83,726. One effect of this was the building of smaller, cheaper houses: it was a condition of loans from the Public Works Loan Board that they be used for houses of a low rent, and this accounts for the smallest houses (17–22 Brunner Road), letting at six shillings and sixpence per week, and, later, the great preponderance of small houses in Fowlers Walk, in particular.

Only 63 houses were completed in 1909, fewer than in 1908. In that year there had been some empty houses, which necessitated taking out advertisements in the *Middlesex County Times* and the *Richmond Herald*. The houses built in 1909 were in Neville Road, the eastern part of Meadvale Road, all of Ludlow Road and Ruskin Gardens, 1–7 Winscombe Crescent, and number 2 Brentham Way, built for the vice-chairman, William Hutchings.

The year 1909 also saw the acquisition of the final portion of land from the Millards – the westernmost portion of Brentham on which Holyoake Walk, Denison Road and North View were to be built. Unlike with the acquisition of the other major portions of land, no objections seem to have been raised by the members. Despite the slackening of the pace in building, some over-supply of houses remained: by February 1910 there were 41 houses waiting to be let, and advertisements were placed in Great Western Railway's magazine and in W.H. Smith's shop at Ealing Broadway station – a clear indication that Ealing Tenants were aiming to appeal to commuters. This over-supply was not so much a miscalculation on the part of the Ealing Tenants committee as a reflection of conditions in London as a whole: the 1890s' building boom was well and truly over, and 'To let' signs were going up all over the capital.

But that year of 1910 was an important one for Brentham because it saw the commencement of the building of the Institute on Meadvale Road, and a consequent expansion of the tenants' social and sporting activities. The year also saw a further shift of emphasis away from Ealing Tenants, to Co-partnership Tenants. Vivian had first suggested a centralised architectural department in 1908, and in November 1910 George Lister Sutcliffe, who had taken over from Frederic Cavendish Pearson as Ealing Tenants' architect in March of that year, was taken on as Co-partnership Tenants architect, employed to supply designs not just to Brentham, but also to the other societies affiliated to Co-partnership Tenants. Thereafter Ealing Tenants used Sutcliffe's services only through Co-partnership Tenants, and the relationship, and the tenants' input into the designs, was necessarily more distant.

The demand for houses picked up over 1910 and by the end of the year a further 76 houses had been completed, with 20 more in the course of construction. These were all in Meadvale Road, apart from the houses at the junction of Brunner Road and Neville Road, the last houses built to designs by F.C. Pearson. The peak year for construction was 1911, with 84 houses completed in Brentham Way, Denison Road, Holyoake Walk and Pitshanger Lane (at the end of Denison Road).

It was apparently the success signalled by this prodigious increase in building that led Vivian, finally, to resign his position as chairman of Ealing Tenants in December 1911. He had occupied the position from the beginning, and, he admitted, 'for the first five or six years of the society's life I confess there were times when I felt very anxious about its future'. Now he observed a very satisfactory balance sheet, 'of which we have

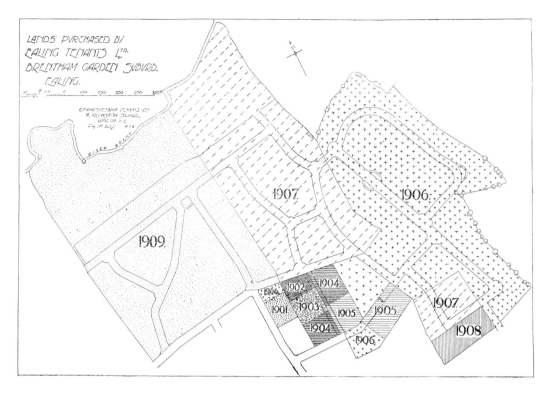

every reason to be satisfied'. He had wanted to resign two years earlier, but felt obliged to stay on to see the society through the purchase of the final part of the Pitshanger estate and the building of the Institute. Vivian was replaced by his deputy, William Hutchings, who was promptly voted an annual salary of £100.

Despite Vivian's triumphalist tone, his resignation seems to have been connected to a major upheaval among the tenants that Ealing Tenants Ltd almost succeeded in airbrushing out of history. In June 1911 an Association of Ealing Tenants had been set up, although exactly what they wanted at that time beyond 'more

ABOVE: *Map of Brentham showing when the land was acquired, 1911. This map graphically illustrates the piecemeal nature of land purchases before 1906, in Woodfield Road, Avenue and Crescent. Unwin and Parker's plan was largely restricted to the land bought in 1906 and 1907; the earlier part was laid out at the time it was bought; the later part (1909) was laid out to a plan by the architect F.C. Pearson.*

information' about the society is not recorded. William Hutchings, the chairman of Ealing Tenants, proposed to ignore the new Association, on the grounds that any individual member could have any information they wanted by asking the committee: Hutchings was a firm believer, with Vivian, in the 'leadership of the best and wisest'. As early as 1905 he had taken issue with a comment made at a public meeting by E.C. Duchesne, a former committee member, that there should be 'collective responsibility' and that 'far too much power was placed in the hands of the committees'. Hutchings' opposition was based on the palpably disingenuous belief he expressed that 'the committee could hardly have too much power if the society were founded upon a democratic basis'.

But, whatever Hutchings' view, this hostile attitude to the tenants' right to association was striking in a society set up by working men and which had had strong trade union links. By November 1911, the discourtesy of the Ealing Tenants Association was noted with distaste in the minutes, and in January 1912 a report that was thought to libel the committee was published by the Association. The prime movers were two tenants R.O. Smith and E.A.R. Lee, and by the beginning of 1912 a clearer picture of their grievances begins to emerge, when the writer of a column of Brentham Notes in the *Ealing Gazette* took up their cause. Their main complaint was a serious one: that Ealing Tenants Ltd were effectively freezing out the tenant members from control of the society. The *Gazette*'s correspondent, who lived in Brentham, pointed out that new tenants, who originally had been obliged to buy shares, had since 1907 been encouraged to buy loan stock, which carried no voting rights. He described a particularly

fraught special general meeting in January 1912 when the Association was treated very peremptorily by the Ealing Tenants committee, despite the fact that a number of outside shareholders at the meeting expressed

their willingness to sell their shares to the tenants. The problem was not restricted to Brentham. Around the same time an Association of Hampstead Tenants was also active. Leaflets issued by this body survive which refer to the 'the wilful or careless neglect' of the 'true principles of co-partnership' by the tenant societies in Hampstead, the specific objection being once again that fewer and fewer tenants were now shareholders; indeed,

that share acquisition was being made more difficult for tenants. And they were quite correct – as early as May 1906, only 40 out of 67 Brentham tenants were shareholders. The result, they felt, was that tenant power in the administration of the estate was eroded to virtually nothing.

The position of tenant members had already been weakened in Brentham in March 1908 when the

STRAIGHT FROM THE COW
THREE DELIVERIES DAILY.

Whither with that milk, my pretty maid?
Direct to **Hornby's Dairies**, Sir, she said!

ABOVE: *Advertisement for Hornby's dairies, Ealing, 1912, demonstrating how rural Ealing still was at this time.*

LEFT: *Payday for Ealing Tenants building workers, late 1909 or early 1910. This photograph, taken on what is now known as Ludlow–Denison Green, shows that at this date Ealing Tenants Ltd were employing around 80 men – 76 houses were completed in the year 1910. In the background are 1–31 (from right to left) Ludlow Road, then nearing completion, and at the far left, in a bowler hat, is Harry Perry, the works manager. The rails in the foreground carried trucks of bricks across the site.*

difference in rents between members and non-members was abolished. In an attempt to reverse this, Ealing Tenants Association attempted in August 1912 to get non-tenant members 'extinguished'. It got them nowhere: the motion was defeated and the rule for calling a special general meeting was changed. In future the prerequisite for calling such a meeting was changed from the signatures of 20 members, to the signatures of those who between them held one-tenth of the society's paid-up share capital. Since more than 6,000 shares were now held by Co-partnership Tenants Ltd, and many tenants, especially those who had arrived in the past three or four years, held loan stock rather than shares, this effectively withdrew the right of ordinary tenant members to call special general meetings. All in all it was a long way from the picture of the sunny co-partnership housing future painted by Vivian only eleven years earlier.

In that year, 1912, the rate of building dropped sharply, with only 23 houses in Holyoake Walk and North View completed, along with the 24 flats in Holyoake House. In 1913 progress picked up somewhat, with 42 houses completed in the central section of Brentham Way, the south side of Winscombe Crescent and the south end of Fowlers Walk. This progress came despite the partial absence of the works manager, Harry Perry, who now spent half his time advising Co-partnership Tenants.

The following year, 1914, saw 34 houses completed, all, apart from two houses in Brentham Way, in Fowlers Walk, and by the end of the following year a further

# Houses Building and to Let
## at Rentals from £25 to £40 per annum.
### AT THE
# BRENTHAM GARDEN SUBURB
## OF THE EALING TENANTS, LTD.

*Sketch in Ludlow Road on the Estate.*

12 Acres Recreation Ground with Cricket Ground, Tennis Courts, Bowling and Croquet Greens. Institute with Club, Reading and Billiard Room, etc.

SOCIAL PLEASURES FOR TENANTS.

'PHONE, WRITE OR CALL AND SEE FOR YOURSELVES.

SECRETARY EALING TENANTS, 7, Winscombe Crescent, Brentham, Ealing. Telephone, Ealing 388

47 had been built, all in Fowlers Walk. By this time, the estate was all but complete. Only the north and south ends of Brentham Way and the north part of Fowlers Walk remained to be developed. In 1930 the latter part was sold off to the developers of the Greystoke estate on Brunswick Road and the streets to the east and south.

What called a halt to the development was, of course, the First World War. It is striking that for those charged with completing the estate, the war's significance did not dawn for quite some months. There is eerily little reference to the conflict in the society's minutes until

1915. By the middle of that year, as the increasing pace of enlistment leached away the building workers, and the cost of materials soared, it became obvious that it was impossible to continue.

But by that time Brentham was a flourishing community, with a population of more than 2,000. This achievement was all the more remarkable when one realises that although the Edwardian decade had been one of modest economic growth generally, the period had also, following a boom in the late 1890s, seen a major slump in the building industry. Ealing as a borough had been protected more than almost

anywhere else in London from the effects of this because of the continuing expansion of its population, which soaked up much of the oversupply of housing created by the boom.

In Brentham in particular the financial viability of the estate was due in part to its appeal to a wider social mix of residents than had perhaps been anticipated in 1901. By the time building stopped, the population was already predominantly clerical and professional, and it is important to realise how early this process began, that is, long before the first sales of houses in the

ABOVE: *Henry Vivian at Wavertree, Liverpool's Garden Suburb, c. 1912. This was one of at least 30 co-partnership garden suburbs that had come into existence by this date, organised after the model of Ealing Tenants Ltd.*

LEFT: *Slum children, East End of London, 1912. Urban poverty was still a major problem at this time.*

RIGHT: *Harborne estate, Birmingham, 1998. The Harborne estate, opened by Vivian in 1908, has similar hedged paths or 'twittens' to those found at Brentham and Hampstead Garden Suburbs.*

RIGHT: *Harborne estate, Birmingham, 1998. The Harborne estate, opened by Vivian in 1908, has similar hedged paths or 'twittens' to those found at Brentham and Hampstead Garden Suburbs.*

1920s. For an explanation of this we might look to Letchworth around the same time, or Brentham in the present day. In Letchworth many of the small houses designed for workers at W.H. Smith's, J.M. Dent's or Spirella were being taken by middle-class tenants, sometimes as a second home. The houses were the victims of their own success in terms of their architectural design and general visual amenity; the same argument applies to Brentham houses in the present day, which sell for higher prices than houses of equivalent size elsewhere in Ealing. The main difference between then and now

is that then the rents were not driven purely by market forces: the co-partnership organisation of the estate meant that Ealing Tenants Ltd did not charge the highest rents for each house that the market would stand, and skilled artisans could still afford to live there, even if most of their neighbours worked in offices.

And the success of co-partnership housing was not restricted to Ealing. Ealing Tenants enjoyed the position of pioneer in a co-partnership housing movement that encompassed more than 30 societies, which by 1915 had built 7,000 houses all over the country. Of these

LEFT: *Henry Vivian and a group of MPs and supporters at Hampstead, 1912. Vivian is explaining the plans for extending Hampstead Garden Suburb beyond Unwin's original plans. By this time Hampstead, with three co-partnership tenants' societies and property worth £380,000, had far outstripped Brentham as the main centre of co-partnership housing.*

societies, 14 were affiliated to the Co-partnership Tenants Ltd, which by the time war broke out had more than £300,000 in shares and loan stock. And the wider garden city movement was also thriving, with the foundation in 1913 of an International Garden Cities and Town Planning Association. Garden city and suburb associations and developments had appeared in all the major European countries, and Germany was especially active, with a nascent garden city founded at Ratshof, near Königsberg, and with garden suburbs in Hellerau, near Dresden, and in Strasbourg (now in France).

But the co-partnership societies had achieved a unique distinction. Although the tenants might have lost much of their power, Brentham was still entirely owned by the co-partnership society of Ealing Tenants, and this collective ownership of land and houses was closer to the spirit of Ebenezer Howard's little book than anything ever achieved at Letchworth Garden City or Hampstead Garden Suburb. All in all it was a formidable success following the modest start made by those twelve Ealing pioneer shareholders in the Haven Arms public house 13 years earlier.

# 4

# Social life in Brentham, 1901–1914

*. . . he was sane enough, after a fashion. I knew the type. Vegetarianism, simple life, poetry, nature-worship, roll in the dew before breakfast. I'd met a few of them years ago in Ealing.*

GEORGE ORWELL, *Coming Up For Air*, 1939

AREFULLY DEFINED and limited in scope though it appeared, the proposal that Henry Vivian made in 1901 was to prove highly significant for the growth of Brentham. The aim was to put into practice in housing the co-partnership ideals that he had been promoting for most of the past decade. The first land bought could accommodate only nine houses, and further land on which they had an option would be large enough for an estate of 54 houses. This suggests that there was no intention to realise a grand self-contained new town, on the lines of Howard's Garden City, or even a consciously engineered suburban community, such as Henrietta Barnett set about creating on the edge of Hampstead Heath a few years later.

Yet the very fact that Brentham was to be a co-partnership endeavour carried with it from the start certain implications about what life would be like on the new estate. The co-partnership movement had a rich heritage, with links to diverse progressive groups, from Co-operators and Secularists, to Christian Socialists and Owenite utopians. Co-partnership was not just a simple compact between capital and labour; rather, it was a way of achieving social harmony between the classes, which as well as being a good thing in itself, would act as a catalyst to social progress. That progress would be further enhanced by a range of activities designed to improve the mental and physical well-being of the population at large. This explains the educational facilities provided to employees of, for example, General Builders.

In the case of co-partnership housing, the implications and opportunities were greater than with co-partnership workshops, factories, and so on. Of course, the improvement in housing was important. Better housing made for better people, and giving people a stake in their housing via co-partnership ensured the better housing remained better: self-interest and community interest thereby became one and the same. And that community interest could be further cultivated to a far greater degree than was possible with co-partnership workshops by the establishment of a vibrant social life. Brentham's diverse social, educational and sporting life up to the First World War, especially after the opening

Woodfield Road). Like the classes and lectures held by General Builders in Notting Hill, subjects of co-operative and co-partnership interest dominated – although 'interest' might be stretching the point. Discussions in the period 1903–5 included 'Tariffs Reform' and 'The co-partnership iron foundry at Guise'. Lectures also tended to be improving or educational in character: Baillie Weaver, barrister-at-law, on 'How to help the less fortunate', and Councillor Cuthbert Paistowe on 'Sugar' (an attack on the protectionist Brussels Sugar convention of 1905), are typical.

*LEFT: Interior of the office and institute at 73 Woodfield Road used by Ealing Tenants between 1901 and 1905. Two rooms were converted into one to provide more space for meetings and lectures.*

*BELOW: Cartoon lampooning the arguments about free trade, from the Ealing Gazette, 16 May 1908. Those in charge at Ealing Tenants were strong supporters of free trade.*

of the Institute in 1911, is usually said to follow the garden city ideals after the social model of Letchworth and Hampstead. Yet long before the opening of the Institute, or even before the estate was firmly yoked to the garden city movement (by the employment of Raymond Unwin and Barry Parker to produce a new site plan in 1906), these collective activities are evident at Brentham. By that time Brentham had already evolved a distinctive social character, and it was the pursuit of the wider aims of co-partnership that helped shape that character.

Even before Ealing Tenants celebrated its first birthday, when only nine houses had been built, Brentham had begun its first tentative moves towards an organised social life. In November 1901 a discussion class that ran for several winter seasons, was started by Mr H.M. Conacher. It was held in the estate office, which until the office moved to 32 Woodfield Crescent in 1905, was in the front room of 2 Vivian Terrace (now 73

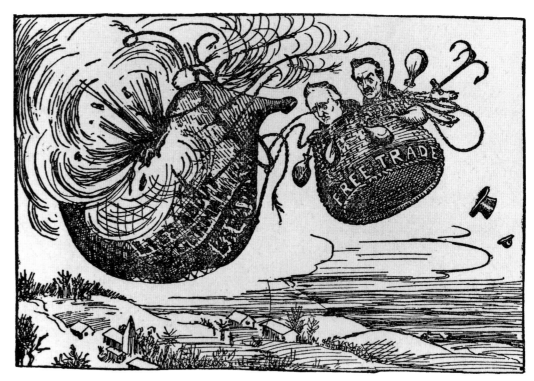

ABOVE: *Ealing Co-operative Stores, 50–2 Pitshanger Lane, c. 1906. Before this shop opened the first local co-operative store was run from the offices of Ealing Tenants in Woodfield Road.*

a rousing speech by Vivian, in which he would congratulate the society on its success in the past year, and would emphasise the financial soundness of the business – which in the first couple of years was being economical with the truth. The dinners concluded with 'capital songs, pianoforte, banjo and mandolin selections', in which Vivian was known to take part.

The dinners were an opportunity for Ealing Tenants to spread the co-partnership gospel around Ealing and beyond. Journalists from the *Ealing Gazette* and *Middlesex County Times* were invariably present, and their reports could hardly have been more favourable had Vivian written them himself. The dinners were also an opportunity to invite local dignitaries and interested parties from further afield. In 1903 J. Ben Johnson, the headmaster of St John's School, was invited to address the dinner, and he spoke approvingly of a cricket shield that Ealing Tenants had supplied for competing local schools – and which St John's team had won. Many pious words were uttered about the physical and moral uplift provided by team games and competitions, but the minutes of Ealing Tenants meetings record a less altruistic aim: presenting the shield 'will be good propaganda'.

The propaganda was perhaps too good. It cannot have been an entirely restful experience being a tenant in Brentham in the first couple of years of its existence. Vivian's spirited campaign of publicity brought visitors from all over London to peer into houses and gardens and ask questions of workmen and tenants. Representatives of the Christian Social Union, the Ethical Society, the Royal Oak Benevolent Society, the Rambling Club, the National Housing Reform Council and the Mildmay Park Radical Club all came trooping

In case those attending missed the point about being good co-operators, the company used the first season of discussion classes to display a 'range of co-operative goods' in the office. By the end of 1902 the Ealing co-operative stores had started business in their own premises at 50 Pitshanger Lane, with Ealing Tenants having an interest – possibly a controlling interest – in the business.

Until about 1904 the main social events for Ealing Tenants, workers and tenants alike, were the various annual dinners and half-yearly meetings, the former usually held in the Lyric restaurant at Ealing Broadway, the latter on the estate. The dinners invariably involved through. Co-partnership housing had certainly caught the imagination of a wide diversity of interest groups.

No doubt the tenants and workmen got used to the interest that their experiment had stirred up. They had to get used to being looked at, and having their homes scrutinised. By 1903 Ealing Tenants had institutionalised this by starting garden competitions. These, like several of the social and educational activities at Brentham, were not an Ealing Tenants innovation – Tenant Co-operators had been taking part in competitions since the 1890s – but Brentham was to prove more consistent than most in pursuing this, as garden awards are still made today in the suburb. The shield for which they were to compete before the First World War was made by metal-worker and pioneer Edmund Roe.

The first judging took place at the half-yearly general meeting that took place on the estate on 22 August 1903. The judge for the garden competition was Richard Dean, a Fellow of the Royal Horticultural Society, and author of a *History of the Dahlia* and *The Culture of Sweet Peas*. His task was much easier than it is for today's judges: there were only 22 gardens to look at then. Dean took the judging very seriously, giving marks for both back and front gardens. His detailed criteria included 'culture' (the way plants were placed according to size and how they were tended and staked), quality of flowers on space cultivated, the effect of the gardens (including tidiness of paths), and harmony of colours. His remarks reveal that vegetables were being grown as well as flowers. The first winner was Harry Perry of 7 Vivian Terrace (83 Woodfield Road). Although he was the works manager, there was no suggestion that it was a 'fix'.

The competitions were only one of the ways in which Ealing Tenants encouraged tenants to cultivate their

gardens. From as early as 1902 trees were supplied for the front gardens of the houses in Woodfield Road 'to form an avenue', and the following year, trees were planted in the back gardens of the Woodfield Avenue houses. What species these trees were is not recorded, but from the evidence of trees supplied a few years later, and the fact that the tenants were encouraged to grow vegetables as well as flowers, it is likely they were fruit trees. A number of apple trees survive from the early years of the estate, and plum trees, pear trees and even, so one resident recalls, peach trees were known.

ABOVE: *Henry Howard FRHS (left) judging a garden competition at Hampstead Garden Suburb, 1909. Howard also judged the garden competitions in Brentham, following the death of Richard Dean who had judged the first competition in 1903. The competitions were part of a drive by Ealing Tenants Ltd to encourage tenants to look after the estate.*

RIGHT: *Brentham garden, 1906. This illustration from* Garden Suburbs, Villages and Homes*, a booklet about the co-partnership housing movement published in 1906, is labelled 'A typical garden on the Ealing Tenants Estate' – it seems doubtful, however, that every garden featured a wigwam.*

In the months following the general meeting held in August 1903, Vivian first started articulating his hopes for the social side of the estate, calling on the members to 'make the social life of the estate all that the idealists hoped for'. By early 1904 a separate social and educational committee had been formed with ambitious aims that included setting up 'a library, arranging debates, lectures and social and other meetings, a choir, garden parties and festivals and to co-operate with similar organisations'. The library was the first item tackled, with donations of books arriving from Vivian and Greenhalgh in January 1904, and the following year from Richard Dean, who gave some gardening books and magazines shortly before he died.

Debates and lectures continued, but the organisers seemed to have adopted a lighter approach after the first couple of seasons: the various improving, politically correct co-partnership lectures were leavened by 'An Evening with Tennyson', a lantern lecture on India and Richard Dean's 'Pleasant Chat about Common Flowers'. The formation of a choir under the baton of J.E. Fox also suggests that life in a co-partnership estate could be enjoyable as well as improving. The choir, which rehearsed on fine evenings in the open air, performed at various meetings, including a party held for 50 of the workmen at the Haven Arms in March 1905. At this stage there is no sign of the folk revival that was to manifest itself in Brentham from the following year in May Day celebrations and pageants: the music reflected the popular taste of the time, the composers most often mentioned being Michael Balfe (perhaps best remembered for his operetta *The Bohemian Girl* featuring 'I Dreamt I Dwelt in Marble Halls', recently revived by Enya) and Arthur

Sullivan (of Gilbert and Sullivan fame). At one party in 1906 a spoof song called 'The Ealing Tenants' to the tune of 'The Old Folks at Home' was greatly enjoyed.

The party at the Haven Arms was just one of a number of 'beanfeasts' and outings arranged to 'cultivate friendly feelings with the workers'. In July 1906 a party of 50 went to Box Hill in Surrey, 'conveyed there by brakes, while others cycled'. They were favoured by the proverbial good 'Ealing Tenants' weather', and

LEFT: *The first Brentham tennis court, c. 1905. This court was laid out on ground to the east of Woodfield Avenue in the summer of 1904, when the tennis and cricket clubs were founded. The smart dress of the player and crowd suggest this occasion was one of the public meetings held by Ealing Tenants Ltd to show off their new estate to potential tenants and investors. The 'match' was probably staged for the benefit of the camera – certainly the quality of the court seems to leave something to be desired.*

during the day a cricket match, in which the carpenters competed against the bricklayers, was played. The bricklayers won.

Sports of various kinds were greatly developed by the new social committee, and by the summer of 1904 cricket and tennis clubs had been formed. The lack of land held up the laying of a cricket pitch, although impromptu matches were held from time to time around what is now Brunner Road. The tennis players were luckier. During the summer of 1904 at least one court, and a small shelter, was set out on the land to the east of Woodfield Avenue on the site now occupied by the house called Rookery Nook. That same summer a sports day or 'gymkhana' was held on the estate, featuring a programme of tennis, quoits and athletics contests, and culminating in a hard-fought tug of war between the tenants in Woodfield Road and those in Woodfield Avenue. After a plucky struggle, Woodfield Avenue

ABOVE: *Sybella Gurney, c. 1906. Gurney, a university graduate, was one of the few women who held prominent positions in the co-partnership movement. She organised a children's bank and library in the early days at Brentham.*

RIGHT: *A children's 'treat' on Dog Kennel field, 1903–4. In the background is Vivian Terrace (now 71–87 Woodfield Road). These swings were temporary (the land did not belong to Ealing Tenants), but permanent swings were soon erected for the children.*

came from behind to pip Hubert Brampton's Woodfield Road team. Music, singing and dancing brought the day to a close. So successful were the social committee's efforts that it was claimed that on the estate 'people do not go away on holiday, but spend time cultivating their gardens and in playing various outdoor games'.

Children were also expected to take part in this burgeoning Brentham social life. Vivian and his supporters stressed that 'it is worth while to make the children understand and care for our aims' and it was noted approvingly that 'with the exception of a few toys, books of a sound educational value had been selected' for prizes at the gymkhana. In 1904 Sybella Gurney from the Labour Co-partnership Association organised a penny bank (a children's savings bank), and the following year she set up a children's library. In 1905 'a collection of articles for use in case of sickness or accident' was started.

But the children had more fun than all this suggests. In fact they made it abundantly clear that they were not perfect little co-partners. In August 1904 Harry Perry was busy erecting swings for the children to try to keep them off the building sites, as 'more than £1-worth of damage was caused by children knocking down brick-work'. However, the building sites continued to be an attraction to the children, even the well-behaved ones. Ninety years on, Doris Palmer (b. 1906), whose parents were the first tenants of 52 Meadvale Road, still remembers the pleasures of clambering around the half-built houses on Denison Road and Holyoake Walk.

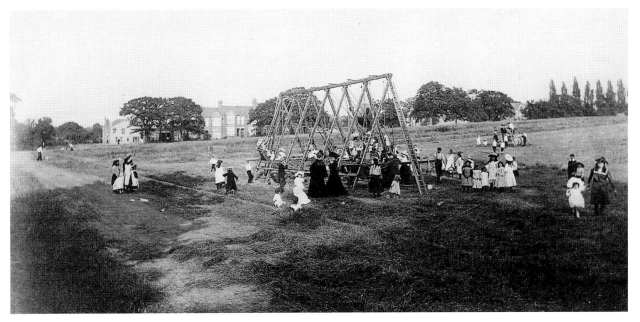

As the estate developed, so did activities for the children. From 1904 a Christmas party with songs, games, 'gramophone selections' and presents on a tree was organised for the first time. This traditionally took place in January – not so unusual at the turn of the century – and the first year 80 children were entertained at the co-operative shop at 50–2 Pitshanger Lane. The following year the recently acquired Pitshanger farmhouse was used.

The stores and the farmhouse were just two of several venues off the estate – the hall of St Stephen's School on Pitshanger Lane was another – that Ealing Tenants used if a meeting was likely to attract more than 40 people. Although the accommodation at Ealing Tenants' office in Woodfield Road had doubled with the removal of the wall between the front and back rooms, it was still only one room in a house. If the estate's social life was to expand in a coherent and cohesive way, more spacious accommodation would be needed.

A purpose-built but temporary institute was what they decided on. It is interesting that even in 1905, Ealing Tenants had in mind to build a large, permanent institute, which can be seen marked on Unwin's plan of the following year. The decision to build this permanent institute explains why the interim institute that they built took the form it did. In 1904 the committee had debated buying a temporary, presumably prefabricated, iron building, but by September 1905 they had decided to build a house in Woodfield Crescent (number 33) that could be used as an institute.

On the outside it looked like a normal house; it was more like the houses at the other end of Woodfield Crescent than the smaller houses immediately adjoining it, as it had unrendered red brick with a bay rising

through two storeys. But on the inside it was left empty of both dividing walls and staircase. That created two substantial rooms, the upper one reached by an iron staircase, like a fire escape, on the outside. This arrangement meant that when the institute proper was built, 33 Woodfield Crescent could quite easily be turned into a house by the insertion of interior walls and staircase, and then let, an arrangement that would avoid being wasteful. The new institute was set up with a billiard room on the ground floor (J.H. Greenhalgh supplied the billiard table) and with 'every convenience for catering'. The upper room, which could accommodate a hundred people – although that must have been quite a crush – was to be used for concerts, dances and lectures. New ventures included a first aid class and a weekly Saturday-night dance.

The opening of the new Woodfield Crescent institute early in 1906 coincided with the final negotiations over the new land that Raymond Unwin and Barry Parker were asked to lay out for building that autumn. What the acquisition of this new land meant was that a proper recreation ground could be created, on nearly five acres that had been earmarked for the purpose, down by the River Brent. This land encompassed the part of the recreation ground as it exists today, east of Denison Road. It was not until late in 1907 that the recreation ground was actually laid out, mainly because of wrangling over how it was to be used.

The general committee of Ealing Tenants was especially keen on a good cricket pitch, and Vivian suggested only two tennis courts be laid out, until it became clear how much demand there was. There was a certain amount of argy-bargy with the social committee, who claimed that 'football was being neglected' in plans for

ABOVE: *Cricket at Brentham, 1906. Although a proper pitch was not laid at Brentham until 1908, a cricket club was started in 1904, and many impromptu matches were held on land that was soon to be built on near Brunner Road.*

RIGHT: *Children on the recreation ground at the Brentham Institute, c. 1912. The children are listening to a gramophone (its horn is visible behind the man sitting on the end of the bench), which was often used to entertain children and adults alike.*

laying out the recreation ground. It is striking how little this traditional working-class man's recreation features in Brentham before the First World War. The general committee of Ealing Tenants could be intolerant of dissent, as was evident in a change in the rules in 1907: the general committee would now elect four of the eight members of the social committee.

In fact the first sports ground to be laid out after the institute opened was a bowling green. It lay to the east of the institute, roughly on the site of 34–5 Woodfield Crescent and their gardens. It was declared, 'a more lovely spot than this it is difficult to imagine . . . well sheltered by stately oaks . . . with views to Harrow'. The ground immediately behind the institute was used for social gatherings on fine days, and it was here, in 1906, that the first maypole in Brentham's long history of celebrating May Day was erected.

It was also here, in July 1906, that Ealing Tenants children entertained nearly 90 visitors from the London County Council Invalid School in Paddington. This was the acme of the co-partnership spirit of brotherhood in 'helping those who cannot help themselves'.

Lunch was served in the concert room, as the upper room was now known, and a concert laid on in the grounds with more maypole dancing, songs, and a Punch-and-Judy show. 'It may be safely stated that during this show bodily ailments were forgotten,' a report claimed. The afternoon also featured one of the earliest appearances of the Ealing Blackbirds, a troupe of boys in black face, whose 'merry antics' brought 'uproarious merriment'. The basic premise of the Blackbirds, which sustained a varied line-up through at least ten years, was that because they were black they had trouble in telling one another apart. No one seems to have found it offensive; brotherhood and the resolution of class differences were conceived as white aspirations.

They were also largely male aspirations. Although Sybella Gurney and a small number of other middle-class women took leading roles in the Labour Co-partnership Association and Co-partnership Tenants, in Brentham and the other estates women generally took the traditional roles of supplying catering

ABOVE: *John Burns's car at the top of Brentham Way, 8 June 1908. Burns, who was a government colleague of Henry Vivian (elected an MP in 1906), was arriving to open the new recreation ground in Meadvale Road. The sight of a motor car would have been a novelty in Brentham in 1908.*

of feminine behaviour, for instance in taking part in sport, this 'caused endless amusement'.

By the autumn of 1907, decisions had finally been reached about how to lay out the recreation ground by the Brent, and 6,800 yards of turf was laid. The issue had become more pressing because Vivian had arranged for an opening ceremony to take place on Whit Monday, 8 June 1908, and it was important that the recreation ground should be in good condition for the event. A suggestion that an open-air swimming bath be built down by the Brent was put on hold; four tennis courts (on the ground nearest Meadvale Road, probably close to the present institute) and a cricket pitch were the limit of their immediate ambitions.

Vivian, and no doubt the rest of the estate, was keen to make an impression because he had succeeded in persuading a very prominent person to open the estate. John Burns was President of the Local Government Board, a senior colleague of Vivian's in the House of Commons. As the first working-class man in Britain to have made it into the Cabinet, Burns was a particularly apt choice to open the estate, a walking example of the philosophy of self-help and self-improvement. He was also in the throes of shepherding through Parliament what would become the landmark 1909 Town Planning Act.

Burns, as befitted his status, arrived by motor car at the entrance to the estate at the top of Brentham Way, accompanied by his wife and son, and by J.F.L. Brunner, the MP son of Brentham's benefactor, Sir John Brunner. On a platform erected on the land between Brentham Way and Winscombe Crescent, Hubert Brampton presented Burns with the 'Freedom of Brentham'. The party proceeded on foot to the recreation ground,

for sports and social events, singing at concerts and looking after the children. Only one woman occupied a place on an Ealing Tenants committee before the First World War, and that was on the social committee rather than the works, finance or general committee. Women were also concerned with 'good works' such as the Paddington children's party. By 1906 a Women's Work Party was meeting weekly to make clothes and remake old clothes 'for distribution to local and other charities'. When women stepped outside the normal boundaries

contrived to convey all the right co-partnership messages. He spoke warmly of Henry Vivian as a 'practical mystic'. He commended 'rational recreation' and 'good old-fashioned English games, such as tennis, bowls, cricket and quoits', while condemning 'gladiatorial spectacles' such as football: 'He did not like to see 120,000 men, without a woman among them, watching 22 players developing the wrong end of their anatomy (*laughter*). Where the woman and child were not, there the beast was (*great cheering*)'.

LEFT: *John Burns (1858–1943), c. 1900. Burns was the first working-class man in Britain to join the Cabinet.*

BELOW: *John Burns and guests inspect one of the smaller cottages –18 Brunner Road – on their way to the opening of the recreation ground, 8 June 1908.*

stopping to inspect, and ceremonially unlock, 18 Brunner Road, the first of the cheaper cottages for rent at six shillings and sixpence per week.

At the recreation ground Burns participated with enthusiasm in a cricket match, and watched the children performing sports. But before this, Burns climbed to the balcony of the newly completed cricket pavilion where he addressed the crowds. In his speech he

ABOVE: *Queen's Parade, 108–24 Pitshanger Lane, c. 1911. This block, built in 1909–10 for Alfred Frazer, a one-time member of the Ealing Tenants committee, was designed by F.C. Pearson, Ealing Tenants' architect. It included a dairy at the far right, and several shops – Kay's, Sims, and Stowell's among them. In 1910 F.S. Stowell was refused a beer licence by the council after Ealing Tenants Ltd objected. Later he was successful, and the shop is still an off-licence today.*

And he offered advice on the arrangement of the home. He hoped tenants would not make their rooms overcrowded 'like furniture repositories', and that 'they would have no best parlour . . . The room into which no one entered but the doctor and the undertaker's man'. He gave an amusing sketch of his mother's parlour, with its antimacassars and wax flowers. It could have been Raymond Unwin talking. Burns also alluded several times to the evils of drink, one of the Englishman's 'besetting sins'. He looked forward to the day when a Licensing Bill would 'get rid of 25,000 or 30,000 public houses (*applause*)'. As he succinctly concluded, 'if we had more cottages and fewer public-houses, we could do with fewer asylums'.

Nowadays it is perhaps hard to understand the Victorian and Edwardian horror of drink. The temperance movement in its various forms was a mass movement right up to the First World War; its adherents were from every part of the political spectrum, followers of every creed – or lack of creed. There was an underlying terror in the nineteenth century of the unruliness of the masses, a conviction that revolution was never far away; and nothing, it was felt, could more surely unleash that unruliness than drink. Temperance was, therefore, essentially a form of social control.

The enthusiasm for it on co-partnership estates is therefore dubious, especially at Brentham, which had been conceived in a public house. It is notable that Vivian took to writing that Ealing Tenants owed its existence to a meeting in 'the Haven Assembly Rooms', thereby cleansing its history of the taint of drink. Brentham remained resolutely dry – as Hampstead Garden Suburb still is – for 35 years after it was founded. The banning of drink was written into the first set of rules for the Institute, and several times Ealing Tenants opposed attempts in the district to open pubs. In 1910 they also successfully opposed the application by F.S. Stowell for a beer licence for a shop in Pitshanger Lane, just off the estate, although he was successful later. Indeed the shop remained Stowell's until after the Second World War, and it is still an off-licence (108 Pitshanger Lane). The lack of drink appears not to have worried the early tenants unduly. The sons and daughters of several recall their parents walking to the Fox and Goose at Alperton. Another tenant, J.G. Taylor, looking back to these days in the late 1940s, recalled that bottles were routinely, if discreetly, smuggled into the Club.

LEFT: *Temporary allotments, Winscombe Crescent, c. 1909. Ealing Tenants had created more than 30 allotments by 1910, mostly in the back land between Ludlow and Denison Roads and Ludlow and Neville Roads. The allotments in this photograph were soon built over by 2–12 Winscombe Crescent. Fruit, vegetables and roses, for which Brentham's gardeners became famous, were the usual crops.*

One of the 'healthy' distractions from drink was gardening. The gardening competitions continued, with various judges including Henry Howard, like Richard Dean a Fellow of the Royal Horticultural Society. From early in 1909 the possibilities for cultivation were extended by the development of allotments. The first of these were three temporary allotments, on land that was soon to have 2–12 Winscombe Crescent built on it. By the end of 1909 nine further allotments had been created on the land between Ludlow and Neville Roads, and by the following autumn a further 20 allotments had been created between Ludlow and Denison Roads, and between Brunner Road and Brentham Way, all the plots being between five and seven rods (126–77 m²) in size. The rents were ten shillings a year for members, and eleven shillings a year for non-members. By the end of 1910 such was the demand for allotments that eligibility was restricted to members. It was reported before the First World War that there were 2,000 rose trees in Brentham, as a result of which the suburb became famous locally for its roses. The first Rose Show was held in 1910.

By 1904 a Horticultural Society had been formed to assist gardeners, and seeds and other gardening essentials were made available at favourable prices. Early in 1911 the gardeners' society – it is not clear if this is the same as the Horticultural Society – had taken over an acre of land near the Brent to demonstrate which species of plants would flourish in Brentham. They were also given partial use, at a nominal rent, of Pitshanger farmhouse which, since the last land acquisition in 1909, had belonged to Ealing Tenants. Various forms of 'intense cultivation on the French method', which involved cultivation under glass, were tried; mushrooms were grown in the dark, favourable conditions of the farmhouse's basement – until it was discovered that rats are partial to mushrooms.

The gardeners and the rats were not the only occupants of Pitshanger farmhouse. In July 1909 Arts and Crafts classes had been started on the estate. These took various forms. Carpentry classes were especially popular, and early in 1910 the carpenters were given the use of the lower rooms in Pitshanger farmhouse, where woodworking benches were fitted. A painting class led by an artist, Wilfrid Walter, met at the institute in Woodfield Crescent. Its main achievement was the decoration, early in 1910, of the walls of the institute. The decor consisted of a frieze round the walls, of 'a running pattern of holly against which are relieved, every few feet, light medallions containing a flower and bird alternatively, painted on a blue ground, one of each for every month of the year'. Mr Walter stressed the importance of decoration as a collective endeavour. Both the type of decoration and the way it was produced were models of Arts and Crafts practice – at least, until the art class lost interest and disbanded in November 1910. The carpentry class was more popular, and by 1912 they were producing what was described as 'garden-suburb-style furniture'. It is significant that although the houses being built by this time were Arts and Crafts in style, the building workers were attending technical classes in Chiswick rather than the craft-based classes arranged for the tenants, which were essentially a leisure activity.

As Pitshanger farmhouse was pressed into service, so was the cricket pavilion. In July 1910 a kindergarten school was started for children aged four to eight. Healthy and happy conditions were stressed, with 'all lessons and exercises to be taken in the open air'; the changeable British weather meant that this latter aim was rarely achieved, as one of the kindergarten's first pupils, Doris Palmer, recalls.

All this varied social and sporting activity made it increasingly evident how much the new permanent institute was needed. Building work on the new site in Meadvale Road started in the autumn of 1910, and was completed by the following spring. Number 33 Woodfield Crescent was duly turned into a house by the insertion of walls and staircase, then let. The accommodation in the new Institute was prodigious in comparison with the old one – even with the Hampstead Garden Suburb Clubhouse, or the Pixmore Institute in Letchworth. There was a large hall for concerts, lectures and plays, on the ground floor. Above this was a billiard room with three full-size tables, and in the long walls of this room were inglenook-style 'recesses for the enjoyment of quiet games of draughts, chess, cards etc'. At the end of the building, towards

Meadvale Road, was a reading room on the ground floor, to house the growing library; above this was a 'ladies' room' (meaning a room for ladies, not a lavatory). The tower contained committee rooms, and at the other end of the building, overlooking the new recreation ground, was a flat intended for a caretaker.

ABOVE: *The Brentham Institute in Meadvale Road, c. 1911. The possibilities for education and entertainment were greatly enhanced when this much larger building was opened in 1911.*

RIGHT: *The opening of the Brentham Institute, 27 May 1911. This was a great day in the history of Brentham, as royalty – Queen Victoria's youngest son, the Duke of Connaught – had agreed to open the Institute. This guard of honour at the front door was composed of 14 little girls, each carrying a wand with the name of a co-partnership estate. Doris Palmer (third from left) remembers the day as exceptionally hot – especially as she was wrapped up in several layers of winter petticoats.*

The day fixed for the opening of the Institute was 27 May 1911, and not content with a cabinet minister, Ealing Tenants had this time succeeded in attracting royalty to do the honours. Prince Arthur, Duke of Connaught, was Queen Victoria's youngest son, and was soon to replace Earl Grey, who had persuaded him to come to Brentham to open the Institute, as Governor General of Canada. The Duke had already taken an interest in town planning, a subject on which he had corresponded with John Burns in recent years. The opening of the Institute was a much grander affair than

the opening of the recreation ground had been three years earlier, and one newspaper reported a crowd of 10,000 people – which seems implausible. The Duke and Duchess arrived with Princess Patricia, their daughter, and Viscount Howick, who was Earl Grey's heir and the future chairman of Co-partnership Tenants. The Mayor and Mayoress of Ealing, Mr and Mrs J. Roose Francis, also turned up in their finery.

On arrival at the Institute the royal party was greeted by a rendition of the national anthem by the Brentham Choral Society, and by a group of 14 little girls, each carrying a wand inscribed with the name of a co-partnership estate. One of those 14 little girls, Doris Palmer, recalls the unseasonably hot day, when she felt stifled in the layers of her winter petticoat. The architect G.L. Sutcliffe then presented the Duke with a gold key with which to unlock the Institute. Following the performance of a specially composed 'Ode to the Duke and Duchess' by G.T. Fairweather and H.W. Pierce, the party proceeded to the balcony, where the Duke addressed the gathering. His speech was encouraging rather than stirring, as John Burns' had been, and he noted approvingly how the scheme was commercial rather than charitable in spirit. He concluded by saying that he was 'looking forward to seeing all those who enjoy sports, as Englishmen ought to do, hard at work at them . . .' Unlike John Burns he did not offer to take part in them. The party descended to the recreation ground and duly watched the good Englishmen at their sports – tennis, bowls, cricket and croquet – and the good English girls plaiting the maypole. A display was given by the Women's Sick and Wounded Convoy Corps, a body that had been set up by J.H. Greenhalgh's new wife, the formidable Mabel St Clair Stobart. The party rounded off the day with an inspection of one of the houses, 'Cornwood', 11 Neville Road.

The opening of the Institute was important for Ealing Tenants, as the event was widely covered and brought the estate much publicity. A commemorative booklet was produced in time for the opening in 1911, and in 1912 a further edition was produced, with additional photographs of the events of 27 May. In fact, on the estate itself, the opening of the Institute had more of a consolidating than a formative effect on the social life of the tenants. Its main purpose was to expand existing social and sporting activities, rather than to spawn a range of new ones.

The recreation ground – expanded to the west by seven acres from 1909 after the last land was bought – and new Institute were particularly beneficial to sport. By 1913 there were twelve tennis courts, and the tennis club had a membership of 130 who regularly played competitively against other local clubs. The cricket club had nearly as many members, and fielded a first and

ABOVE: *The royal party approaches the Institute, 27 May 1911. Fred Litchfield, left, is talking to the Duchess of Connaught. The Duke, doffing his bowler hat, is behind her with Ealing's Mayor, J. Roose Francis. To the right are the magnificently attired Mrs Roose Francis, and a slightly bemused Princess Patricia, the Duke and Duchess's daughter.*

RIGHT: *A display by the Women's Sick and Wounded Convoy Corps at the opening of the Institute, 27 May 1911. The Corps, for transporting wounded troops to hospital, was founded and organised by Mabel St Clair Stobart (in helmet, talking to the Duke), who had recently married J.H. Greenhalgh, Brentham's long-time benefactor. In 1912 the Corps travelled to Bulgaria and the Balkan War, and then to France and Serbia during the First World War.*

second XI, who played clubs from all over London, as well as such teams as the GWR cricketers. The bowling club continued to be popular with older members, although the green was generally acknowledged to be 'a bit of a curate's egg'.

There is no doubt that sport was already the dominant recreation at Brentham by the time the First World War broke out, but this does not mean that the co-partnership quest for a better world had been forgotten.

Educational classes in French conversation and economics were started. One of the tutors of the latter was Hugh Dalton, later a Labour Chancellor of the Exchequer. Lectures and debates continued, the programmes for these showing the usual pragmatic mix of the serious and improving, in various forms, and topics of local or natural interest: subjects included 'Proportional Representation', 'Savonarola', a 'debate on the abolition of poverty from the viewpoints of

Liberal, Labour and Conservative', 'A Middlesex Stream' and 'Birds of Middlesex'. The 'Brentham Parliament', however, a debating society mimicking the procedures of Parliament that had started in the old institute, faltered for a while because of 'difficulties forming the parties'. The committee occasionally complained that insufficient interest was shown in some of the lectures, but this could not be said of the more conventional social activities. There were whist drives and a chess club, and the weekly dance was especially popular.

All this is not to suggest that there were not new activities, both sporting and social. The golf club, which admitted women as well as men, had been in its infancy when the Institute opened, and an 18-hole putting course had been established around that time. This was replaced in March 1914 by a nine-hole pitch-and-putt course – 'the first of its kind in London' – on the north-west side of the recreation ground. A croquet lawn was also laid out, and by 1912 the section was competing against other clubs. A hockey club begun in 1911 was also fielding a team against other London clubs (including Argyle, Kensington, Ealing Wesleyan and Bentinck) by the following summer. Rambling and cycling clubs were also started, making regular trips around the district, to Ruislip and beyond.

Among non-sporting recreations that grew after 1911 was the camera club. A darkroom was set up in the pavilion, with lockers for equipment and an enlarger. By 1912 it was reported that 'a good start has been made in recording the history of Brentham in pictures' – several of the photographs in this book are Brentham Camera Club productions – and by 1914 room number 4 in the Institute had been turned into a portrait studio with lights all round and a backdrop.

It was not just the Institute that changed life in Brentham in the year or two before the First World War. In 1912 Brentham became more accessible, and therefore more attractive to commuting tenants, when Brentham Halt station opened at Hanger Lane, a shorter walk than Ealing Broadway station, although the services were never as regular.

Another innovation that was not brought about by Ealing Tenants Ltd (although they did subsidise it) was the publication of *The Brentham Magazine*. The magazine, which was edited by a schoolteacher,

ABOVE: *The new bowling green on the recreation ground, c. 1916. The bowling club was one of the few clubs that flourished throughout the First World War – most of the members were too old for military service. The man on the left with the beard is John Allport, long-time committee member and a stalwart of the club and Institute.*

ABOVE: *Harold Allport and Elsie Roe, c. 1912. This couple had a co-partnership romance: Elsie's father was the pioneer Edmund Roe, and Harold's was John Allport, a fellow committee-member of Roe's. Motorcycles were a popular form of Brentham transport, increasingly so after the First World War, when many tenants were given permission to erect a cycle shed in their gardens.*

W.E. Reading, provides a valuable record of the years between 1913 and 1925. Mr Reading was his own man, and although many of the articles are parochial and made obscure now by 'in-jokes', the tone is much less 'pollyanna-ish' than most contemporary newspaper and magazine reports. These latter were effectively controlled by Ealing Tenants' general committee, who would respond to journalists interested in the goings on in Brentham.

So far, with the exception of some of the lectures, so conventional. But what of Brentham's putative

reputation for cranks, alluded to in the quotation from George Orwell at the beginning of this chapter? Were Brentham folk seen, as the early inhabitants of Letchworth were, according to contemporary cartoons, as sandal-wearing vegetarian exponents of free love? The answer seems to depend on whom you asked. Yes, if you were to believe C.G. Harper, the author of a book called *Motor Rides Round London*, published in 1919: 'The village seen away to the left is the new "garden suburb" of Brentham, inhabited by quaint people who subsist upon lentils and mental injections of Fabianism, administered at the local institute which dominates the place'.

But however much they affected to believe this, the rest of Ealing appeared to know that Brenthamites were not so odd really. According to a column in the *Middlesex County Times*, 'although Ealing people pretend to regard the suburb as a community of cranks, yet they appear most happy when showing their "town" friends around its gardens and recreation grounds . . .' The crankiness extended to debates at the Institute on the merits of vegetarianism, but when it came to the vote, the flesh-eaters won.

Although Brentham may never have attracted a middle-class hard core of Simple Lifers, as Letchworth did in its early days, there were other ways, apart from the highly developed social life and the picturesqueness of its houses and gardens, in which it differed from an average London suburb – notably in attitudes to religion and politics.

Although he did not reveal his beliefs in print, it is fairly clear that Henry Vivian was not a practising Christian. Despite his concern not to antagonise potential supporters, he could not help letting slip an occasional anti-clerical sentiment. As he expressed it in 1905, 'My hope is that we shall be equal to our growing opportunities, that we shall not regard the highest conceptions of human conduct and life as only fit to be . . . talked about by ministers to congregations once a week . . .' Of the other prominent pioneers and other early supporters, the majority appear to have been followers of one or other of the non-conformist churches – Methodists, Baptists and Congregationalists.

One thing is certain, though; that there was a slight coolness towards the established church in particular and to the idea of Ealing Tenants building a church on the estate. In 1907 an offer by Messrs Kerby & Sons to erect a cross on the estate met a lukewarm response from the committee, and was not pursued. The following year a request from a tenant, J.D. Hawkin, to build a 'hall for religious purposes' was turned down flat. By 1911, however, the attitude to building a church on the estate had softened a bit. When Ealing Tenants were approached by the vestries of St Stephen's and St Peter's churches about building a church at the corner of Denison Road and Pitshanger Lane to replace the iron church (also called St Barnabas) that had been built in 1908 on Pitshanger Lane, their response was equable enough. The Church was willing to pay a substantial sum – more than £1,000 – for the land, after all. The Ealing Tenants committee's main concern seems to have been bell-ringing, and how to restrict it. But a circular sent round Brentham by the Rev. Walter Mitchell shortly before the foundation stone was laid in June 1914, indicates his awareness that Brentham was hardly a staunch Anglican community. He wrote that although he was a resolute 'churchman', he was 'no bigot' and

was keen to 'keep in touch' with people in Brentham. As the *Middlesex County Times* commented: 'This is just the spirit to command respect in a suburb where so many varieties of opinion are represented'.

This variety can be seen in the various groups that hired the hall or other rooms in the Institute. Wesleyans, under the Rev. Odery, held a regular Sunday evening service and Sunday school there from 1911. In 1914 Quakers held a meeting in Brentham to explain their aims. These were specifically religious meetings, but the Institute also had Ethical Society meetings for adults and Ethical Sunday school for children. Despite the religious overtones of the name 'Sunday school' (perhaps intended to soothe more conventional tastes), the Ethical Society was a secularist organisation.

One of the most popular meetings – and symptomatic of co-partnership pragmatism in contriving to give a platform to both religious and secular views (and various shades of each) – was the Brentham PSA meeting. The initials stood for Pleasant Sunday Afternoon. These were first organised in 1910 at the old institute by S.B. Hocking, a civil servant who had moved that year into 9 Meadvale Road. Services were ecumenical in the extreme. The meetings always had the same format, with an address on a particular subject and musical solos with piano accompaniment. The speakers ranged from Church of England vicars, to non-conformist ministers, to local worthies. Several speakers were members of the Brotherhood Church, founded in 1891 by the Rev. J. Bruce Wallace, a friend of Ebenezer Howard. Wallace had helped found Topolobampo, an Owenite colony in Mexico, in the 1890s. Brotherhood Church meetings consisted of a short service followed by an improvised vegetarian meal and a discussion that could go on for

"The most graceful bicycle of the day."
—*The Cycle Trader.*

"The HUMBER cannot be surpassed for ease of running."
R. J. MECREDY, Esq., in the *Daily Graphic.*

FOR TOWN OR COUNTRY.
**HUMBER CYCLES,**
Built by the King's Cycle Makers
Prices from £8 8s.
Easy Payments 9/- per month.
Call and inspect the latest Models.
Catalogue Free.

UXBRIDGE—T. S. ROSE, 43, New Windsor St.
HIGH WYCOMBE—J. C. WOODBRIDGE, 8/10, Queen's Square.
NORTHWOOD—HUTSON and MURRAY, Church Road.

ABOVE: *Advertisement for Humber Cycles, 1907. Cycling was an affordable form of recreation for most residents of Brentham. The estate's position on what was then the green fringes of London, meant there were ample opportunities for pleasant cycle rides locally, and a cycle club for men and women was in existence by the First World War.*

ABOVE: *On the recreation ground, c. 1912. The 'rec', as it was always known, became the focus for leisure activities for residents of all ages.*

several hours. The Brentham PSA was clearly less outré, but addresses were as diverse as the speakers. Sir Julius Benn spoke on 'Life', Mr H. Davis on 'Hope'. Rev. Austin Thompson spoke of his experience of 'a living personal God', while Mr T. Weeks of Northampton Brotherhood gave an address that was both anarchistic and pacifist, on 'the growing demand for the suppression of war'. Perhaps it was not so surprising, therefore, that Brentham Garden Suburb was suspected, by the rest of Ealing, of harbouring cranks and subversives.

Political views on the estate also differed from those of the rest of the Ealing electorate. Ealing Tenants as an organisation was staunchly Liberal, and mildly suspicious of socialism that tended to the collectivist. Despite this, there is evidence of considerable socialist activism in Brentham before the First World War. F.J. Gould, the writer who lived at Armorel in Woodfield Avenue from 1910 to his death in 1938, was secretary of the Ealing branch of the Independent Labour Party; he organised meetings in the Institute and at schools in North Ealing in support of causes such as women's suffrage. In the local elections of 1912, two Brentham tenants, Miss D. Nesbitt of Brunner Road and J. Connor, stood as candidates of the short-lived British Socialist Party in Mount Park and Castlebar wards respectively. It is telling that despite their suspicion of both socialist parties, Ealing Tenants Ltd offered support to these candidates; they may have been socialists, but they were *our* socialists, the Brentham connection apparently outweighing political considerations.

Perhaps this is the key to Brentham's social life before the First World War – co-partnership was a pragmatic philosophy, the union of labour and capital for the resolution of class differences, and tolerance of political and religious difference was merely an extension of this. But the pragmatism of co-partnership also meant it was not necessarily prescriptive. However much Ealing Tenants Ltd might think they knew what was best for their tenants and workers, they were sufficiently steeped in the idea of self-help and democratic self-determination – or perhaps it was that they were just becoming increasingly wrapped up in the business side of the estate – to let the tenants get on with it themselves. Which is, by and large, what they did.

# 5

# Brentham May Day before 1914:
## the origins of a twentieth-century custom

*You must wake and call me early, call me early, mother dear . . .*
*For I'm to be Queen o' the May, mother, I'm to be Queen o' the May.*
ALFRED TENNYSON, *The May Queen*, 1832

A S THIS BOOK GOES TO PRESS, preparations are under way for Brentham's leading annual event, the May Day procession. Dance steps are being learnt, a May Queen is being chosen and the maypole is being taken out of storage. On a Saturday in late May, a procession of characters that include a 'Jack-in-the-green', Britannia and May Queens past and present, will set off from the Brentham Club to parade round the streets of Brentham, before returning to the Club grounds. There, the new May Queen will be crowned, the maypole will be plaited by little dancers dressed in white and country dances will be performed. The care devoted to these preparations is partly inspired by the idea that this activity is traditional, that it has taken place in Brentham since before the First World War, and elsewhere in the villages of England since 'time immemorial'. But is there any truth in this idea?

The notion that traditions are passed down to us intact by some kind of folk memory is very attractive.

It is also very tenacious. But the truth is that traditions evolve, become established then slowly die out, only to be revived in a way that owes little in form or meaning to the original. So it has been with May Day. But many of the ideas about May Day and its customs that people have today, and indeed had 90 years ago when Brentham first celebrated May Day, derive from two sources that do not always relate to any historical facts. The first is the nineteenth-century notion of 'Merrie England', of an 'olden time' (any period between the Middle Ages and Tudor times) before cities and factories, when in England's villages rich and poor knew their place and lived together in harmony. A crucial part of this social cohesion was the regular participation in communal festivities, including 'bringing in the May' with feasting, dancing and plaiting the maypole. This nostalgic vision became entrenched in the nineteenth century as the population became increasingly urbanised and the countryside became an environment known only at one remove by the majority of people.

FACING PAGE: *The road to Brentham Halt station, c. 1914. This station opened in 1912, and provided an alternative route into London for Brentham commuters. Many, however, preferred to make the longer trip down to Ealing Broadway, which provided a much more frequent service. This path, known as 'China Alley', was popular with courting couples.*

The second source, influential at the end of the nineteenth century and the beginning of the twentieth century, was Sir James Frazer's vast compendium of folk custom, *The Golden Bough*. The suggestion was that in Britain a native pagan religion survived the arrival of the Romans and of Christianity in a covert form, in legends, dances, rites and superstitions. This notion of the significance of folk customs was propagated with great success by the English Folk Dance and

Song Society, and by the Folk-Lore Society; so much so, that throughout most of the twentieth century it was taken as a given truth.

But what is the truth about May Day and the way it was celebrated in the past? Although it is probably true that from 'time immemorial' the arrival of summer has been celebrated, the historical evidence for 'bringing in the May' goes back in Britain only as far as the thirteenth century. Over the following two or three hundred years, the term in literary sources and historical documents seems to refer to a gathering of flowers and young foliage to celebrate the coming of summer. A common feature was the making of garlands of foliage or flowers. These were used to decorate houses or were carried around as the focus for appeals for money.

Between the fifteenth and seventeenth centuries, the Church, always keen to control and benefit from mass festivities, instituted 'church ales'. These generally included a procession with a 'mock king' or 'summer king' to preside over the occasion or, much more rarely, a May Queen; May games were another feature. These games (which did not just take place at church ales) took a wide variety of forms. An important aspect, and a focal point of revived May Days in the nineteenth and twentieth centuries, is the maypole. The earliest recorded ones date from the fourteenth century, and there seem to have been two principal types. There were large permanent maypoles (although they could be taken down and stored), and two examples in London are well recorded: one in Cornhill in the City (the church of St Andrew Undershaft was so called because the pole was higher than the church), and another in the Strand. The second kind would be erected anew each year. The poles could be painted or decorated in

*LEFT: 'The maypole in the 16th century', by Joseph Nash. This image probably tells us more about the 'Merrie England' imaginings of the early nineteenth-century artist who created it, than it does about May customs in the sixteenth century. Historical records indicate that the occasions were often less decorous than this image suggests.*

ABOVE: *Milkmaids dance with a pile of silver objects on May Day. The headdress of greenery and silverware evolved in time into the wicker frame covered in greenery worn by the 'Jack-in-the-green' character associated with May Day.*

a variety of ways, with flags, flowers or garlands. Although they were a focus for dancing, there is no evidence that the ribbons attached to the maypoles were anything other than decorative. The dancing seems to have involved circling by dancers holding hands, and the complex plaiting of the ribbons came later, an innovation of the nineteenth century. Nor is there any evidence that maypoles were seen as phallic fertility

symbols (an idea popular in the twentieth century), or that, as Sir James Frazer suggested, they were believed to be inhabited by 'tree spirits'.

Common features of May revels until the sixteenth century were ballads, plays and processions involving the legendary English hero Robin Hood and possibly the figures of Friar Tuck and Maid Marian. These Robin Hood plays sometimes included the morris, a dance that has come to symbolise English folk dancing. It has, perhaps, been the most misrepresented of English folk customs, as throughout the twentieth century it was seen both as a rural, 'peasant' dance and one that had an unbroken descent from 'an ancient folk rite to induce fertility'. In fact, research since the 1950s has revealed that the morris began as an entertainment at the royal court (first recorded in the fifteenth century), and that it was 'a miniature romantic drama, in which a set of young male dancers competed for the hand of a lady, who chose instead to give her favours to a fool'. The dancers, liberally bedecked with bells, made movements characterised by great energy. From the court, the dance moved to the rest of London in the sixteenth century, then to other towns, and only later to the countryside, where numerous local variants were established by the eighteenth century. The morris is therefore urban and royal in origin.

Although May revels often formed part of Church-controlled festivities, by the sixteenth century they were attracting disapproval from Protestant commentators who saw them as occasions for debauchery by the young men and women who went to the woods to collect the greenery. One spoke of 'divers dirty sluts' wandering the countryside and cavorting in ditches. This disapproval reached its height in 1644, when an ordinance of the Long Parliament directed that maypoles be removed. The restoration of the monarchy in 1660 saw a revival of maypoles as the focus for dancing and May revels, and they remained common well into the eighteenth century. By around 1800, however, the various activities associated with them were in decline, and maypoles were often neglected and left to rot.

Yet, even as the traditional May revels were dying out, a new form of May Day was developing. From the early nineteenth century antiquarians began to take an interest in folk customs, and write about them, often with scant regard to historical fact. At the same time, the novelist Sir Walter Scott was popularising a vision of the Middle Ages as a time of chivalry, with bonds between rulers and ruled cemented by traditional festivals. Writers such as Tennyson, whose hugely popular poem *The May Queen* was published in 1832, took up the topic, and plays with May themes proliferated on the London stage in the 1830s and 1840s. These productions included May Queens, morris dancing and maypoles, and it was in one of these – *Richard Plantagenet* staged at the Victoria Theatre in 1836 – that the first recorded instance took place of maypole plaiting by dancers holding ribbons attached to the top of the pole. From the stage, displays involving May Queens and maypole dancing spread, and in the 1850s and 1860s they were a common feature of many types of popular urban entertainment.

Although this May revival was urban in origin, it was the rural revival of May ceremonies as a specifically children's activity that became more influential. From the 1840s a number of country squires began to see revived May revels as a wholesome and enjoyable way of enhancing social accord between the classes. One

of these squires was Roland Eyles Egerton-Warburton, whose seat was at Arley Hall in Cheshire. From the 1840s to the 1860s he presided over an event that included the crowning of a May Queen and maypole dancing. The popularity of this event led to numerous others in the following half century in neighbouring northwestern counties. These established the basic format of May Queen coronation, procession and dancing that was used into the twentieth century. One of these, at Knutsford, which included a Jack-in-the-green figure, survives to this day. It was probably one of these northwestern May Days that John Ruskin witnessed in the 1860s and that inspired him to collaborate with the principal of Whitelands College, a women's teacher-training college in Chelsea, to introduce a May Queen ceremony there in 1881. Teachers from Whitelands took the ceremony with them, and as a result May Queen ceremonies became a feature of school life nationally in the late nineteenth and early twentieth centuries.

It was at this period that Frazer's *The Golden Bough* popularised the belief that customs including May revels represented a survival of pagan ritual. These ideas in turn became associated with the notion that folk customs were a democratic expression of popular culture, and this helps account for the enthusiasm for revivals of May revels in 'progressive' circles. The early years of the twentieth century also saw renewed interest in folk song and dance generally, as members of the Folk Song and Dance Societies (they later merged) 'collected' examples from performers around the country. These 'collected' songs and dances came to be seen as immutable traditional forms, despite the fact that some of them later turned out to be nineteenth-century inventions created for revived May Days and other festivities.

RIGHT: *An early nineteenth-century Jack-in-the-green. Despite the widely held fanciful view that the Jack-in-the-green owes its origin to pagan customs associated with 'tree spirits', all the historical evidence points to it as an urban custom of seventeenth-century origin, which came to be identified mainly with chimney sweeps' parades. This sketch captures the boisterous antics of the characters – they include a lord and lady – that drew disapproval from the authorities in the nineteenth century.*

A common feature of the revived May Days in the twentieth century that has been reinterpreted out of all recognition, is the figure of the Jack-in-the-green. A man in the May Day procession wears a conical or bee-hive-shaped wooden or wicker frame, densely covered in greenery. Under the influence of *The Golden Bough*, and later writings by Lady Raglan, this figure has come to be seen as 'a vegetation spirit' or 'green man', and associated with the carved heads, entwined with branches, found in late medieval churches. But research by Roy Judge, who has exposed many of the nineteenth- and early twentieth-century suppositions about May Day as fanciful, has revealed a more recent origin for the Jack-in-the-green.

In the seventeenth century London milkmaids would dance to earn money on May Day, with their pails and heads crowned with flowers. Later in the century the headgear had evolved to include ribbons, flowers and silverware. The style was copied by chimney sweeps, who gradually monopolised the activity. Throughout the eighteenth century the frame for the headgear gradually grew in size, and greenery replaced the silverware. In the nineteenth century the capering antics of the Jack-in-the-green, who was often accompanied by a lord and lady, was a common sight in May Day sweeps' parades in London and the surrounding area, but the custom was all but extinct by the end of the century. By that time, however, it had attracted the attention of the May Day revivalists, who embraced it as a supposedly ancient custom.

The revived May Days continued successfully as a children's event, with pretty accoutrements such as the May Queen coronation, maypole plaiting, white costumes and floral decorations. And while the

self-conscious nostalgia of the May Day revivalists continued, so too did the tendency for customs to evolve and change out of recognition. Some of these survivals, such as the Helston Furry and the Padstow Hobby Horse in Cornwall, retained their 'folk' quality. Others were more responsive to social changes. For example, church ales, which were no longer ecclesiastical festivities in the seventeenth century, survived as secular occasions. By the nineteenth century they were often controlled by bodies such as friendly societies or temperance groups. There might be Whitsun parades with colourful banners that would end, as in the church ales, with feasting and games – by this time often just for the benefit of the children.

A local example of a May Day event that owed nothing to folk revivalists was the Ealing tradesmen's

ABOVE: *The first Brentham maypole dancers, 1906. Many of the features of children's May Days at this time were derived from Whitelands College in Chelsea, which had started a May Day celebration in 1881, under the guidance of John Ruskin.*

parade that took place on or around 1 May each year, from the 1890s up to the First World War, and revived in the 1920s as an RSPCA-run horse-and-dog show. The parade included the council's fire engines and local delivery vans (all horse-drawn) and ended on Ealing Common, where prizes were awarded for the best-turned-out horses. The only feature that might have owed something to 'folkery' was the way the vans, even the fire engines, were decorated, usually with ribbons, but sometimes with flowers.

It was against this rich and varied background of survivals and revivals that Brentham's May Day celebrations were instituted in the early years of the twentieth century. In fact, the first May celebration in Brentham did not take place in May at all, but in June 1906. The previous year, in May 1905, the committee of Ealing Tenants Ltd had decided to have a 'May day concert' with 'sports, maypole, tea, etc.' on 27 May 1905, to celebrate the fourth anniversary of the society. However, although the party went ahead that day, with children participating in sports, the maypole was absent. No reason is given. Perhaps no one could be found to teach the dancing.

The following year, for the fifth anniversary, the maypole appeared for the first time. On 9 June 1906 a party was held under the 'spreading oaks' behind the old institute at 33 Woodfield Crescent. There a 30ft maypole 'with a gaily decorated top' had been erected. At 5 o'clock, after the sports had concluded, 15 'gaily dressed maidens . . . handled the parti-coloured ribbons and after a display of part singing, gave an exhibition of intricate movements, composed of alternate march and dance, and covered the pole with a plait, the process being reversed, it was unplaited without a hitch'. Later that evening, by popular demand, the dancing was repeated by the light of Japanese lanterns. The *County Times*, in reporting the event, stressed the notion of tradition and continuity, by suggesting that the scene brought 'back pleasant memories to some of the older spectators who can recollect when May-day festivities were the rule and not the exception'. Six weeks later, on 21 July 1906, the maypole dancers were at work again, entertaining the children of the Paddington school for disabled children on their visit to Brentham.

What is notable here is that at this date there is no sense that the plaiting of the maypole was part of a wider May Day celebration. The dancers were there to celebrate a specific Ealing Tenants anniversary, or to entertain their guests. The rest of the entertainment on these two occasions – sports, the Ealing Tenants Blackbirds boys, Punch and Judy – did not have a particular folk-revival resonance, and was typical popular entertainment of the time. There was no May Day procession, no Jack-in-the-green, not even a May Queen. And this continued to be the case, with one exception, until after the First World War.

The next time the Brentham maypole dancers were seen was not in Brentham at all, but at the 'cutting of the first sod' by Henrietta Barnett at Hampstead Garden Suburb on 2 May 1907. There the Ealing children braided the maypole while singing 'May songs' – apparently a new feature of their repertory. *Co-partnership* reported that 'although the wind blew very roughly with consequent ill-effects on the ribbons, the children's dances went with plenty of spirit'. Gladys Bateman, one of the Brentham children, presented a bouquet of flowers to Mrs Barnett, but there was still, apparently, no May Queen. The children had been taught the songs and dances by Mr and Mrs Ernest White; it was Ernest White who later ran the wood-work classes in Brentham where residents could learn to make 'garden-suburb-style furniture'.

The Hampstead ceremony seems to have been the only May event celebrated that year by the Ealing children. But the next year, 1908, saw the children back at work on their home turf, and it also saw the first

Brentham May Queen. The occasion was, again, not a specific May festival, but the official opening of the recreation ground by John Burns, on Whit Monday, the workers' holiday that had gradually evolved from the medieval church ales.

This spirit is reflected in the programme of sports, maypole dancing and 'feasting on the recreation ground' that day. The May Queen first made her appearance

ABOVE: *Cutting the first sod at Hampstead Garden Suburb, 2 May 1907. As Henrietta Barnett wields the spade Henry Vivian (behind her) and Fred Litchfield (far right) look on. Brentham maypole dancers Gladys Bateman (left) and William Hutchings's daughter, Winnie (right), are in front.*

when John Burns arrived at the entrance to the estate at the top of Brentham Way. There Hubert Brampton presented Burns with the 'Freedom of Brentham' and an album, while Gladys Kelly, the May Queen, presented Mrs Burns with a bouquet. How and when the Queen was chosen is uncertain, but a photograph taken on the recreation ground suggests she may have been 'crowned' earlier the same day. The party of Brenthamites and visitors then walked from Winscombe Crescent to the recreation ground. This was not an organised procession as in later years, although one report mentions a 'children's procession' later in the afternoon, when the children also danced and braided the maypole.

There then followed a gap of three years, when May revels were apparently forgotten in Brentham. And when they were next celebrated – at the opening of the Institute by the Duke of Connaught on 27 May 1911 – once again the maypole braiding was subsumed into a programme of children's sports and games, warranting only a passing mention in reports of the occasion.

Although Gladys Kelly in 1908 was the only Brentham May Queen before the First World War, other May Queens were being crowned in the Borough of Ealing as part of the wider revival of May Day festivities in schools. From 1908 Drayton Girls' School was staging a May Day revel on the first Wednesday in May, with a May Queen elected by the pupils, a festival that survived at least into the 1920s. By 1914 this had become a much more complex affair than the isolated instances of maypole dancing in Brentham; it included a procession round the playground with Jack-in-the-green and sweeps, and Robin Hood accompanied by his Merry Men and Maid Marian; it also included maypole plaiting and the coronation of the May Queen.

In Acton, from 1910, the boys and girls of Acton Wells School elected a May Queen and organised a procession of May Queen and Maids of Honour, as well as an extensive programme of May songs and dances. This was still an annual event in the early 1930s, by which time, a May King was being crowned alongside the May Queen. Whether this was an expression of sexual equality, or an acknowledgment of the historical significance of the King of the May, is not recorded.

These May Day activities around Britain, of which the Brentham and Ealing festivals are just a sample, were a further manifestation of the revival of Merrie England. They are another expression of the same impetus that inspired Raymond Unwin in his preference for rustic forms in his planning and architectural design; or, before him, William Morris, in his vision of England remade as a series of villages organised along the lines of medieval guilds. But just as Morris's nostalgic vision was allied to a socialist programme of economic and social reform, so too did the celebration of May Day have its radical and progressive manifestations. And this was not simply in the way that 1 May has become the workers' holiday. The holiday on 1 May is a red herring as far as May revels are concerned, as it commemorates a strike in the United States in 1890 that was supported by workers in France. But Merrie England and May Day also found radical expression, not least in the garden city and suburb movement, Brentham included.

From 1906 the garden city of Letchworth had a May Day celebration that combined features of both the Ealing civic May festival and the later Brentham May Day. These included a procession, a horse-and-cart competition, a baby show, maypole dancing on

PREVIOUS PAGE: *The first plaiting of the maypole at Brentham, 9 June 1906. Although reports of maypoles and maypole dancing go back several hundred years, the plaiting of ribbons only dates from the 1830s, when it was done in a London stage show. At Brentham the plaiting of the maypole on this first occasion was a one-off, performed at a party at the old institute at 33 Woodfield Crescent, to celebrate the fifth anniversary of Ealing Tenants Ltd. There was no parade and no May Queen.*

BELOW LEFT: *May Queen crowned. This is almost certainly the coronation of the first Brentham May Queen, Gladys Kelly, on 8 June 1908, the day John Burns opened the recreation ground.*

BELOW RIGHT: *The opening of the Institute, 27 May 1911. To the left in the distance the children are plaiting the maypole.*

Westholm Green, and a May Queen. Initially Letchworth May Day was no more overtly progressive than the Brentham maypole dancing of the time. But in 1909 and 1910 Letchworth staged a more ambitious May procession. This was intended to 'symbolize the forces, activities and interests of Garden City', with sections emblematic of House (May Queen, mothers, children and schools), Civic (the company, workers and the Parish council), National (various national bodies) and, ever conscious of the grander ambitions of the garden city idea, Universal (although 'university

graduates and the rest' seem a rather feeble symbol of the Universal). This was a step beyond the nostalgic aims of most May revel revivals, as the Letchworth local newspaper, *The City*, made explicit in its report: 'We find our feet placed on a new path, which may lead us, in the future, to who may say what varied goals in the realms of Art and Fellowship'.

The organisers of the Letchworth procession were partly inspired by the example of the historical pageants that became increasingly popular from the 1880s, particularly just before the First World War. In

Brentham, too, there was enthusiastic support for pageants. Such pageants, like May Day processions generally, could serve as vehicles both for this nostalgic longing for Merrie England, and for the progressive goals expressed by *The City*. In the words of Louis Parker, who was responsible for popularising this new type of pageant, pageants were a way of 'bringing rural life in England back to its old-time innocent gaiety while reviving . . . the noblest sort of patriotism'. Parker put on six pageants between 1905 and 1914; his example was widely followed, and generally these included an episode of May revels as a standard feature. Pageants of various kinds were performed at Hampstead Garden Suburb between 1910 and the 1930s.

The grandest pageant of the period just before the First World War was the Festival of Empire at Crystal Palace in 1911. 'The London of Merrie England: May Revels in the Days of Henry VIII' was performed, arranged by a group including Cecil Sharp, doyen of the English Folk Dance and Song Society. It is clear from Sharp's later comments that such May revels were generally regarded as a form of fertility ritual, a 'thanks to the earth spirit of fertility' – an echo of the ideas of James Frazer's *Golden Bough*. Others who took up pageantry with a May festivities' element were attracted by its progressive possibilities. In 1912 the anti-militarist 'Merrie England Corps of Young Citizens' performed 'May-pole revels' in Islington. And Brentham was not the only co-partnership estate to embrace the revived May Day. Harborne Tenants in Birmingham had May revels before the First World War, while Wavertree, the Liverpool garden suburb, celebrated midsummer with a Rose Queen festival.

It was against this varied background that an article by Eversley Hampton appeared in the May 1911 issue of *Co-partnership*. In it he commended the present revival of pageantry for the way that it broke down 'distinctions of social class' during rehearsals: 'All are working for the beauty of the ensemble, and anything but the Democratic or associative spirit is out of place'. As well as a social balm, pageants were an educative tool, stimulating 'new thoughts and ideas' and 'a larger sense of patriotism'. But Hampton had in mind a new type of pageant for a specific occasion. He felt that pageants could be 'utilised in the

ABOVE: *Children's maypole cart at the Hampstead Garden Suburb employees' festival, 3 May 1913. May Day celebrations were a common sight on all the co-partnership estates before the First World War, but very few were revived after 1918. The decorated 'babies' carts' made it possible for children too small to walk in the procession to participate in the celebrations.*

RIGHT: *Advertisement for the 1906 Co-operative Festival. These huge celebrations, often orchestrated by G.J. Holyoake, were a key event in the Co-operative calendar from the 1880s up to 1910.*

BELOW: *Coronation of the Rose Queen, Wavertree, Liverpool, c. 1910. Rose Queen festivals were a north-western variant on May Queen celebrations.*

development of the Co-partnership Idea', by presenting scenes from co-operative history, or demonstrating the 'before' and 'after'. By 'before' he meant the terrible conditions of the factory system in the early nineteenth century, by 'after' he meant the 'happy printer with his 48-hour week' and 'the well-nurtured women operatives'. Such a pageant served, therefore, not just as a sentimental evocation of old England, but to offer a picture of how things might be in the good time that was to come, so that 'what is now the dramatic insight may become the real life of the workaday world'.

This, then, was the new type of pageant. And Hampton suggested that such a pageant might be presented at the exhibitions that accompanied the Co-operative congresses. A co-operative pageant would liven up meetings, encourage social intermingling and provide inspiration for the future. The biggest of these events had always been the Crystal Palace Co-operative Festival that took place every August from the mid-1880s to 1910; G.J. Holyoake had been a guiding influence. From 1911 the festival was reinvented as the Co-partnership Festival, and was held that year in Hampstead Garden Suburb. The pageant performed, *Three Scenes from History*, was written by a suburb resident, Kate Murray. Mrs Murray was a university extension lecturer, a close friend of Henry Vivian's colleague Sybella Gurney, and a translator into modern English of classics such as Langland's *Piers Plowman* and Spenser's *Faerie Queen*. *Three Scenes from History* was evidently a success, as the next year, when Brentham hosted the Co-partnership Festival, Kate Murray was asked to write a new pageant.

The work she came up with, *Merrier England: A Pageant of Progress*, was a model of what Eversley Hampton had imagined for a co-partnership pageant.

And as the title suggests it combined rural nostalgia with co-partnership utopianism. Like her previous effort, the play had three scenes. The first represented a village in the year 1409, with cosy cottages, a village green and 'English craftsmen, happy, wise and gay'. Comic relief was provided by a jester who ended up in the stocks. The second scene was set in 1809, with 'Industrialism at its height. The starving populace for justice cry'. The imagery employed was 'on one side a dreary factory wall, on the other the backs of a street of mean houses'. This scene ends with an address by a character called the Reconciliator, who tells an incredulous worker that 'Masters and men must have the same interests in the end . . . You must firmly insist on your right to share in the profits your hard work makes for them . . . Every worker in a business should be a shareholder too.' To which the worker responds

ABOVE & LEFT: *Most of the cast (above) and Frank Hender (left) with a fellow forester in the* Merrier England *pageant, Brentham, August 1912.*

RIGHT: *In the first scene of the* Merrier England *pageant (above), set in 1409, 'the boy Alison' (W.H. Collinson) is led astray by 'Light of Love' (Ena Brampton) and her cohorts 'Vain Imaginings' (left, Ethel Brampton) and 'Dalliance' (right, Mrs Patten). In the final scene (below), Todd Carter wakes after 200 years asleep to find that the year is 2009, and the glorious co-partnership future has dawned.*

'Oh, my 'eavens'. Patronising in tone, and turgid in its dialogue, its co-partnership credentials were nevertheless immaculate. The final scene was the happy realisation of the Reconciliator's words, in 'a beautiful English town in the year 2009'. In fact, the scene bore a strong resemblance to a garden suburb in 1912.

The staging of *Merrier England* was a great achievement for Brentham, for it required 25 speaking parts and twice as many walk-ons. The latter were supplemented in the final crowd scene by visitors from Hampstead. One feature that puts the production firmly in the contemporary fashion for pageants with a May theme, is an interlude in the first scene when 'in trip a crowd of little Morris dancers, who foot it merrily in their dresses of heliotrope, telling of a "gaiety that rises in the heart of every man when he beholds the spring"'. What is notable about this is that the morris dancers were trained by a Miss Aschliemann of the Espérance Guild. The Guild was the creation of Mary Neal, a onetime colleague of Cecil Sharp who had fallen out with him over her interpretation of the morris. Sharp saw himself as the arbiter of the morris, and believed that it should only be performed by adult men, according to forms of dance that Sharp himself sanctioned. Mary Neal saw it more as a living form of dance, one that could develop, and one that could and should be performed by children of both sexes as well as adults. By the time the *Merrier England* pageant was performed Mary Neal and her Espérance approach to the morris were on the wane, but the performance of an Espérance morris dance at Brentham in 1912 ensured its survival there for a number of years.

The *Merrier England* pageant was a great success, repeated 'by popular demand' on several occasions in the following weeks. But it was a one-off for Brentham. Nothing on such a scale was performed there again, but two developments did follow. One was the setting up of the Brentham Players from the cast of the pageant. This drama society lasted in various forms into the 1960s, although right from the beginning its aspirations were more mainstream than Merrie England, performing such productions as Oscar Wilde's *The Importance of Being Earnest*. The other result of the pageant was directly related to its content. This was a morris-dancing class that was taught in the Institute over the winter of 1912 by a Brentham resident, Frank Chambers. It seems likely, since Chambers' class was for boys and girls, not adult men, that he followed the Espérance style of morris seen in the pageant, and although his class lasted only a few months, morris dancing occasionally featured in Brentham May Day festivities of the 1920s, thereby prolonging the survival of Mary Neal's approach to morris dancing for more than a decade.

LEFT: *Reprise of the morris dance from scene one of the* Merrier England *pageant, 1912. This style of morris dancing, performed by little girls, was popularised by Mary Neal and her Espérance Guild, and it was one of her pupils who taught the Brentham children the morris for the pageant. Soon this style of morris was eclipsed by the more familiar manner with adult men, but Brentham girls continued to dance the morris in this way at May Day celebrations into the 1920s.*

# 6

## The architecture and planning of Brentham, 1901–1915

*We shall . . . work up a small garden city on our own account.*
RICHARD WHITE, secretary of Ealing Tenants Ltd, January 1903

T IS DIFFICULT to arrive in Brentham purely by accident. Because of the sylvan boundary of the Brentham Club's grounds and the River Brent to the north, and the largely unbroken stretches of Woodfield Crescent and Fowlers Walk, there are really only three main routes into the suburb – Pitshanger Lane from the west, Eaton Rise from the south, and Brunswick Road from the east. Ironically, the route that is least likely to be chanced upon – from Mount Avenue – was conceived as the original entrance to the estate. But whichever route is taken, the visitor is bound to be struck by the contrast between the streets he has just left – the mix of thirties' and Edwardian terraced houses, postwar blocks of flats and large but conventional Victorian detached houses – and the rustic charm of Brentham with its characteristic small Arts and Crafts houses, low privet hedges and gently curving street pattern.

There is a conventional wisdom that Brentham has only two types of houses: the standard Edwardian terraces of Woodfield Road, Avenue and Crescent (the 'Woodfields') built between 1901 and 1906, and the picturesque Arts and Crafts houses in the rest of the suburb, the latter designed by F. Cavendish Pearson between 1906 and 1910 and by G.L. Sutcliffe between 1910 and 1915, to a plan by Raymond Unwin. While this is broadly true, the simplifications and omissions of this generalisation distort the picture of Brentham's architecture to a significant degree. For one thing this view ignores the fact that the suburb is not a fly in amber, frozen as G.L. Sutcliffe left it in 1915. A number of houses and flats were built after the First World War, some of which follow the garden suburb aesthetic, some of which followed contemporary architectural trends. And most houses of all periods in the suburb have been altered to some extent over the years.

Most crucially it ignores the extent to which the designing of Brentham was a collective endeavour. There is always a danger in treating architecture – much as art historians of a connoisseurial bent treat easel paintings – as the product of a single artist/architect working in isolation to produce a work of art that is the unmediated outpouring of his creative genius. But at Brentham this approach is especially inappropriate. While the role of the architects involved should not be underestimated, Brentham's appearance owed more than most comparable contemporary estates to the input of the client, which until 1936 was usually the committee of Ealing Tenants Ltd, and beyond them, the tenants themselves.

Just how this interplay of architect and client affected Brentham emerges only in the 'architect-designed' areas built after 1906. But the building of the Woodfields also demonstrates that even where there was no architect, the creation of houses was more than a simple matter of builders following a standard design; rather, it was the result of a complex negotiation between builders, landlords and clients all responding to a variety of conditions and demands. The situation was further complicated because the special nature of co-partnership meant that there were considerable overlaps between these three groups of people.

One of the principal factors affecting the design of the Woodfields seems to have been the tenure of the land. The first plots of land in most of the area up to 1906–7, were bought in small leasehold parcels. According to Vivian, writing in 1906, 'on [Ealing Tenants'] first land the lines of development were already laid down; roads were made and stipulations imposed concerning elevations'. There may have been an element of exaggeration in Vivian's words. The Woodfields were beginning to look a little old-fashioned by 1906, compared with Letchworth and what was projected for Hampstead Garden Suburb, and he may have wished to suggest that the apparently conventional appearance of the Woodfields was entirely

due to the caution of Charles and Edward Millard, the freeholders of the land. The Millards certainly stipulated that the houses on their land should have a minimum value per house, as became apparent when they objected in 1904 to the two-bedroom houses in Woodfield Crescent. This was a common requirement with land let for building: it was intended to ensure a respectable social tone (thereby protecting the value of the freehold of the land). It is also true that the houses that went up a few years later on the Pitshanger and Woodbury estate, where the Millards were also the freeholders, are similar in size and appearance to the first houses in Woodfield Road and Woodfield Avenue, which suggests that the freeholders' views were a factor in the design of Ealing Tenants Ltd's houses.

ABOVE: *The first houses built by Ealing Tenants Ltd, 71–87 Woodfield Road, 1901. These nine houses, originally known as Vivian Terrace in honour of the chairman, Henry Vivian, are of a type seen all over London at this time. There are, however, minor differences between the houses – note the alternate timber-framing and tile-hanging in the gables.*

RIGHT: *Typical plan of the houses in Woodfield Road and Woodfield Avenue, 1901–5. Although less picturesque than the later Arts-and-Crafts-style cottages which began to be built in 1907, the houses in the Woodfields are more spacious, with three good-sized bedrooms, upstairs bathroom and two WCs.*

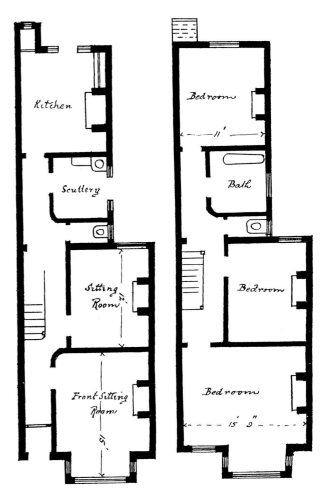

But who, in the absence of an architect, designed the Woodfields? The most obvious answer might be that they designed themselves. General Builders, who started off as contractors, had built similar houses elsewhere in London. The various workmen employed when Ealing Tenants Ltd took over control of the building would have been familiar with this type of house and would have known how to build it without recourse to an architect or even drawings produced as a guide by a draughtsman. So in this respect there is little to mark out the houses in the Woodfields from ordinary speculative building.

The houses may have been produced in an unexceptional style, a late-Victorian metropolitan vernacular that owed little to the 'cutting edge' of architectural thinking and fashion. But this does not imply a lack of interest in design on the part of the builders, committee and tenants. Indeed, sketches of elevations, and suggestions for variations on the plans, were often produced at meetings by various people including Richard White, the secretary, Harry Perry, the works manager, and Lewis Ensor, General Builders' works manager. And it was not just the building-worker members who were involved in designing the houses. At a meeting in 1904 Edmund Roe produced a suggestion for a smaller house, which featured a rendered first floor and a tiled canopy supported on wooden brackets. By the end of that year his design had been approved by the council and built as 16–32 Woodfield Crescent. This awareness of design can also be seen in 9–15 Woodfield Crescent. Although these look earlier than Roe's adjoining terrace, they are not: the works committee took the decision to build them 'in unison' with the earlier houses in Woodfield Avenue, which they face down.

The special nature of the scheme as a co-partnership, in which many of the men building the houses were prospective tenants, also had a bearing on the way that apparently 'off-the-shelf' designs were adapted, especially in the planning and fitting out of the houses. The first houses were Vivian Terrace, now 71–87

Woodfield Road, built in 1901. The plans, like the external appearance of the houses, were on the face of it conventional: upstairs there were three bedrooms and a bathroom, and downstairs were two separate living rooms, a kitchen and a scullery. As they were building for themselves, their designs were for the type of accommodation skilled artisans might expect, with the rent kept to around ten shillings a week.

Yet variations from the standard, speculative expression of this plan appeared from the start. The most striking way this affected the design was in the responsiveness to the specific needs of the tenants. Two houses in Woodfield Avenue were built with the living room at the back and the kitchen in the middle, because that is what the tenants wanted. On one occasion decisions about the plan of another house in Woodfield Avenue were held over because the prospective tenant was away and could not be consulted.

Other special features were introduced as part of the standard designs. Each of the first nine houses in Vivian Terrace had a canted bay window at the back, with a door opening straight from this into the garden; a built-in dresser in the kitchen; and a second, separate downstairs lavatory. Ealing Tenants, however, were not immune from the financial realities that drove speculative ventures. Savings had to be made in the houses built in Woodfield Avenue in 1902–4, which, although virtually indistinguishable from the front from the Woodfield Road houses, have a simplified and therefore cheaper construction to the rear extension.

This varying of the plan behind a uniform façade sometimes had more complex ramifications. In the terrace that Roe designed in Woodfield Crescent (16–32)

some houses (25–32) have a two-storey rear extension and three bedrooms; others (16–24), which are nearly identical from the front, have a single-storey rear extension and two bedrooms. This was done partly because of market forces (there was a demand for cheaper, two-bedroomed houses); partly as a sop to those, such as Roe, who objected to the expensive four-bedroom houses that had been built at each end of Woodfield Avenue; and partly to help achieve a social mix on the estate as a catalyst of the co-partnership ideal of defusing class conflict. All in all, it reflected the mix of pragmatism and idealism inherent in co-partnership.

ABOVE: *Back elevation of Vivian Terrace, Woodfield Road. These first houses were unusual in having a rear bay window. Similar houses built in the following three years in Woodfield Avenue have a simpler, cheaper construction at the back. The garden in which the three girls are standing belonged to the 'pioneer' Hubert Brampton.*

ABOVE: *17–26 Woodfield Crescent nearing completion, with 16, to the right, just begun, 1905. These smaller houses were built to a design, with wooden porch, tiled canopy and rendered first floor, by the pioneer Edmund Roe. While they all appear to be the same, those to the right of the wall plaque have two bedrooms, those to the left three.*

horizontality, Roe's design shows him responding to current architectural trends, as do the wooden porches and roughcast here, and at the slightly later terrace at 211–23 Pitshanger Lane.

This responsiveness to contemporary developments was not restricted to design matters. In June 1903 an interesting exchange took place at a committee meeting about the desirability of wiring the houses for electric light (heating by electricity was not considered). The fact that the committee even considered the issue is worthy of note, as at this date it was highly unusual for houses of this size to be wired. Electricity for private use had only been available since 1882, and that only in a small part of central London; by 1920 there were still only one million consumers of electricity in Britain.

The Ealing Tenants discussion reflected every shade of opinion. Vivian was all in favour, seeing electricity as a healthy alternative to gas. His attitude was perhaps unsurprising, given his faith in progress and the fact that through his propaganda work he moved in elevated social circles where he would have seen electric light in private houses. But even among the tenant members there were supporters. Richard White took the utilitarian line that after three years electric wiring would have paid for itself, as electricity was cheaper than gas. Richard Meyer thought electricity better in all respects, especially from the view of cleanliness; Richard Williams and Harry Perry took the pragmatic view that electricity was better for light but gas was better for cooking, so a choice should be offered. Edmund Roe, perhaps predictably, thought electricity 'a luxury and outside the requirements of the average workman', while others against electricity, who included Hubert and Albert Brampton, mentioned safety and the need for gas for

But Roe's modest design for 16–32 Woodfield Crescent illustrates the fact that Ealing Tenants was beginning to move with the times architecturally. These houses are wider in proportion to their height than the other Woodfield houses. The horizontal emphasis applies to the entire terrace, which has no gables and (except where the road falls slightly) no visible party walls. This was a concession from the formidable borough surveyor Charles Jones, as it contravened a local bye-law intended to improve fire safety, that the party walls should be higher than the roofs; and it proved to be crucial to the later development of the estate. In this

By 1906, Ealing Tenants Ltd was swiftly running out of building land. The last building on the original portions of land was the terrace at 1–12 Brunner Road. But by the middle of 1906 the protracted negotiations over the Fowler's Hill estate had finally been concluded, and decisions had to be made about how the new land was to be laid out. The crucial difference between the new land and the old was that the new was freehold, and untrammelled by the Millards' hidebound notions of house value and regular street layout. It represented an opportunity to Vivian, who had close contact with the garden city movement, to achieve something more dynamic in terms of planning.

And that awareness of the garden city ideal extended to the Ealing Tenants committee, of which Vivian was chairman from 1901 to 1911. Hubert Brampton had represented the society at the first meeting of Garden City Tenants in March 1906. A particular enthusiast was Richard White, who as early as January 1903, before the land at Letchworth had even been bought, wrote to the *Daily News* that 'we shall go in for a larger estate and work up a small garden city on our own account'. In October White wrote again, this time to the *Daily Chronicle*, that 'We cannot all, even if we so desire, move into the first garden city, but that is no reason why the development of residential property around our big cities should not be carried out on a more rational plan, with better provisions for healthy surroundings and the prevention of slums in the future'. Here in essence, in 1903, when Hampstead Garden Suburb was still no more than a vision in Henrietta Barnett's mind, is the statement of intent for Brentham Garden Suburb.

At this early date it was far from certain that new land would be bought, but from the time the decision

LEFT: *Interior of a kitchen, probably in Woodfield Crescent, 1906. This room, which is now usually used as a dining room, was fitted with a cooking range and a built-in dresser, a feature of all the Ealing Tenants houses at Brentham. Food preparation and washing up was done in the scullery, which in most of these early houses was behind the kitchen. The decoration and furnishing is typical of houses of the period, with no hint of any fashionable Arts and Crafts features.*

cooking. In the end a compromise was reached: tenants would be given the choice to have electricity if they wished. However, Ealing Tenants clearly favoured electricity, as electric fitting was provided free while gas fitting had to be paid for. The availability of electricity was made a feature of Ealing Tenants advertisements. It is interesting that many tenants opted for gas, notwithstanding the cost, and that many new tenants and, later, purchasers, had to have their houses wired for electricity in the 1930s and even in the 1940s.

to buy was made in 1904, to the time that negotiations were finally concluded in 1906, the calls for more imaginative planning became more urgent. In December 1904, Thomas Adams, manager of First Garden City Ltd and later an important figure in the development of town planning, predicted of the Ealing Tenants estate that the new land 'being freehold and unrestricted, something novel in the manner of laying out may be expected'. By May 1905 Vivian was outlining, apropos Ealing, 'how it is possible to form a little garden city venture on the outskirts of London'.

As Vivian pointed out, Ealing Tenants' estate already had many of the features dear to the heart of Ebenezer Howard and the more practical proponents of the garden-city ideal. It had an institute (at 33 Woodfield Crescent) offering a library, billiards and lectures 'to stimulate the moral and social well-being of the tenants'; and it had sporting facilities in the form of tennis courts (on the site of Rookery Nook, to the north of Woodfield Crescent) and a bowling green next to the institute (on the site of 34–5 Woodfield Crescent). Tenants were encouraged by garden competitions to tend their gardens and to grow their own produce. The estate was also organised on co-operative lines, a central feature of Howard's book.

But the planning of the houses, while they differed in significant points from ordinary speculative housing, and the estate as a whole, fell short of the garden city ideal, as conceived by Raymond Unwin. The estate was still largely surrounded by open land, mainly hayfields and pasture (so much so that until 1909, significant damage was being inflicted on gardens by marauding cows belonging to Mr Bartrupp, a neighbouring farmer), but Ealing Tenants had no control over this, and the

The Garden City Method of Development.

FRONT GARDENS TO HOUSES UNDER TOWN PLANNING.

The By-Law Method of Development.

ORDINARY SUBURBAN VILLAS, SHOWING AMOUNT OF SPACE FOR FRONT GARDEN.

environment was bound to change as more land was sold for building. With a new freehold estate they could at least control what went on in their own land, and Vivian promised in 1905, 'the question of planning to leave open space will receive serious consideration'. More specific architectural commitments were made

in February 1906, that 'the houses will be built in blocks', the existing streets being referred to as 'somewhat monotonous crescents and avenues'.

What the Ealing Tenants committee made of this dismissive attitude to their design efforts is not recorded, but they seemed quite satisfied with what they had done. Indeed once the question of the land was settled, Richard White, the secretary, was all set to lay out the new land himself (including the extra 16 acres of the Pitshanger estate leading down to the Brent – roughly the site of Ludlow Road, Neville Road, Ruskin Gardens and most of Brunner Road – which was still being negotiated). White was, of course, a long-standing garden-city enthusiast but it is doubtful that he was equipped to lay out the estate according to principles that were so novel, and this accounts for the fears that were expressed that Ealing might fall behind Hampstead in the planning of its estate.

Vivian who, as well as being chairman of Ealing Tenants, was a director of Hampstead Garden Suburb Trust Ltd, expressed this with a tinge of frustration in April 1906: 'The Ealing Tenants Society has not yet done much in this direction [i.e. planning], but it has a great opportunity before it [in the new land] . . . It is earnestly to be hoped that the society will realise the importance of this planning, which is all the more important because, if it is neglected, the superior advantages of the Hampstead planning will draw away many who might otherwise have come to Ealing, and so the progress of the society will probably be hampered'. Vivian, ever the practical mystic, saw that good planning meant more than larger private gardens, the limitation of houses to ten or twelve to the acre, and the retention of open spaces: it made good business sense.

LEFT: *Illustration from Raymond Unwin's* Nothing Gained by Overcrowding, *1912. These photographs contrast the varied cottage style of garden city developments, with conventional terraced houses, to the detriment of the latter. The monotonous design of the 'By-Law' houses shown here bore an uncomfortable resemblance to the houses in Woodfield Road and Avenue, and in 1906 the Ealing Tenants committee made the decision, when they bought new land to expand Brentham, that Raymond Unwin's ideas about planning and housing would be reflected in the next phase of development.*

RIGHT: *Raymond Unwin and Barry Parker's first plan for Brentham, September 1906. This drawing was made in Ealing Tenants' offices from a sketch supplied by Unwin. A plan made in 1905 by Frederick Hall-Jones before Unwin became involved shows a completely different layout of streets, whose names included Mazzini Road, after Vivian's hero Giuseppe Mazzini, and Lloyd Avenue, after Henry Demarest Lloyd, the American radical journalist who had attended the first public meeting of Ealing Tenants Ltd in April 1901. That plan was rejected. Unwin's plan, sketchy though it is, shows the broad outline of many of the streets as they were eventually laid out. Features of note include (1) the original tennis court behind Woodfield Avenue, (2) the first bowling green on Woodfield Crescent, (3) the school that was projected for a while on Fowlers Walk, (4) a cul-de-sac at the south end of Fowlers Walk, (5) the retention of existing field trees and (6) the 'vistas' to Harrow that Brentham Way (still 'main avenue' on the plan) and Neville Road were laid out to provide.*

This fear no doubt prompted J.H. Greenhalgh, still a committee member, to propose that Ealing Tenants accept 'a member's offer' to pay for 'expert advice as to the laying out of the estate and the houses thereon'. Who that member was is not certain, but it is likely to have been Greenhalgh himself, as he had given regular financial support to the society following his 1901 loan to buy the first plots of land.

What 'expert advice' meant was advice from someone more professionally versed than Richard White in the garden-city ideals of Letchworth and Hampstead, and the greatest of the experts was Raymond Unwin. Unwin was an obvious choice, not just because of his experience at Letchworth and Hampstead. He was, despite his Fabian sympathies, a supporter of co-partnership, and had been consulting architect to the Co-partnership Tenants Housing Council since 1905. The basis for his enthusiasm was that collective ownership of land allowed planning for the whole site: 'Advantage may be taken of spots of interest or beauty on the ground. Houses may be grouped around these spots, around open greens; or in many other such ways may be arranged to take advantage of aspect and outlook . . . and . . . it becomes easy to arrange for the tenants to share also the enjoyment of open spaces . . . and particularly beautiful spots or views which could not be secured to a series of detached individuals'. Of course Ealing Tenants were already to some extent sharing the common enjoyment of open spaces in the form of the tennis courts and bowling green, and had made provision for further development of this by retaining the northern part of the new site, down to the River Brent, for a new, commodious recreation ground.

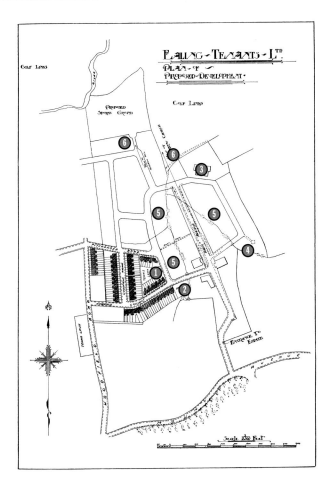

Unwin attacked the task with gusto, and after a preliminary meeting in August 1906 he produced two alternative plans of the street layout by 19 September. These were basic plans intended to allow Ealing Tenants to choose one for inclusion in the publication *Garden Suburbs, Villages and Homes*, but the lines of the final plan were already in place in the plan that survives.

Unwin did not publish *Town Planning in Practice*, the systematic formulation of his ideas about town and site planning, until 1909, but he had been gathering information, giving lectures and publishing pamphlets on the subject for several years by the time he came to Ealing, and he had been putting them into practice at New Earswick, Letchworth and in the preliminary plan for Hampstead. Aspects of the chosen plan at Ealing that he had been using since his plan for New Earswick in 1904, include the informal curving pattern of some of the roads, such as what became the northern part of Brunner Road.

Another feature of the first Ealing Tenants plan was the retention of existing trees, which are clearly marked on the 1906 plan, notably in the back land between Brunner Road and Brentham Way. Unwin's argument for this was that 'nothing so helps the early appearance of a building site as the preservation of existing trees', but more generally he believed in sensitivity to natural features and preserving such links with the landscape's past. Another feature is the laying out of the roads with regard to the natural boundaries of the estate, as can be seen in the way the cul-de-sac in Fowlers Walk projects into the spur of land to the east.

In some ways this was only logical, and the notion of planning according to the landscape had not been entirely ignored at Brentham before Unwin's plan. The laying out by the Millards of the Woodfields was not really the type of rigid grid that is usually cited as a feature of 'monotonous' pre-garden-city developments. Woodfield Crescent follows the line of the southern edge of the Lower Wood Field (and the southern part of Brunner Road the eastern edge of the adjoining field),

in much the same way as Unwin's cul-de-sac in Fowlers Walk follows the edge of the Fowler's Hill estate. Moreover, the ends of the gardens of the houses on the east side of Woodfield Avenue follow an old division, visible on the 1865 map (page 58), along the east side of the old Lower Wood Field, which was still marked by a right of way and a row of ancient trees that were preserved along the backs of the gardens.

This theorising by Unwin of site planning that had more or less taken care of itself until this time, also applies to some extent to the use of 'vistas'. Clearly marked on the 1906 plan are vistas north down what became Neville Road and Brentham Way (here called 'main avenue'). Yet from the start much had been made, by those promoting Ealing Tenants' estate, of the sloping site with views to Horsenden Hill and Harrow Hill in the north. To some extent Woodfield Road, Woodfield Avenue, and Brunner Road before it was extended, also took advantage of this. But although the use of vistas was not invented by Raymond Unwin, it was systematically worked into the planning in a way the Millards had not done.

One major departure on Unwin's plan from the original conception of the estate is the creation of Brentham Way. Where the estate had until then been purely residential, Brentham Way is introduced both as a principal thoroughfare and as a social centre: 'A wide avenue is made to serve as the central feature; one or two public buildings are arranged at points where the cross roads [Woodfield Crescent and Fowlers Walk] lead into this, and the avenue is laid out in such a way as to afford space for seats and wide shady promenades'. These public buildings are placed to provide 'terminal features' along the vistas of Fowlers Walk and

ABOVE: *Illustration from* Town Planning in Practice, *1909. The pavements at many Brentham street corners are treated in this way.*

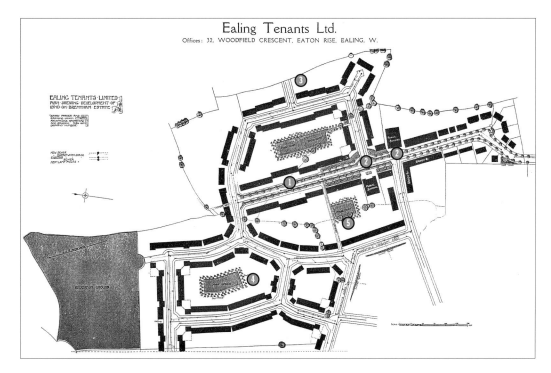

Ealing Tenants Ltd.
Offices: 32, WOODFIELD CRESCENT, EATON RISE, EALING, W.

ABOVE: *Unwin and Parker's revised plan for Brentham, February 1907, showing the arrangement of blocks of houses. Brentham Way (1) is the 'main avenue', with blocks of houses arranged formally, and public buildings and shops (2) at the junctions. There is a new road leading east from the middle of Fowlers Walk (3). The back land is for open space (4) and tennis courts (5). Unwin has virtually ignored the Woodfield houses, so much like the monotonous 'By-Law' houses he abhorred.*

Woodfield Crescent (which, unlike as built, are offset from one another). They are also located on relatively high ground, which both affords them vistas and helps them to serve as a focal point.

The notion of the 'centre or enclosed place' as a feature of any plan was central to *Town Planning in Practice*, but the combination on this plan of the formal and informal on such a small scale was an innovation for Unwin, and one that he would put into practice with his plan for Hampstead Garden Suburb in 1907. This first Brentham plan also featured a school at its northeast corner (on Fowlers Walk), intended to replace the inadequate buildings of St Stephen's School in Pitshanger

Lane. (This never materialised as the council chose a site further west, which became North Ealing School.)

On this first plan the school, public buildings and shops are the only buildings marked, apart from the houses that had already been built in the Woodfields. But part of Unwin's duties as site planner was to provide block plans, showing the disposition of the houses that would be built on the roads. Once Ealing Tenants had provided him with a detailed site survey, he delivered this new plan of Brentham, as it was now called, in February 1907. The details of public buildings, shops, and 'wide shady promenades' in Brentham Way are filled in, and a type of central square is created around the centre of the street, with extra tree planting and front gardens made part of the public space. As Unwin pointed out in *Town Planning in Practice*, this is an equivalent to the 'subsidiary centre' he created at Willifield Green in Hampstead Garden Suburb, site of the clubhouse.

Further refinements on the February 1907 plan were the creation of 'framed views' towards Harrow – these can be seen from the end of Neville Road, through the narrow gaps in the blocks opposite the north ends of Brentham Way and Ludlow Road – and the open spaces behind the houses. In time these would be cultivated as allotments, but here they are marked variously as 'tennis courts' and 'open space'. These spaces fulfilled a number of purposes, including Unwin's belief that houses should have 'a pleasant outlook both front and back', and also provided for the shared 'enjoyment of open spaces'. Also marked are one or two footpaths, a network that was later much extended, giving access to the open spaces. But the open space indicated between Ludlow Road and

Brunner Road appears to be for the use of occupants of houses whose gardens back on to it. This can be explained by Unwin's suggestion in *Town Planning in Practice* that, rather than have lots of 'useless strips' of private garden 'diminishing in width almost to a vanishing point', these 'could be thrown together to produce a small orchard, a lawn, a hazel copse'.

Perhaps what is most striking about this new plan is the way the Woodfields have been air-brushed out of the picture. The original plan had been prepared in Ealing Tenants' office from a sketch by Unwin, for publication in the booklet *Garden Suburbs, Villages and Homes*, and every house in the Woodfields had been carefully drawn in. The new plan came from Unwin's office in Hampstead, and the Woodfields appear merely as 'existing houses'. The reason is that, as far as Unwin was concerned, these were the wrong kind of houses.

What was most wrong with them was probably the back extensions, also carefully drawn in by Ealing Tenants in the 1906 plan. The back extension, usually containing a kitchen and scullery on the ground floor and a third bedroom on the first floor, had become a standard feature of the urban terraced house throughout England in the nineteenth century. It was the accepted way of expanding the amount of space that could be included in a house without resorting to a wider plot of ground. But since at least 1902, when he wrote a Fabian tract on *Cottage Plans and Commonsense*, Unwin had been campaigning against 'the wretched prefix back'. Dispensing with the back extension meant that a wider and more expensive plot of land was needed for the same amount of accommodation, but this was compensated for by the lower construction costs of bringing all the rooms in the house under the

one roof. This also offered a greater flexibility in the way those rooms could be arranged.

On a larger scale, Unwin's plan did away with what he had called the 'dreary rows of miserable tenements that we see in all our small suburbs'. His plan, although it lacks details, shows a varied selection of short terraces, and what are apparently semi-detached pairs and a few detached houses. This met a number of his site-planning criteria, one of which was picturesqueness: 'where many buildings of various characters and size are gathered together . . . a picturesqueness of grouping is rarely absent, even when individual buildings have in themselves no special beauty'. This variety was enhanced by shifting the building line of each terrace or pair, both in relation to one another and to the street. In long straight streets such as Brentham Way and Meadvale Road, this served to break up the visually tiring vanishing perspective caused by long, unbroken rows of buildings, and also made for small impromptu squares along the road. In curving streets such as Brunner, Neville and Ludlow Roads, it enhanced the homely informality of this purely residential part of the plan.

LEFT: *Illustration of broken and unbroken building lines, from Unwin's* Town Planning in Practice, *1909. This diagram illustrates why Unwin preferred a building line that broke back and forth along the line of the street (on the left) to a straight line (right). The former was picturesque, with visual interest, the latter dull, with 'vanishing perspective'. Hence the preference for varied blocks of houses in Brentham after 1907.*

An important aspect of the creation of 'street pictures' was the manner in which houses were arranged at road junctions. Unwin had a particular abhorrence of the way typical modern terraced houses created ugly junctions, with back extensions and blank end walls built up to the building line. This was due in part, he acknowledged, to building regulations requiring a minimum depth of open space behind all houses: terraces could not just meet at corners as the end houses would have no back gardens. He devoted an entire chapter in *Town Planning in Practice* to ways around this problem, but his February 1907 plan for Brentham features two solutions in particular. At the junctions that were roughly right-angled – the north end of Neville Road and at both ends of Ludlow Road – he proposed an arrangement, which he was also to use at Letchworth, where 'the ends of the buildings should be considered as front elevations [i.e. not left as towering blank walls] and the erection of a high wall, with arched opening through to the rear, might serve to link the houses together and help the architectural effect'. Where roads met at an obtuse angle, such as the junction of Neville and Brunner Roads with what became Brunswick Road, and also the junction of Ruskin Gardens with Brunner Road, he proposed what appear to be semi-detached pairs built forward and across the junction, forming a terminal feature of the vista down the roads opposite.

One way in which Brentham, at least as it was built, did not conform to Unwin's planning ideals was in the planning density. Unwin came, by trial and error, to the conclusion that twelve houses per acre was the ideal density for housing. As well as providing the requisite sunlight and fresh air, such a spacious arrangement

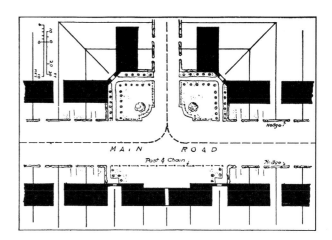

allowed for each house to have a garden sufficiently large 'to be worth cultivating seriously for the sake of the profits'. Gardening was also felt to be a wholesome and worthwhile activity in itself. Unwin later came up with a complicated economic argument to suggest that it was actually cheaper to build with this lower density because fewer roads were needed, an argument that only worked when the building land could be bought at agricultural prices. Even with careful negotiation Ealing Tenants had paid much more than agricultural prices for their land, so the density at Brentham is up to twenty houses to the acre.

Unwin, however, cited Brentham in *Town Planning in Practice* as an example of a suburb that was 'healthy' despite its higher density of building. Vivian himself, when he came to offer his views nine years later on the subject of site planning to the readers of *Co-partnership*, stressed the need for flexibility in housing density, particularly in co-partnership estates where 'the smallest type of house' was concerned. While fresh air and green space were desirable, tenants did not want gardens that were too large. He reported gloomily on one estate where 'some of the gardens are derelict', and the others 'indifferently cultivated'. 'The site planner should not on this matter be carried away by abstract ideas, but have careful regard to the characteristics of the probable residents': Vivian was not about to let theory, however attractive, overrule practicality.

The tension between the ideal and the pragmatic was one thing, but in Unwin's plan there was tension between two different ideals. On the one hand there was Unwin's socialist, egalitarian leanings, on the other his sentimental attachment to the social hierarchy of the villages of 'old England'. One of Henrietta Barnett's main aims at Hampstead Garden Suburb was that it should encompass a wide range of social classes, but from Unwin's first plan for her in February 1905, it had been clear that the classes would be accommodated in distinct areas of the suburb. At Brentham, by contrast, although Ealing Tenants Ltd had not yet achieved as wide a social mix as Barnett projected, or as they themselves wished, there was a wider range of occupations represented than might have been expected on an estate of fewer than 120 houses. And crucially the £1-a-week houses and the 13-shilling ones, the civil servants and the bricklayers, were all living cheek by jowl. Unwin's new plan, however, suggested grouping the new larger detached houses together at the top, south end of Brentham Way where it joins Mount Avenue, which was perceived as the entrance to the estate.

Vivian, in the annual report of the Co-partnership Tenants Housing Council in September 1906, had explained that 'As the land is immediately in the rear of houses of a high rental value [i.e. the houses on

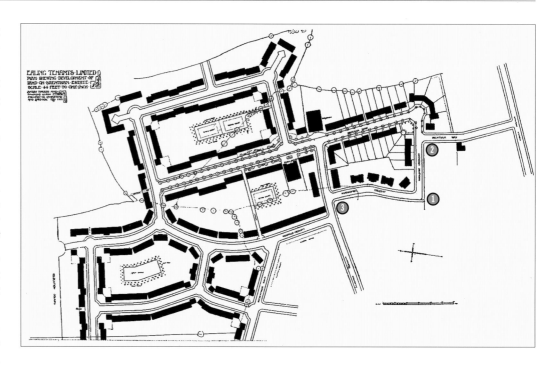

Mount Avenue], the committee will no doubt arrange to erect a good class of house at the entrance to the Estate.' The creation of an area specifically designated for 'a good class of house', while it chimed well with the aim of creating a socially diverse estate, tended to create more distinct class divisions in the layout of the estate than had existed before Unwin was employed. But the creation of a good impression, and attracting good tenants, made sense from a business point of view, a factor that assumed greater importance as power shifted from Ealing Tenants to Co-partnership Tenants Ltd after 1907.

Ealing Tenants appear to have been happy with their new plan, but the borough surveyor was not. The

ABOVE: *Unwin and Parker's revised plan for Brentham, from* Town Planning in Practice, *1909. Unwin and Parker produced a new design in April 1907 (which this 1908 plan incorporates), after the borough surveyor rejected the previous plan: Brentham Way, at 600 ft long without a cross road, contravened a local building bye-law. The purchase of more land allowed Unwin's design to incorporate Winscombe Crescent (1), so that Brentham Way (2) connected with Woodfield Crescent (3) and effectively became two roads.*

RIGHT: *Frederic Cavendish Pearson (1882–1963), c. 1930. Pearson was taken on by Ealing Tenants as an assistant to the works manager, Harry Perry, in October 1906. Between 1907 and 1910 he designed almost all the new houses in Brentham, typically cramming numerous Arts and Crafts features into a single design.*

BELOW: *The Pearson family on holiday on the Isle of Wight, 1925. Pearson is in the front of the charabanc with his younger daughter, Hazel, on his lap.*

problem was Brentham Way which, because it was more than 600 ft long without a cross road, contravened a building bye-law. The difficulty was soon overcome when Frederick Goodenough of Winscombe Court, Mount Avenue, sold the society a piece of his land. A new plan was produced in April 1907, featuring a new road, Winscombe Crescent, which connected Brentham Way with Woodfield Crescent. The south part of Brentham Way now counted as a separate street, for bye-law purposes.

The issue now, for Ealing Tenants, was who would design the new houses on Unwin's plan. Unwin was later to say that wherever possible it was best for the site planner to be employed as the architect but,

although he and his partner Barry Parker were to design five houses in Brentham, Unwin was too busy with his work at Hampstead Garden Suburb to take on any other extensive architectural work. In anticipation of the expansion of the estate, therefore, Ealing Tenants had, in October 1906, advertised for a draughtsman to act as assistant to Harry Perry, the works manager.

The man chosen to act as Perry's assistant was Frederic Cavendish Pearson, who was born at Shipley, just outside Bradford in Yorkshire, in 1882. It may be significant that Pearson's father, James, was a manager at Sir Titus Salt's mill at Saltaire, the village built from the 1850s near Shipley by Sir Titus for the workers in his great alpaca mills. Although it was built in a conventional manner of terrace houses on a grid pattern, Saltaire included some of the social facilities that were to be a feature of Brentham and, later, Hampstead Garden Suburb and Letchworth. Although it was an example of paternalism rather than co-partnership, Saltaire was a precedent in several ways for Brentham, and the fact that Pearson was familiar with such a venture could have helped in his selection for the job by Ealing Tenants.

Another factor would have been his experience as a local-authority architect. Pearson had completed his education at Furness College in Morecambe, Lancashire, and had been apprenticed there around 1900 to an architect, A. Lancelot Lang. Although Lang was only a few years older than he was, Pearson (so his daughter Hazel remembers) considered him a very competent teacher, and when Lang moved to the south of England in 1905 to take up an appointment as architect to the Heston and Isleworth Urban District Council, Pearson went with him as his assistant. In the meantime, Pearson had been continuing his education, and in 1904 he had been elected a Professional Associate of the Surveyors' Institution (now the Royal Institution of Chartered Surveyors). This practical background in local authority work and surveying was probably just what Ealing Tenants were looking for, but unglamorous as Pearson's architectural background was, the fact that Ealing Tenants employed an architect is surely significant.

At the age of 24 Pearson was young when he was appointed, but he had a few years' experience as well as a professional qualification. It therefore seems unlikely that he would have taken the job with Ealing Tenants had it not been proposed that he would be given an opportunity to design houses. If Ealing Tenants were merely proposing to carry on designing for themselves and to adapt the existing 'metropolitan vernacular' manner of the Woodfields to Unwin's

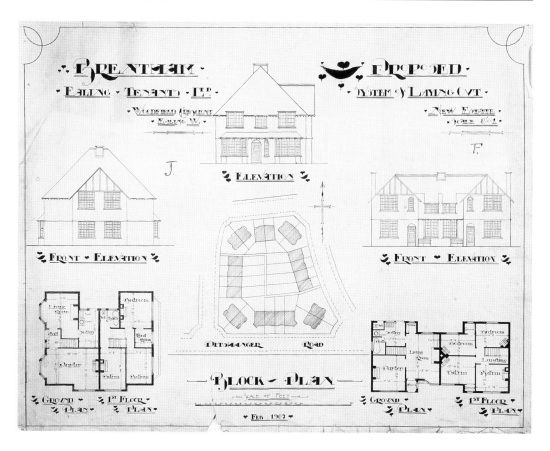

plan, it seems unlikely they would have needed an architect to act as the manager's assistant.

Whatever the society had in mind when they took Pearson on, events rather took over. Just before Pearson arrived in Brentham, Richard White, the former secretary, who had been estate manager since April 1906, was suddenly dismissed. Pearson was quickly pressed into service in estate management duties, such as collecting rents. This diversion from architectural duties

ABOVE: *F.C. Pearson's first architectural designs for Ealing Tenants Ltd, February 1907. These semi-detached houses, which were built to a different design, were intended for the sites at the junctions of Pitshanger Lane with Ludlow and Brunner Roads. Pearson often indulged in this fashionable Art Nouveau lettering.*

plans. In fact, the only result seems to have been the decision to roughcast the four houses in the centre of the first terrace in Brunner Road, which was then in the course of construction. Moreover, from his very distinctive style of drawing, replete with fashionable Art Nouveau lettering, we know that Pearson prepared the drawing for this alteration, and from this time onwards, he prepared drawings for all new houses built.

But the habit of designing collectively was not easily given up. The first drawing that Pearson produced of houses in pairs appeared in February 1907, and there are interesting differences between this design and the houses as they were built. This was for the semi-detached houses on the corners of Pitshanger Lane and Ludlow Road, and Pitshanger Lane and Brunner Road. On paper the designs owed quite a lot to developments at Letchworth. One bears a close resemblance, down to the rustic seat built into the return wall of one of the bays, to the prize-winning pair of cottages built for Garden City Tenants and supervised by Ealing Tenants, on Eastholm Green, Letchworth, for the Cheap Cottages exhibition of 1905 (page 45). But the designs as built (218/20 Pitshanger Lane and 2 Ludlow Road/208 Pitshanger Lane), which were based on the other semi in Pearson's drawing, owed less to the garden city aesthetic. In place of the central gable with timber-framing, there is a parapet to the central two-storey bay that the houses share, which gives it a more formal quality, more in keeping with the existing houses in the Woodfields.

Pearson's design for the group of four houses in between (210–16 Pitshanger Lane) was similarly adapted in execution, with a central parapet added

was compounded in January 1907 when Mr Cooke, the caretaker secretary of Ealing Tenants Ltd, resigned, and Pearson was appointed in his place.

With Pearson diverted from designing houses, it might have meant that the collective manner of house design, employed in the Woodfields, would continue for a while. Certainly, Harry Perry seems to have been closely involved in the earliest designs after Unwin produced his plan. In September 1906, before Pearson arrived, Perry had agreed to prepare 'plans for some pairs, fours, and sixes, and a single one or two', that is, the varied types of houses suggested by Unwin's 1907

WHY WAIT?

BUY or BUILD your HOME NOW !
WITH THE HELP OF THE
CO-OPERATIVE PERMANENT
BUILDING SOCIETY
WRITE FOR PROSPECTUS. FREE. TO
22 RED LION SQUARE. LONDON. W.C.1

during construction (although this has since been removed). In fact, all the houses designed during 1907 (13–16 Brunner Road, 208–20 Pitshanger Lane, 2 Ludlow Road, 18–38 Winscombe Crescent and

37–40 and 53–6 Woodfield Crescent) display this curious hybrid of the progressive and the conventional. There are certainly more Arts and Crafts features, with a greater variety of building materials such as tile and roughcast, and the planning is more varied, especially in the semi-detached pairs. But overall the blocks of two and four houses are still quite formally conceived and planned, most of the groups of four terminating with a double-height bay with plain or castellated parapet.

These 1907 houses represent Ealing Tenants' unwillingness to relinquish control of architectural design to a purely garden-city aesthetic, and this independence is also evident in the way they adapted Unwin's plan.

ABOVE: *Ludlow Road, c. 1910. This photograph demonstrates Pearson's ability to range his blocks of houses along a curving street to achieve the 'street pictures' that were an aim of Unwin's planning. The block of houses on the left is at an angle to 'turn' the corner, and beyond is one of two unusual blocks of 'rhomboid houses'.*

LEFT: *Advert for the Co-operative Building Society, 1920s. Co-operative societies had all but given up building houses themselves by this time.*

RIGHT: *Illuminated album presented to John Burns when he opened the recreation ground, 1908. The cottages illustrated were, in, fact, in Letchworth.*

BELOW: *Adaptation of Unwin's Brentham plan, late 1907, probably drawn by F.C. Pearson. The main changes are the dropping of the cul-de-sacs in Fowlers Walk (although one was later re-instated) and the road in the middle of Fowlers Walk, and the different treatment of houses at road junctions. Pearson replaced all the proposed houses linked by arches with houses angled across the junction.*

From the start, the houses built to the new plan in Pitshanger Lane departed from Unwin's suggested disposition of houses. The corner treatment suggested by Unwin, involving an angled wall, with an arched opening, joining the two corner houses, was never used at Brentham. For example, in its place at the eastern corner of Ludlow Road and Pitshanger Lane, they used an angled pair; that is in keeping with Unwin's theories, but not exactly what he had suggested. This may have been because there was a potential problem with bye-laws: Unwin's suggested treatment would have reduced the amount of space behind the two corner houses to an unacceptable degree.

Anticipation of a problem with the bye-laws probably explains another feature of a revised plan, based on Unwin's plan but produced by Pearson at the end of

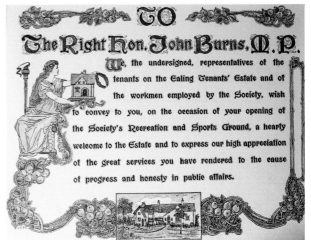

1907, and included in the first book about Brentham, *The Pioneer Co-partnership Village*, published in 1908. In Unwin's plan of February 1907 he had included a short cul-de-sac at the south end of what became Fowlers Walk. Cul-de-sacs became a favourite feature of Unwin's, and appear extensively in *Town Planning in Practice* in 1909. He had included them in his 1905 plan for Hampstead Garden Suburb and they had first been built at the Bird's Hill estate at Letchworth in 1906. However, they worked best, producing one of his favourite 'enclosed spaces', with a narrow carriage road in the centre with a turning place at the end. The problem was that Ealing's bye-laws, in common with many boroughs', demanded a minimum road width of 40 feet. Hampstead Garden Suburb had resorted to an Act of Parliament in 1906 to get round this problem, as a result of which a 20ft width was permitted there for minor or access roads. This explains the preponderance of this feature there, both along the edge of the Heath extension

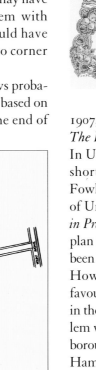

EALING TENANTS·LIMITED
PLAN SHEWING DEVELOPMENT · OF
LAND · ON · BRENTHAM · ESTATE ·
SCALE 44 FEET· TO· ONE· INCH

and in the Artisans' Quarter down Erskine Hill. Although the feature did eventually form part of Fowlers Walk, the bye-law problem probably explains why Pearson dispensed with it in this interim plan.

The following two years were the zenith of Pearson's contribution to the architecture and planning of Brentham. In January 1908 he was finally relieved of his duties as secretary, and appointed surveyor to Ealing Tenants, allowing him to concentrate on design. Almost immediately there is a perceptible change in the houses built, which is exemplified by the block of six small houses at 17–22 Brunner Road (page 104). These are in a full-blown Arts and Crafts style, that goes well beyond what was being built at Letchworth in terms of artistic expressiveness and – there is no other word – quaintness. It is almost as though Pearson, finally unfettered, decides to cram in every feature he can think of: there is a mansard roof to the central four houses, with tiled dormers; there are straight sloping buttresses; there are tall, roughcast chimneys; there are square oriel bays to the outer two houses, with a tiled canopy; there is tile-hanging and roughcast; and there is a porch for the two outer doorways, with another, this time hipped, tiled canopy. Pearson has clearly been looking at what is going on at Letchworth, but he has also incorporated features – every feature, one might think – from mainstream Arts and Crafts pioneers such as C.F.A. Voysey and M.H. Baillie Scott, whose work he would have seen in such publications as *The Studio*. The difference is that Voysey and Baillie Scott were using such features in greater moderation and on much larger houses.

Although Pearson toned down his manner for later houses, it is this hectic proliferation of features that characterises his work at Brentham. He rarely uses one

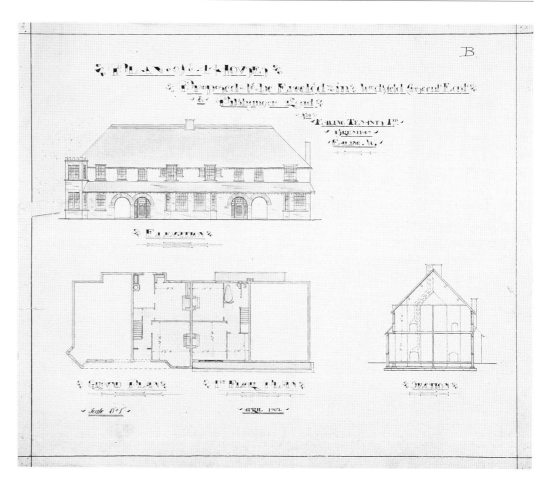

angle of roof when three will do. In larger houses, such as the semi-detached pairs on the east side of Winscombe Crescent (9–23) and in the four pairs that make up Ruskin Gardens, the larger scale means the overall effect is less frantic. But on occasion, the striving for effect can produce some alarming results. The quintessence of this must be the two blocks of four he

ABOVE: *F.C. Pearson's design for 13–16 Brunner Road, April 1907. This design is a transition between the earlier houses and the full-blown Arts and Crafts designs. The front doors are rather close for comfort to the stairs, because they are set back in a porch.*

RIGHT: *Ruskin Gardens, c. 1912. This type of pavement corner arranged in an arc was illustrated by Unwin in* Town Planning in Practice *(page 142).*

BELOW: *Winscombe Crescent, c. 1910. The first houses in Brentham to have hedging to the front garden were in Winscombe Crescent. Hedging was planted in front of the houses on the right, and added behind the Voysey-style garden walls opposite. The street trees are alternating acacia and lime.*

designed at 12–18 and 28–34 Ludlow Road in 1909. The four end houses are rhomboid in plan, as a result of which there is hardly a right-angle in the house.

It has to be added that there are some infelicities of planning, even in the houses that are less obviously exotic, and where problems could have been avoided if Pearson had been less wedded to creating architectural effects. For example, sometimes the stairs are too close for comfort to the front door, yet this problem arises because the front door is set back within a porch. Dispensing with the porch might have diminished the charm of the design, but it would have allowed for a more spacious and convenient hall.

Another instance of this triumph of style over convenience is the introduction into small two- and three-bedroom cottages of features that were evolved for much larger houses. This is most striking in a block (admittedly unexecuted) that Pearson designed for Brunner Road, where in a living room that is only 11 ft by 15 ft, he introduces an inglenook around the fireplace that takes up around a quarter of the floor space. Inglenooks were popular with Arts and Crafts architects, including Unwin and Parker in their larger houses, but they were intended to create warm, intimate spaces in an otherwise large hall-cum-living room. Even where they were used in smaller houses, they often occupied an end wall so that the floor space would be reduced as little as possible. In other designs Pearson achieved something of the cosy inglenook effect without compromising the use of space to the same degree, by introducing an arched feature in the parlour. Examples of this are the cottages at 21 and 31 Ludlow Road, and the larger semi-detached houses, built across the corner, at 9 and 11 Winscombe Crescent.

But there was one factor that had a bearing on the planning of the houses that was outside Pearson's control. By 1908 Ealing Tenants Ltd was increasingly dependent on loans from the Public Works Loan Board, which meant that they had to build more cottages clearly aimed at 'working-class' tenants, which in turn meant building small. Among the earliest of these is the terrace of four cottages at 23–6 Brunner Road, which displays a number of features typical of small Ealing Tenants' cottages designed by Pearson. Upstairs he manages to squeeze in three bedrooms, a bathroom and a separate lavatory. Downstairs there is an L-shaped living room, but also a small separate parlour. One concession to the limited space in these houses are the stairs, which rise

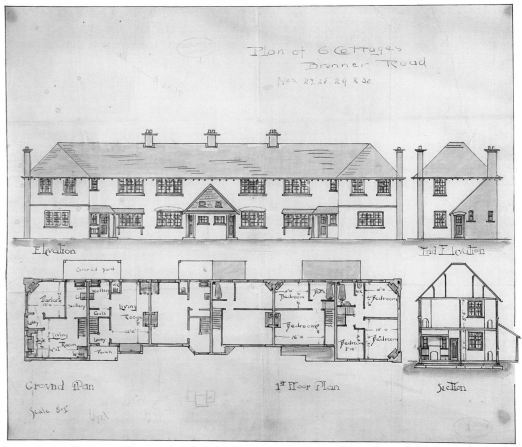

directly out of the living room; this is also a feature of 21, 23, 29 and 31 Ludlow Road.

Space limitations could also affect the location of two features found in most Brentham houses, the built-in dresser and the pantry or larder. Typically these were located in or off the scullery, which would also normally contain, at this date, a cooking range set within an

ABOVE: *Unexecuted design by F.C. Pearson, 1908. On the left of the plan is an unfeasibly large inglenook.*

LEFT: *11 Winscombe Crescent. An arch creates an inglenook effect without unduly compromising the living space.*

RIGHT: *F.C. Pearson's design for 41–9 Ludlow Road, 1909. Ealing Tenants made a great play about the fact that their houses had upstairs bathrooms, and by this date Pearson had become adept at achieving this, even here in two tiny two-bedroom houses, which have a compact bathroom and separate WC. The steep gables, single-storey canted bays to the end houses, and the treatment of the porch with window on one side and door on the other, are typical Pearson features.*

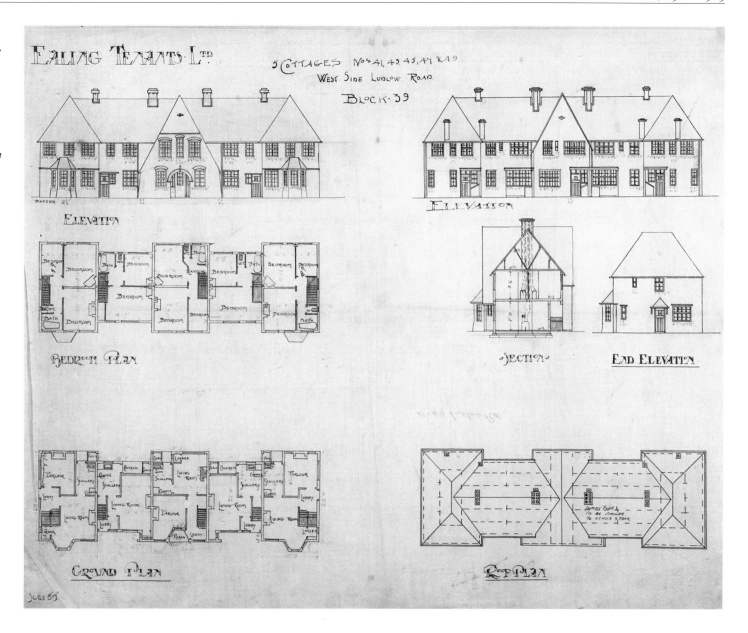

overmantel, some wooden shelves supported on metal brackets, a Belfast sink, a wooden draining board and a 'copper' (a large metal tub usually made of iron, rather than copper, that was in a brick housing and was used for heating water). The work surface, as we now know it, was virtually non-existent, although there might be a wooden, fold-down flap. At 23–6 Brunner Road the scullery is very small; the dresser is built in, and the pantry leads off the living room instead; the pantry here is located right at the front of the house, the opposite side from the scullery. In other houses such as 52 and 54 Brunner Road, the pantry is located off the parlour, which seems an odd arrangement in a room traditionally 'kept for best'.

Many of the small Pearson houses reflect Unwin's belief that all the house's facilities should be located under cover, in that they have a small brick-and-wood lean-to or 'covered yard' at the back. These typically contained a coalhole (although in some very small houses, such as 17–22 Brunner Road, and the blocks in Ludlow, Neville and Meadvale Roads that were built to the same design, the coalhole was located under the stairs, off the scullery). In houses such as 3 and 7 Meadvale Road and 17–22 Brunner Road, too small for a separate w.c. adjacent to the bathroom upstairs, the lean-to might also contain an outside lavatory. This explains why some bathrooms were not originally equipped with basins. (On the architect's plans, the word 'lav' sometimes appears in the bathroom, but this did not indicate that the lavatory and bathroom were combined – 'lav' is short for 'lavatory sink', i.e. basin.)

Brentham's early residents must have found that Pearson's houses, with their unusually arranged

**HOUSE-PLANNING.**

Sometimes internal comfort has to be sacrificed to external beauty, and this is the cause of some slight inconvenience— when the Plumber comes into your bedroom to examine the cistern at 6.30 a.m. when the Bathroom and the Scullery are combined ; when the Dustman's only way lies through the Drawing-room ; when the roof-lines of the picturesque Study get in your way ; and when the Larder window faces South.

ABOVE: *'Ealing Garden Suburb', c. 1920: Brunner Road looking towards houses at the junction with Neville Road. Pearson's design for these houses was unusual in incorporating three separate houses on a 'butterfly' or 'suntrap' plan usually used for single houses.*

LEFT: *Cartoon of 'House-planning' by George Morrow, c. 1912. Morrow, a Punch cartoonist, is lampooning the small size, low ceilings and unconventional planning of typical garden suburb houses.*

rooms, rooms with corners cut off to accommodate corridors, and sloping ceilings created by the complex roofs, took a bit of getting used to. But that they seem to have regarded them with affection is reflected in a humorous story that appeared in *The Brentham Magazine* in June 1914. It tells the tale of the ill-tempered 'Mr Grouzer', who relates his unhappy experience living in 'the suburb at Crankton', where the houses 'look all right outside, but I found that, by clever architecture, the houses, which looked like one, were really two. I was told that the place which I thought was the pantry was the drawing-room, and as for bedrooms, why all the ceilings were walls, and the only place to put the looking-glass was on a small square patch of ceiling, so that one had to lie on his

back to shave'. Eventually Mr Grouzer decides to leave and set up his own colony.

Pearson may by 1908 have been devoting all his time to architectural design, but this did not mean that Raymond Unwin had entirely severed his links with Brentham. Indeed, in May 1908 Unwin produced another new plan for the suggested layout of Brentham Way. This is probably the plan, reproduced in *Town Planning in Practice*, which shows a more formal treatment of Fowlers Walk, with cul-de-sac features at either end (despite the doubts of Ealing Tenants Ltd about this feature). This plan still shows 'public buildings' marked on Brentham Way, but a more detailed plan of the south end of Brentham Way shows that the idea of including shops in the street had been dropped.

It may be that Ealing Tenants had given up the idea of building shops here, because shops were beginning to appear on the north side of Pitshanger Lane, to the west of their estate. One of these blocks, 108–24 Pitshanger Lane, was built in 1909 by Alfred Frazer, proprietor of the New West End Brick Company and sometime member of the Ealing Tenants committee, and he used Frederic Cavendish Pearson as his architect – the perilously steep gables recall some of Pearson's designs in Neville Road and Meadvale Road. A few years later, in 1913, Ealing Tenants contemplated building shops and offices themselves in Pitshanger Lane (presumably the north side between Holyoake Walk and Denison Road), but this came to nothing. The decision made in 1908 not to build shops in Brentham clearly diminished the role of Brentham Way, as Unwin had conceived it, as the 'main avenue' and focal point for the estate.

An interesting feature of Unwin's plan of the south end of Brentham Way is the treatment he suggests for the corner where Brentham Way turns sharply into Winscombe Crescent. The plan shows a circular 'summerhouse' fronted by a small public green, which links the houses at the corners. An adaptation of this feature was used at Asmuns Place in Hampstead Garden Suburb, but it never left the drawing board at Brentham.

This block plan of Brentham Way was produced at the same time as the block of four houses (page 247) designed by Unwin and Parker at 1–7 Winscombe Crescent (although these houses were not built until 1909). As the site faces the 'entrance' to the estate, the short stretch of Brentham Way that leads from Mount Avenue, it was an especially sensitive one, and this may explain why Unwin was invited to design the houses. Rather like a group of cottages Unwin designed the following year in Temple Fortune Hill, Hampstead Garden Suburb, they are red-brick, quiet and low-key, in contrast to Pearson's exuberant use of mixed materials. The hipped roof hints at the stripped-down Germanic manner of the Brentham Institute designed by G.L. Sutcliffe three years later.

Equally unassuming is Widecombe, 2 Brentham Way, the only other house in Brentham designed by Unwin and Parker. It was built in 1909 for William Hutchings, vice-chairman of Ealing Tenants, and is an example of the 'good class' of house Vivian suggested would be built at the entrance to the estate. Although the outside is plain to the point of reticence, the house features both an inglenook in the drawing room and a wooden balcony over a veranda, with French doors opening from one of the bedrooms and from the dining

**A £650 HOUSE ERECTED BY EALING TENANTS, LTD.**

room. This reflects Unwin and Parker's shared enthusiasm for creating flexible spaces, for breaking down the distinction between inside and outside space, and their Simple Life passion for fresh air. When he designed a house for himself at Letchworth, Parker was to build a tower with a 'sleeping platform' that could be left open to the air.

Although these five houses were the extent of Unwin and Parker's architectural design at Brentham, their influence is evident in one other way all over the suburb: this is in the preponderance of hedges. In the first houses built at Brentham, in

ABOVE: *Parker and Unwin's design for a 'good class' of home, 2 Brentham Way, 1909. On top of the price of £650 were costly extras such as oak parquet flooring.*

RIGHT: *Plan of Brentham Garden Suburb, 1911. Although this was drawn by Brentham's second architect, G.L. Sutcliffe, it incorporates F.C. Pearson's 1909 plan for the new land on which Denison Road, North View and Holyoake Walk were built.*

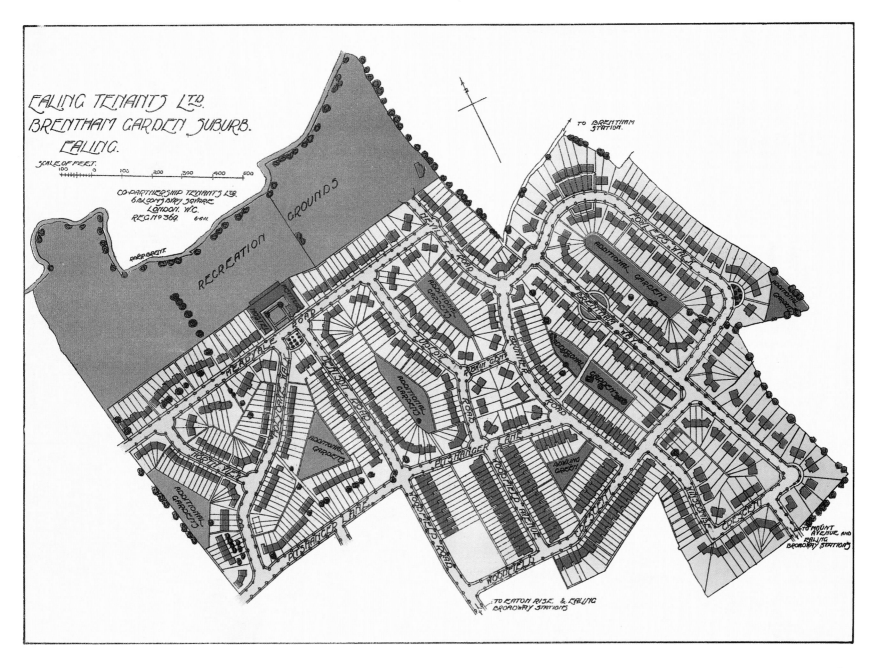

EALING TENANTS LTD.
BRENTHAM GARDEN SUBURB.
EALING.

SCALE OF FEET.
100    0    100    200    300    400    500

CO-PARTNERSHIP TENANTS LTD.
6 BLOOMSBURY SQUARE
LONDON. W.C.
REG. Nº 369.    6-6-11.

RIVER BRENT.

RECREATION GROUNDS

TO BRENTHAM STATION.

FOWLERS WALK

ADDITIONAL GARDENS

ADDITIONAL GARDENS

ADDITIONAL GARDENS

ADDITIONAL GARDENS

BRENTHAM WAY

ADDITIONAL GARDENS

ADDITIONAL GARDENS

ADDITIONAL GARDENS

RUSKIN GARDEN

GROVLER ROAD

MEADVALE ROAD

DENISON ROAD

LUDLOW ROAD

NEVILLE ROAD

NORTH VIEW

ADDITIONAL GARDENS

PITSHANGER HILL

PITSHANGER LANE

WOODFIELD ROAD

WOODFIELD ROAD

WINSCOMBE CRESCENT

BRUNNER CRESCENT

BOWLING GREEN

TO MOUNT AVENUE AND EALING BROADWAY STATIONS

TO EATON RISE & EALING BROADWAY STATIONS

159

Woodfield Road and Woodfield Avenue, the front gardens had been edged by dwarf brick walls topped by cast-iron railings of a mildly baroque character, while chestnut palings were used for the back gardens. Beginning with Woodfield Crescent, the houses had close-boarded fences to the front – perhaps because they were cheaper than brick walls, perhaps in keeping with the more informal style of the houses – and, once again, chestnut palings behind.

This tendency of the English to build houses, 'each with its little garden securely railed', was an arrangement likened by Unwin in *Town Planning in Practice* to the creation of 'cattle-pens', and his ideal solution was to throw the front gardens together into a single strip of semi-public green space. But he acknowledged that 'English people desire some privacy in their garden', so a compromise was suggested in the form of hedges and shrubberies, preferably only to the front with little or no demarcation between the individual plots.

But as with the architectural design, Ealing Tenants took some time to put this suggestion into practice. All the houses built in 1907, after Unwin had supplied his estate plan, were built with the same boarded fencing that had been used in Woodfield Crescent. It was only with 18–38 Winscombe Crescent (designed in 1907 and built in 1908) that hedging was introduced, and this was behind the roughcast dwarf walls with Voysey-manner gateposts designed by Pearson. Starting with the larger semi-detached houses opposite, built in 1908, the front gardens were demarcated by short wooden posts joined by chains, with hedges planted along the line of the posts, the idea being that the posts would be removed once the hedges had grown to maturity.

One point that should be made is that not quite everything that was built before 1915 within the Brentham conservation area, as it was determined in 1969, was built by Ealing Tenants. The two terraces of houses at 41–69 Woodfield Road that adjoin Vivian Terrace (71–87 Woodfield Road) were built by a commercial builder in 1902–5. These houses take their cue from Vivian Terrace to which, with the exception of some additional carved decoration, they are similar.

Nearby, even before Ealing Tenants had started building Woodfield Crescent, another commercial builder who owned the eight plots at the west end of the Crescent, began building a terrace of conventional three-bedroom terrace houses (1–7). The first two to be built (5 and 6) provide an interesting contrast with the rest of the houses in the Woodfields, as they are truly conventional, being built of pale brown bricks known as London stocks, and with double-height canted bays. It was a type of house (with the exception of the more modish red-tiled gables) that had been built all over London since the 1870s and, as such, it brings home the variety and colour of the Woodfield houses, which are themselves so often dismissed as entirely conventional. However, the end house of this terrace, number 7, is slightly different. This house, completed in 1909 by Frederick Hill, a builder, for himself, was built on two plots. It is double-fronted and, most unusually for the early date and old-fashioned style of the house, it had an integral garage or 'motor shed' beneath the left-hand bay (since converted to domestic use).

It is often stated that estates such as Brentham were built 'before the motor car', but this is not strictly accurate. Clearly motor traffic was very light at this time, and 7 Woodfield Crescent was built for a wealthier

ABOVE: *'An imaginary irregular town' from Unwin's* Town Planning in Practice*, 1909. One of the effects that Unwin hoped to achieve in his planning was the appearance of a settlement that had grown up over many years.*

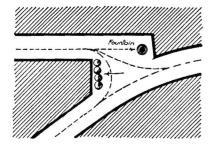

ABOVE: *Illustration of a treatment of a junction where a curved road meets a straight road, from Raymond Unwin's* Town Planning in Practice, *1909. F.C. Pearson adapted this for the junction of Holyoake Walk with Denison Road opposite the Institute.*

class of person than most residents on the estate. However, garages began to be built on the Ealing Tenants estate before the First World War: the very first one, also built in 1909, was for the tenant of 2 Neville Road (it has also been rebuilt since).

Although Unwin was responsible for the plan of the Fowlers Hill estate and the general disposition of the houses in Brentham, as well as the adoption of hedges, it would be a mistake to underestimate F.C. Pearson's contribution. Between the middle of 1907 and the middle of 1909, 140 new houses had been built in Brentham, all but five of which were his work as an architect. Moreover, although he had departed from Unwin's suggestions for the layout of the blocks of houses, the alternatives he had produced were still very much in keeping with Unwin's ideas about planning.

The blocks he designed in 1909 at the corner of Ludlow Road (1/3) and Pitshanger Lane (204/206) were a textbook example of one of Unwin's ideas about buildings turning a corner. The 'butterfly' houses he designed later that year for the junction of Neville Road, Brunner Road and what is now Brunswick Road, were an adaptation of a type of house much favoured by Arts and Crafts architects. Pearson's design is an early example of the adaptation of this form to three small houses, and although he did not entirely overcome the problem of planning three separate houses within the confines of the plan (partly because bye-laws required a straight party wall between the houses, so that the two end houses have some awkward, nearly triangular rooms), the restraint in the use of materials shows him maturing as an architect – so much so that when Professor Nikolaus Pevsner visited the estate in the early 1970s, he suggested that Unwin might have designed the houses.

In fact Pearson's contribution to the planning of Brentham went further than this. It is usually assumed that Unwin planned the whole of Brentham, apart from the Woodfields, but when he produced his various plans, Ealing Tenants had yet to buy their last tranche of land from the Pitshanger estate. This was the roughly square area that contains the western part of Meadvale Road including the Institute, Holyoake Walk, North View and Denison Road. The purchase of this was not finalised until 1909, but so enthusiastic was Pearson about the matter that he produced a plan for it in his own time.

While the detailed planning of the blocks was almost certainly the work of George Lister Sutcliffe, who succeeded Pearson as architect in 1910, the layout of the new roads – Denison Road, Holyoake Walk and North View – was Pearson's work, and in planning them he reveals his sure-footedness in applying Unwin's ideas. Holyoake Walk and North View are examples of the gently curving informal roads that give ample scope for the creation of street pictures, while Denison Road leads straight on from Woodfield Road, providing a vista of the site for the new Institute. Ealing Tenants had finally decided not to build the Institute in Brentham Way but rather, for convenience' sake, next to the recreation ground created from 1907 onwards on the land north of Meadvale Road. The junction that Pearson suggested for Holyoake Walk and Denison Road appears to have been taken straight from *Town Planning in Practice*: a curve meets a straight, and there is a small green at the end. Furthermore, when viewed with the Institute, which had yet to be built, the junction creates a small *place* in the Unwin manner.

Pearson's enthusiasm did him no good. By this time the long-projected creation of a centralised architectural design department, for all the estates federated to Co-partnership Tenants Ltd, was in hand, and in April 1910 he was given a month's notice by Ealing Tenants to quit his job as surveyor. In the last couple of months that he worked for Ealing Tenants he produced designs for several more houses, at the south end of Brentham Way. These are of the 'good class of house' that Vivian had promised for the entrance to the estate, and one design, in particular, for a detached house that might have been built next to Widecombe, is especially appealing.

In the event, G.L. Sutcliffe was not taken on as Co-partnership Tenants' architect until November 1910, but he started work for Ealing Tenants in March 1910, and the delay was probably purely administrative. There is no suggestion that Pearson's replacement was due to anything other than this desire for centralisation, and that he was not chosen for that job was probably because a more experienced man was being sought: Pearson was still only 28. For all the vagaries of Pearson's house planning, he had an instinctive understanding of the way that Unwin's plan worked, and the result is 'street pictures' unequalled in charm, if not sophistication, in either Hampstead or Letchworth.

Pearson stayed on in Brentham as a tenant until 1912. His next post was as architect to a new garden suburb, organised initially as a co-partnership, planned for Sutton, south London, under the initiative of the sausage magnate Thomas Wall. Although only three streets were ever built, as the First World War effectively put paid to the scheme, the plan Pearson produced confirms his understanding of Unwin's ideas. His tendency to cram in every possible feature, as in some of his house designs at Brentham, is still in evidence. There is a wood, as at Hampstead, an institute with recreation

ground as at Brentham, and there are many gently curving roads, which take account of the sloping site. Then there are cul-de-sacs, and several small greens with houses arranged around on three sides.

One unusual feature that Pearson takes from Unwin are the traffic roundabouts projected for Aultone Way: the first example in Britain was designed by Unwin at Sollershot Circus, Letchworth, only two years before Pearson's Sutton plan. Pearson's house designs at Sutton are a mix: there are small terraced cottages that are much more sober than most of his Brentham designs,

BELOW: *F.C. Pearson's plan for Sutton Garden Suburb, 1912. Pearson's plan incorporates most of the features developed by Unwin in his planning – curving streets, cul-de-sacs, village greens, woodland, even what appear to be traffic roundabouts, which were used for the first time in Britain only two years previously. Only the Y-shaped section to the right of the plan was built – the First World War ended development.*

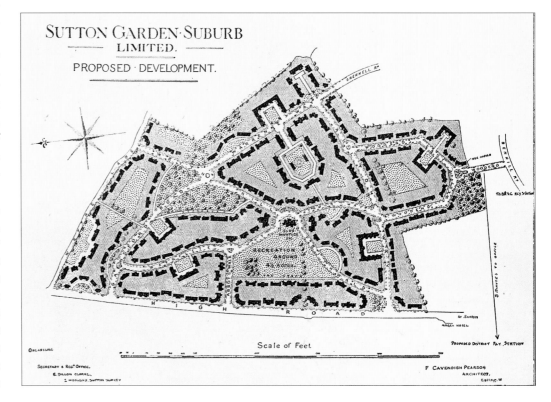

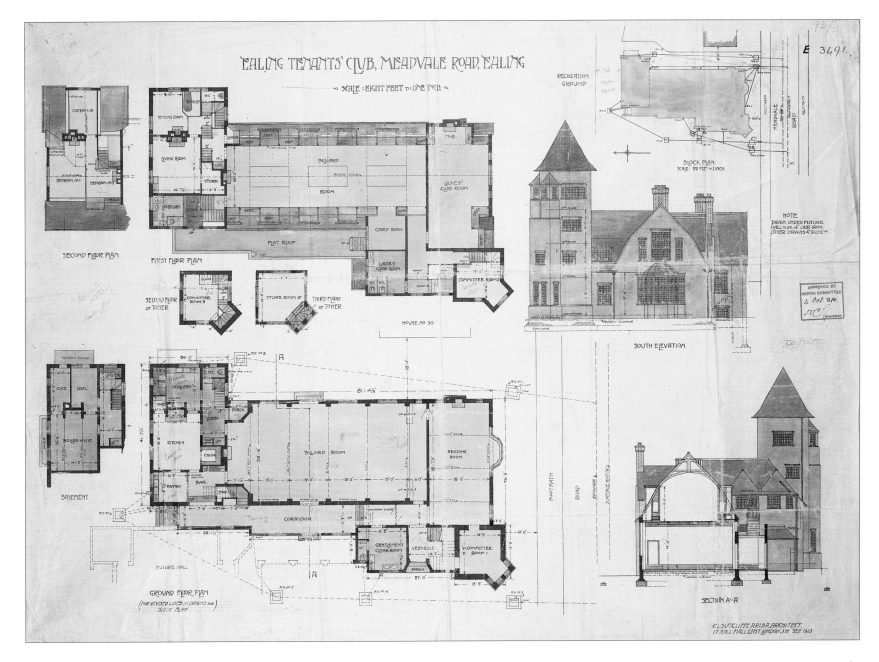

# EALING TENANTS' CLUB, MEADVALE ROAD, EALING

~ SCALE : EIGHT FEET TO ONE INCH ~

E 3491.

SECOND FLOOR PLAN

FIRST FLOOR PLAN

SECOND FLOOR of TOWER

THIRD FLOOR of TOWER

HOUSE No. 38

BASEMENT

GROUND FLOOR PLAN
(FOR REVISED LINES OF DRAINS SEE BLOCK PLAN)

BLOCK PLAN
SCALE : 22 FEET TO 1 INCH

RECREATION GROUND

SOUTH ELEVATION

NOTE
DRAIN UNDER FUTURE HALL TO BE 4" CAST IRON OTHER DRAINS 4" STONE WARE

APPROVED BY WORKS COMMITTEE
4 Oct 1910
CHAIRMAN

SECTION A-A

G. L. SUTCLIFFE ARIBA, ARCHITECT.
17 PALL MALL EAST LONDON, S.W. SEP. 1910

163

and would not look out of place alongside Unwin's cottages in Letchworth; and there are flamboyant corner houses, full of impossible angles, that make his Ludlow Road rhomboid houses look quite tame.

After Sutton, Pearson went on to work mainly as a local-authority architect, employed by Wandsworth Borough Council (for whom he designed a reinforced concrete library at Earlsfield in the 1920s) and, from 1927, for London County Council. Two projects he worked on for the LCC were the vast estates at St Helier, south London, and Becontree, Essex. In their use of small terrace blocks and informal layout, these estates are examples of the extraordinary influence (in an admittedly watered-down version) of Unwin's ideas about planning on public housing in the 1920s and 1930s. Pearson finally retired in 1952 and died in a house of his own design at Sutton Garden Suburb in 1963, having long outlived all the Brentham pioneers.

Pearson's replacement as Ealing Tenants' architect was another Yorkshireman, George Lister Sutcliffe. Sutcliffe was 45 when he was taken on by Ealing Tenants in 1910, and had an extensive career behind him as both architect and author. He was born in 1864 at Heptonstall above the Calder Valley near the Lancashire border, to William Mitchell and Rachel Lister Sutcliffe, who together ran a grocer's and draper's shop. The area was notable for non-conformist religion, Liberal politics and enthusiasm for the co-operative movement. Hebden Bridge, the main town below Heptonstall, was home to one of the earliest and most successful of co-partnership firms, Joseph Greenwood's fustian mills. Sutcliffe and his family were Baptists, and George Lister was active in the 1880s and 1890s as secretary and sometime conductor at his local church

LEFT: *George Lister Sutcliffe (1864–1915), c. 1900. Sutcliffe, like Pearson a Yorkshireman, arrived as Brentham's second architect in 1910 and stayed until his death in 1915. He was a much more experienced architect than Pearson when he arrived, with many commissions and several books on house construction under his belt. For all but the first few months of his time working on Brentham, Sutcliffe was architect to Co-partnership Tenants Ltd, as part of the centralisation of services in that body that had begun in 1907. As such, Brentham was only one of several co-partnership estates he worked on.*

PREVIOUS PAGE: *George Lister Sutcliffe's design for the Brentham Institute, 1910 (page 167). This was one of the first designs produced by Sutcliffe after he was made Brentham's architect in March 1910. The impressively large building, its design influenced by the clubhouse at Hampstead Garden Suburb, provided much-needed facilities for Brentham's tenants. The room labelled 'billiard room' on the ground floor was in fact the lecture room. Sutcliffe produced a revised design, incorporating changes suggested by Ealing Tenants, notably more or larger windows to the reading room and the ladies' clubroom.*

at Heptonstall Slack. Like Pearson he had personal experience of a planned community, as he went to the grammar school that had been built as part of the Moravian settlement of Fulneck, at Pudsey, near Leeds.

Sutcliffe was articled in 1880, when he was 15, to an architect in Hebden Bridge, John Sutcliffe (to whom, it appears, he was not related) and his partner James Henry Sutcliffe, and he was to stay with Sutcliffe & Sutcliffe, as pupil and partner, for 25 years. He married Daisy Johnson from Islington in 1897, and moved to London in 1902, where he carried on in partnership with the Sutcliffes. By the time he went to London,

RIGHT: *Birchcliffe Baptist Church, Hebden Bridge, West Yorkshire, 1897–9. This was one of several major commissions Sutcliffe had completed in his native county before he took over as architect at Brentham. It features the arcade that was to be a favourite motif of Sutcliffe's (see page 168).*

Sutcliffe had already built two non-conformist chapels near his home, at Boulder Clough and Birchcliffe, both bold, massive buildings with minimal decoration, in keeping with their prominent sites and the hardness of the local stone. After he moved to London in 1902, Sutcliffe maintained his professional contact with Yorkshire, where his many commissions included St Hilda's church in Halifax and a school at Todmorden.

When he went to London, as well as continuing in practice with the Sutcliffes, he took over the British practice of James Ransome, who had been appointed consulting architect to the government of India. The fact that Ransome left his practice in G.L. Sutcliffe's hands is significant: it reflects well on Sutcliffe as Ransome was quite a well-established London architect who would not have chosen a provincial architect like Sutcliffe had he not had a high opinion of his abilities. From Sutcliffe's point of view it was a great opportunity, as Ransome had an affluent client-base, having built a number of substantial houses in London and the Home Counties.

In a letter to his mother written on 17 October 1902, just five days after he had left his family in Heptonstall, Sutcliffe reported that Ransome had taken him 'to Wimbledon and introduced me to some of his friends', that he was to dine 'with Mr Ransome in company with the High Sheriff of some neighbouring county', and that 'Mr Ransome is very kind, and is putting work in my way, so that even in the first week I have made a good deal more than my expenses'. It was this association that enabled Sutcliffe over the following eight years to build, or substantially alter, more than a dozen major houses, including Blackwood House at Dartnell Park in Surrey, and The Dover at Poling in Sussex.

Although Sutcliffe might have enjoyed a successful career as a minor country-house architect, there were elements in his character and interests that meant this was unlikely to satisfy him. He was clearly a man with a strong sense of social responsibility. He had been active in the church in Hebden Bridge, and had run the 'Band of Hope' there. If this sounds a trifle dull and worthy, he was also an enthusiastic cricketer at Heptonstall Slack and a keen musician. He wrote an opera libretto and designed his own furniture. And, significantly for his future at Brentham, he seems to have been sympathetic to the co-operative movement. He built co-operative stores there – not perhaps surprising, given the strength of the co-operative movement locally – but more tellingly he called his elder son Maurice (so Maurice's son, Michael, recalls) after Frederick Denison Maurice, the co-partnership pioneer who also gave his name to Denison Road.

Despite his impressively varied professional and leisure interests, Sutcliffe still found time to be a productive writer. The design of country houses was not his principal concern: as well as book reviews for the trade press, some of them amusingly waspish in tone, he wrote or edited six books on construction. These include a very early treatise on the use of concrete in building (1893), and *The Principles and Practice of House Construction* (1898–9), which laid great stress on sound, economical construction techniques, and ease of maintenance, for achieving 'healthfulness of houses'. Sutcliffe had ample opportunity for putting his ideas to the test, because as well as the larger houses he had built, he also built many smaller ones, both in his native Hebden Bridge and surrounding area, and in Surrey and Buckinghamshire once he had moved to London.

How he came to the attention of Ealing Tenants is not certain. Sutcliffe had been working on his own since 1908. In 1907 he had severed his ties with Sutcliffe & Sutcliffe, and the following year James Ransome had returned from India to resume his practice in England. The most likely explanation for his presence at Ealing is that he had met Henry Vivian at Hebden Bridge through Joseph Greenwood, a high-profile co-partnership businessman, and Greenwood's son Crossley, secretary of Garden City Tenants.

But Sutcliffe might also have met Vivian – or indeed Parker and Unwin – when he moved to Hampstead in 1908, or from his interest in planning. In 1909 he produced a new edition of his book *The Principles and Practice of Modern House Construction* that has a much-expanded section on house- and cottage-planning, and includes reflections on town planning that suggest a familiarity with Unwin's recently published *Town Planning in Practice*.

Sutcliffe was initially approached by Ealing Tenants merely to provide a new plan for the laying out of

Brentham Way, presumably because the society had finally decided, in February 1910, to dispense with the idea of building the Institute there. This was a major departure from Unwin's plan, and was the final nail in the coffin (following the abandonment in 1908 of the idea of building shops there) of the notion of Brentham Way as the social centre and principal avenue. But it was a practical decision. Brentham's recreation ground, which was now 15 acres in extent following the purchase of the new land in 1909, was some distance from Unwin's suggested site in Brentham Way, and it made sense to build the Institute in Meadvale Road where the social and sporting facilities could be together.

Sutcliffe soon provided a new block plan of the estate, based on Pearson's 1909 plan of Denison Road, Holyoake Walk and North View, and designs for the new Institute. But at no stage did it seem that Sutcliffe would become an 'on-site' architect and tenant, as Pearson had done. He was settled with his family in

ABOVE: *The Brentham Institute, seen from the northwest, c. 1912. The new tennis courts had a rather better surface than the old court behind Woodfield Avenue. Hard courts were added in the early 1920s.*

RIGHT: *The balcony of the Institute, c. 1912. It was from here that the Duke of Connaught addressed the assembled masses when he opened the Institute on 27 May 1911.*

BELOW: *The billiard room of the Institute, 1911. The building has not yet been completed as the electric lights have yet to be fitted. The absence of the billiard tables means that Sutcliffe's fitted window seats can be seen clearly.*

Hampstead, and in November 1910 he was taken on as architect to Co-partnership Tenants Ltd, working from their offices at 6 Bloomsbury Square. This did not, however, affect his relationship with Ealing Tenants. Vivian believed that services, including the raising of capital, should be centralised. A central 'Architects' and Surveyors' Department' would, he argued, be 'a great help to our movement as a whole', and would help to 'accumulate experience in the planning of houses and estates'. It would also help to 'get together information on local building bye-laws and regulations, some of which are not only useless and wasteful, but here and there can only be called stupid'.

One of the main bye-laws that caused trouble for architects working in the garden-city manner was the demand for adherence to the building line. It was part of Unwin's creed that instead of adhering strictly to the building line, houses should break back and forth to create visual interest. Pearson had already applied this rule, but Sutcliffe stretched the point further. This was first evident in his designs for the Institute, which were presented to Ealing Council in October 1910. The borough surveyor, Charles Jones, wrote to Sutcliffe, concerned that the tower of the Institute might constitute

ABOVE: *View from the tower of the Institute, c. 1912, including the small shelter designed by Sutcliffe. Verdant views like this one were an important aspect in the planning of Brentham.*

BRENTHAM INSTITUTE, HALL & HOSTEL.
BRENTHAM GARDEN SUBURB FOR EALING TENANTS LIMITED. G.L. SUTCLIFFE, ARIBA ARCHITECT.

an 'obstruction', because it sits further forward than any of the other houses in Meadvale Road. Sutcliffe wrote back to the effect that this was the point of his design, that the tower should be a landmark on the estate.

He could have added that it was doubly important to draw attention to the tower, because the Institute was built at one of the lowest points of the estate, which meant that giving it the prominence that was desired would present a challenge. Building on the higher ground of Brentham Way, as Unwin had suggested, would have been an easier option. But Jones accepted Sutcliffe's argument anyway. Although he was of an

older generation, and had by 1910 been Ealing's surveyor for nearly 50 years, Charles Jones was not unsympathetic to the planning aims of Brentham: in the 1880s he had laid out the roads on Castlebar Hill to the south, in a manner that can be seen, like Bedford Park in Chiswick, as a forerunner of Unwin's informal planning.

The building of the Institute was a major venture for Ealing Tenants, but it was much needed by this time. For the previous four years, despite the growth of the estate and its social life, a house at 33 Woodfield Crescent had had to serve as the institute, and it was now inadequate. The new Institute was roughly

ABOVE LEFT: *Perspective of proposed Brentham Institute, hall and hostel by G.L. Sutcliffe, 1910. Sutcliffe originally planned to balance the Institute with a men's hostel – a building composed of bedsits. The two would have been linked by an arcade, behind which would have been another large hall.*

BELOW: *52–6 Meadvale Road, c. 1911. This photograph shows how Sutcliffe adopted a rather simpler architectural manner than Pearson. The roof angles are all a standard 45 degrees, the windows are prefabricated in standard sizes, and chimney flues are concentrated as much as possible into a single stack. Note the post-and-chain fencing, which marked front garden boundaries while the hedges were growing (the fencing could be removed later).*

rectangular, with its narrow end towards Brentham Way. Inside, its principal rooms were a large lecture hall, billiard room, a reading room and a ladies' club-room. Sutcliffe also designed fittings such as inglenook seating in the ladies' room, and window seating in the billiard room, in a stripped-down Arts and Crafts manner similar to Unwin's. The tower, which was such a prominent feature at the southwest corner, was largely taken up with committee rooms, and a very narrow stair. At the north end was living accommodation intended for a caretaker.

The Institute was originally meant to be merely the eastern wing of a three-sided complex that would be open to Meadvale Road. To the north would have been an additional hall, with an arcade to the south and a terrace to the north, looking out on the view over the Brent towards Harrow. To the west would have been a building variously described as a 'men's hostel' and 'bachelor flats'. The latter was in keeping with the idea of having as wide a variety of housing as possible on the estate, but it also indicates a desire to experiment with communal living, with shared dining and laundry facilities, on the lines advocated by Ebenezer Howard and put into practice at Homesgarth, Letchworth.

Only the Institute was built, but it still remained a major departure in architectural form from most of Brentham as it then existed. It reveals Sutcliffe's familiarity both with *Town Planning in Practice* and with the latest developments at Hampstead Garden Suburb. The tower and the forms of the roofs are Germanic in type, and bear a close resemblance to the German towns such as Rothenburg, illustrated by Unwin in his book. This manner had already been used the year before at Hampstead Garden Suburb by the architect Charles Paget Wade in his design for the clubhouse at Willifield Green; and in the pair of buildings containing flats and shops, known as Temple Fortune House and Arcade House, designed by A.J. Penty.

The precise form of the tower, with a square bay canted round at 45 degrees, is, however, a personal variant of Sutcliffe's. He had used a similar feature, though only in a single storey, at The Dover at Poling in Sussex, and was also to use it in houses in Holyoake Walk, but the extension of the feature through the whole height of the tower seems to have been a one-off.

What is notable in the Institute, and was to be a feature of all the houses he went on to design, was how much

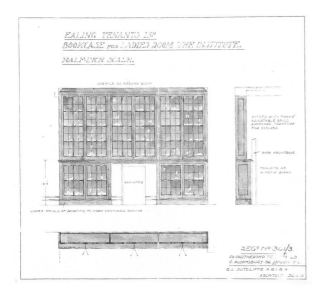

simpler they were in treatment than Pearson's. No longer are there complex roof forms, with several different angles converging to create complicated and expensive constructional problems. With the sole exception of the slight mansard effect on the main roof of the Institute, all Sutcliffe's roof forms are a standard and practical 45 degrees. The simplification is also evident in the restricted varieties of windows. Part of the rationale behind centralising services in Co-partnership Tenants was the saving of money; using fewer types of windows (which were made in Letchworth by Woodworkers Ltd, successors to General Builders) was a way of reducing unit costs. These unit costs dropped ever lower as more and more co-partnership estates took advantage of all the centralised facilities, and Sutcliffe found himself producing designs for estates in Liverpool (Wavertree) and Wrexham, as well as for Hampstead and Brentham.

Sutcliffe's other major building at Brentham was Holyoake House, the block of 24 flats built around three sides of a quadrangle in Holyoake Walk in 1912. Flats might seem anathema to the garden-city ideal of a home for every worker, but they appealed to the sentimental, atavistic yearning of many Arts and Crafts architects for a return to the communal living of medieval times. Howard was especially keen on the idea, and Unwin had offered illustrations for quadrangular buildings, clearly based on Oxbridge college quads, in both *Cottage Plans and Common Sense* and *The Art of Building a Home*. The idea found special favour at Hampstead Garden Suburb, where there are, or were, several examples, including Baillie Scott's Waterlow Court 'for single working ladies', of 1909, and Sutcliffe's Meadway Court, of 1913.

In designing Holyoake House, Sutcliffe reused some of his own ideas. The arcade at ground-floor level, for

LEFT: *Bookcase for the ladies' clubroom of the Institute, 1911. Sutcliffe's interest in fitted furniture – he had edited a series on cabinet-making – is evident here.*

BELOW: *Holyoake House, Holyoake Walk, c. 1914. Holyoake House consisted of 24 small flats originally aimed at single people and retired couples. Although it had a communal laundry into the 1950s, there was no shared kitchen or dining-room, and it never aimed to replicate the co-operative living that Unwin believed would encourage a community spirit.*

example, comes from his original plan for the Institute. Holyoake House was an attempt to provide accommodation for single people and 'elderly couples' unable to afford the rent on even the smallest Brentham house. But it broke one of the cardinal rules of Ealing Tenants, because not all the flats had lavatories; the two projecting bays on the main front, with their elegant, Japanese-looking hipped roofs, housed lavatories on the walkways for the flats behind them.

The Institute and Holyoake House were important designs for Sutcliffe, but most of his time at Brentham was taken up designing houses. The first houses he designed were an addition to one of Pearson's 'butterfly' houses and the house adjoining (now 3 and 5 Brunswick Road), but the rest of his first year he devoted to Meadvale Road. The revised plan he produced for the layout of the houses in Meadvale and Denison Roads, Holyoake Walk and North View, reveals that he had a rather more sophisticated grasp of Unwin's ideas about estate planning than Pearson. Although Pearson staggers his blocks of houses in relation to each other so as to produce a picturesque effect, he does not appear

RIGHT: *The junction of Holyoake Walk and Meadvale Road, seen from the Institute tower, c. 1913. This photograph shows Brentham in the days when a single delivery cart was the only traffic and the street trees were a manageable size.*

to have a sense of an overall picture governing his planning. Sutcliffe, however, keeps in mind variety both within the blocks and in the overall scheme. An early example of this is in Meadvale Road, where numbers 80 and 82 are designed set forward from numbers 84–90. This does three things: it creates variety within that block; it provides a visual stop or 'endpoint' to the three blocks to the east (52–78), so that together the 16 houses work to produce a small, informal *place*; and by setting back numbers 84–90 it acknowledges the houses off the estate to the west, and serves to effect a transition to the more conventional houses beyond.

This awareness of the overall picture is also evident in the way Sutcliffe handles houses that step up a hill. In common with the builders of, for example, Woodfield Crescent, Pearson tended to have his houses step up only slightly. This created a break in the various lines of, for example, the porches and eaves of houses in relation to their neighbours (as at 13–16 Brunner Road). However, when Sutcliffe faced this problem, for example at 10–20 and 9–19 Denison Road in 1911, he kept the eaves line straight through the block, but dealt with the rise in the land by shifting the level of the floors up. To accommodate this shift in internal levels, he used first gables, then both gables and half-dormers, as the houses rise up the hill.

Sutcliffe's sensitivity to the broader picture extends beyond the designing of entire streets as an homogeneous entity, to the whole estate. Where Pearson tended to mix and match features and materials within the one block, Sutcliffe uses variety more sparingly. For example, on the north side of Meadvale Road, there are two blocks entirely of brick, one entirely rendered, and two that are both brick and render. But this variety is

also related to the types of houses, and their setting. These houses in Meadvale are medium-sized by Brentham standards, and the materials relate to the relatively informal conception of the layout of the blocks. In Fowlers Walk, which Sutcliffe designed in 1913 and 1914, the houses are all rendered, a simple treatment in keeping with the small size of the houses. But in the central part of Brentham Way, designed in 1911 and 1913, he uses a more urban vocabulary of wide bands of red brick and pale render, the blocks of eight houses stepping back and forth in twos and fours to create small, formal squares as envisaged by Unwin in 1907.

This sensitivity to Unwin's planning is evident in the way Sutcliffe revised the layout of Fowlers Walk. He reinstated Unwin's cul-de-sac feature at the south end, and got round the problem of the narrow carriageway, by making the road an acceptable 40 feet wide, and by arranging the houses around it as if it were a small central green. Because the decision had been made not

ABOVE: *2, 4 and 6 (right to left) Brentham Way, c. 1911. These are examples of the 'good class' (i.e. large) house Vivian wanted at what was seen as the entrance to Brentham – there are only ten detached houses in Brentham, and most of these date from after the First World War. Number 2, built in 1909 to a design by Parker and Unwin, belonged to William Hutchings, the vice-chairman (later chairman) of Ealing Tenants. Numbers 4 and 6, by Sutcliffe, are detached four-bedroom houses, linked by a wall with an arched opening. Here Unwin's idea about 'framed vistas' is put into practice – the arch is on the axis of Brentham Way and provides a vista towards Harrow.*

to have public buildings on Brentham Way, he was also able to tie Fowlers Walk more into the rest of the estate. This he did by aligning the end of Fowlers Walk where it joins Brentham Way, with the end of Woodfield Crescent; and by designing a pair of houses (123 and 125) at an angle to the road but looking directly along Woodfield Crescent, to which they also form an end-point. Sutcliffe also followed Unwin in placing houses so as to preserve existing trees. This can be seen at 37–51 Meadvale Road where two blocks are angled away from the road so as to accommodate two large oaks (now lost) on the boundary between the blocks.

While Pearson and Sutcliffe were both essentially followers of Unwin as a planner, the varied ways they interpreted his ideas contributed to the obvious differences between streets built with Pearson-designed houses and those that are mainly Sutcliffe's work: the differences lie not just in their different architectural manners. But what of their different approaches to house planning? Is there is a similar contrast here? The answer seems to be yes and, occasionally, no. Although Sutcliffe's architectural manner is more restrained than Pearson's, there are still rooms of unusual shapes, notably in blocks that turn a corner. Sutcliffe, however, makes things easier for himself because he does not always feel the need to have a straight party wall.

There are also occasional oddities over the placing of the pantries. At 21 and 33 Meadvale Road and 50 Denison Road, the pantry is located off the hallway, while at 58 Holyoake Walk, it opens off the living room. And yet there is a logic to this: in each case the pantry is located on the north, and therefore coolest side of the house. There is also a more rational approach to the coalhole. Sutcliffe, like Pearson, occasionally uses the

understairs in smaller houses as the coalhole, but usually only when the stairs adjoin the back wall, so that there is a direct outside opening for the delivery of the coal. A feature that Sutcliffe developed in many of his medium and smallish houses was a small brick-built lean-to containing a larder that opened into the scullery, and a coalhole that opened to the outside. In some of the smallest houses, such as 1–12 North View, he utilises space in three dimensions by accommodating the larder above the coalhole.

Another general difference between the Sutcliffe houses and Pearson's is in the bathroom arrangements. Whereas in the smallest Pearson houses, the lavatory is placed downstairs in the lean-to, in the smallest Sutcliffe houses, such as most in Denison Road and the smaller houses in Holyoake Walk, North View and Fowlers Walk, the bathroom and lavatory are combined in one small upstairs room, although this may have been more

RIGHT: *Interior of a cottage parlour, Bird's Hill, Letchworth, c. 1910. Tenants in co-partnership estates were far less wedded to simple-life rusticity than the middle-class followers of Unwin. This cluttered interior was probably fairly typical of Brentham interiors before the First World War.*

a reflection of the increasing stigma of an outside lavatory than the architect's choice. The only houses that have an outside lavatory are the large houses at 4, 6, 32 and 34 Brentham Way, but these were in addition to a separate upstairs lavatory. In this case the outside lavatory is, paradoxically, a status symbol, in that it is intended for the use of a servant. Sutcliffe was also responsible for a design of a deceptive-looking building at 38 Brentham Way. Although this looked like one house, it was in fact two flats, each of one bedroom and a living room, but the pressure of space meant that the scullery and bathroom were combined: the bath was fitted with a table top when it was not in use.

The large houses at 32 and 34 Brentham Way also display certain constructional novelties. They have wood-block flooring throughout the ground floor (with the exception of part of the kitchen that was tiled), laid on a concrete base. This differs from the usual arrangement of timber floorboards supported on joists suspended over brick foundations. This woodblock, or parquet, flooring reflects the 'good class' of these houses in the upper part of Brentham Way, but the same constructional novelty of the concrete floor was used in the much smaller houses at 39–45 Holyoake Walk. The floor covering here, however, is described on the plans as 'cork carpet', presumably something like cork tiles. These six houses in Brentham Way and Holyoake Walk also share another novelty in the form of integral cycle sheds.

It is interesting to note that houses at Brentham differed from many of the houses designed by architects such as Parker and Unwin for middle-class clients, where the architects' influence extended to the design of interior fittings and decoration. Until around 1910, most houses had such fittings as fireplaces, ranges, door

furniture and baths chosen by the works committee and bought from commercial suppliers. Fittings such as doors, garden gates, and kitchen dressers were made to the works committee's usually fairly conventional designs by firms such as General Builders. After 1910, when Sutcliffe took over, and General Builders had become Woodworkers, based in Letchworth, there was more control and standardisation of such fittings. But the design of them was hardly Arts and Crafts: the standard fireplace design after around 1910 was a sub-Adam neo-Georgian type, typical of more conventional contemporary taste.

This was perhaps because the tenants were less attracted by simple-life rusticity than were middle-class

ABOVE: *Meadvale Road seen from the tower of the Institute, c. 1913. The houses that back on to the recreation ground were protected from flying tennis and cricket balls by high fences. They would have enjoyed rural views towards Harrow – the planners of Brentham believed that such vistas would provide for children 'a healthy and picturesque environment, their minds being trained to see the natural beauties within the shadow of their homes'.*

ABOVE: *Little girl at a garden gate, Meadvale Road, c. 1914. This photograph shows Sutcliffe's skill in stepping his blocks of houses back along the straight road to create an informal and picturesque effect.*

utopian architects such as Raymond Unwin. It is important to realise that the illustrations of house interiors in books produced by Unwin and his contemporaries and in journals, such as *The Studio*, that were sympathetic to their aims, probably bore as much resemblance to the typical Brentham interior before the First World War as the photographs in magazines like *Wallpaper* and *Elle Decoration* do to the typical Brentham interior of today. Just as not everyone now favours beech and steel and glass bricks, neither were Brentham houses then filled with light-painted woodwork, rush matting and simple handcrafted furniture.

A telling illustration comes from Mrs Madeline Jones (b. 1914), whose parents were the first tenants of 41 Holyoake Walk, one of the blocks described above that had a cork-carpeted concrete floor. This house had been an Ealing Tenants show house (which may also explain the constructional novelties), and as such it had what was deemed especially tempting decor. But far from being a model of up-to-the-minute Arts and Crafts rusticity, the house had bright-red distempered walls to the ground floor, green distempered walls to the upper floor and expensive painted graining to the woodwork. This last was the epitome of 'falseness' in design (that is, pretending to be something that it wasn't) that had been denigrated by Ruskin and Morris and their many Arts and Crafts progeny, for the previous half century. Almost as out of keeping with Arts and Crafts taste was the standard finish on woodwork in Brentham houses, a dark brown varnish. An example of this survives (at the time of writing) in the pantry of 3 Meadvale Road. One cannot help seeing it as a quiet subversion of the sometimes overweening wholesomeness of the Arts and Crafts movement.

Perhaps just as out of keeping with the rustic aesthetic of much of Brentham, and with its scale, was St Barnabas Church on the corner of Denison Road and Pitshanger Lane, designed in 1914 and opened in 1916. It was also, perhaps, subversive of some of Brentham's aims. Unlike Hampstead Garden Suburb, churches were not a feature of any of the plans for Brentham. Religious and quasi-religious observance was catered for in the Institute, but Anglicans before the First World War had to make their way up the hill to St Peter's, or make do with the small, iron mission church established by the parishes of St Stephen's and St Peter's on the corner of Pitshanger Lane and Castlebar Park Road in 1908. Although Ealing

Tenants Ltd sold the land to build the new church (at a handsome profit), they do not seem to have had a great deal of involvement in its building, their main concern being that bell-ringing should not disturb the suburb's calm.

The architect of the church was Ernest C. Shearman, assisted by a local man, Ernest Tyler. Shearman is an enigmatic personality, who had spent many years in Argentina. Perhaps this unusual background helps explain the striking originality of the design, a stark late Gothic Revival, offset by exuberant flowing tracery, with odd, stunted towers between transepts and chancel, and a rounded apse. St Barnabas is the first of three very similar churches Shearman designed in west London (the others are St Francis, Osterley, and St Gabriel, Acton): right into the 1930s he stuck by the same vocabulary of forms and materials – dark purple brick outside and pink brick within. But this commission did not end happily for him. Although St Barnabas had been designed with west towers, funds could not be found to build these. Shearman, however, neglected to tell the builders this, and they did not find out until 15,000 bricks had been hoisted to the roof of the west end. In June 1915 Shearman was dismissed, and Tyler took over. Under difficult wartime conditions, the builders completed the church for its consecration on 3 June 1916, when it was so packed that the doors had to be locked.

By the time St Barnabas was consecrated, building in the rest of Brentham had ground to a halt. The last work was carried out in the spring of 1915, by which time George Lister Sutcliffe was beginning to show signs of the congenital heart defect that killed him, at the age of 50, in September 1915. Sutcliffe gives the

LEFT: *G.L. Sutcliffe and some small friends, shortly before his death in 1915. Sutcliffe was only 50 when he died, but he left his mark in the 1,500 houses that were built to his designs in Brentham, Hampstead and several of the other co-partnership estates.*

impression, as did Vivian, of a man with a clear vision of what he wanted to achieve. He combined the prodigious energy needed to realise his aims, with the power to inspire others to help him, and he had worked tirelessly for the preceding five years, during which time 1,500 houses had been built to his designs at Ealing, Hampstead and other co-partnership estates at Liverpool, Wrexham and Stoke. The architectural and planning character of Brentham was already thoroughly established by the time Sutcliffe died, and it forms a tangible memorial to him, and the unshakeable belief that he shared with Parker and Unwin and the co-partners who had dreamed up Brentham, that better lives are led in better houses.

## 7

# Brentham in war and peace 1:
# 1914–1939

*Who would have prophesied six months ago that a European war*
*would have had so little outward effect on our suburb?*

The Brentham Magazine, October 1914

REAT CHANGES might have been expected following the outbreak of war in August 1914, but in the event, it affected Brentham much as it did the rest of the country. There was first of all a flurry of anxiety and patriotic fervour. Around the country thousands of men heeded the call to arms, while the government warned the populace at large against hoarding gold – and food. The railways were taken over by the government, with free travel for men in uniform, and buses were requisitioned to go to the front. Around Ealing some of the war measures now appear slightly farcical, reminiscent of the rumours of 'Storm troopers dressed as nuns' of the Second World War. Garage managers in Ealing were asked to report to the police 'any instance of foreigners taking out cars'. The Ealing Homing Pigeon society was also keen to do its bit, and joined the National Voluntary Pigeon Post. Urging their members to put their 'loft of birds at the disposal of the authorities', they

added: 'In this crisis it is the duty of every patriotic pigeon fancier to answer the call'.

Meanwhile, the *Middlesex County Times* in its first issue after war broke out, was exhorting its readers to 'Keep your heads. Be calm . . . Do not indulge in excitement or foolish demonstrations'. Perhaps mindful of this, the first reaction in Brentham to the declaration of war was eminently practical. At the end of August 1914 the Brentham Protection Association (BPA) was formed to take care of 'the need that may press heavily upon its residents before many weeks'. Supplementing the Ealing Committee for National Emergency Work, it pledged itself to bring to the attention of the Executive anyone in need of financial assistance because of the war – wives of servicemen, principally – and to help those who did not qualify for the Executive's assistance. Residents were asked to subscribe what they could afford, and within a few weeks more than 180 households had committed themselves. The Brentham

Protection Association also made it its business to keep an eye on prices and to report any perceived profiteering. Although conscription did not come in until early in 1916, by October 1914, 41 men had enlisted from Brentham. In Ealing, one of the first tangible signs of the war was the arrival of Belgian refugees. Children in Brentham put on a concert to entertain and raise money for them.

After a few weeks, everything settled down. It really appeared to be that it was, as the popular slogan of the time had it, 'Business as Usual'. That few people could foresee how long and bloody the war was going to be is perhaps no wonder: neither did the government, which largely viewed Lord Kitchener's demand for mass mobilisation as a waste of time and money. It was generally thought that by the time a large army had been raised and sent abroad, economic tactics – blockading Germany – would have secured victory for the Allies.

That this was not going to happen became apparent by the early part of 1915, but the editor of *The Brentham Magazine* could have been forgiven for his comment in October 1914, quoted at the beginning of this chapter: the sporting and social sections of the Brentham Club and Institute certainly took the injunction to 'Carry on' at its face value. The hockey club, conscious that there were some rumblings in the suburb about the advisability of carrying on with games during the National Emergency, sternly quoted the *Infantry Drill Book* that 'Manly games are of value . . . Games and competitions should be used to impress the value of combination as well as of individual prowess'. The problem for some clubs was finding matches, as some of their old opponents were greatly depleted by enlistment. The hockey players and cricketers struggled

on with matches against scratch teams until the winter of 1915 and the summer of 1916 respectively. But other clubs, such as the bowling club, most of whose members were above military age, thrived. A new bowling green was created in 1916 on the recreation ground replacing the old one that had been laid where the original 1904 tennis courts had been, on the site between Woodfield Avenue and Brunner Road.

And new clubs came into being that reflected the 'exceptional times'. A rifle club was started in October 1914, under the tutelage of 'crack shot' Jim Phillips, after Mr L. Roberts of The Grange in Perivale offered the use of a range there, and by the end of the year the club had 73 members. By 1915 Ealing Tenants had built their own range on the northeast of the recreation ground, or 'rec', at the far edge of the cricket field – although it was observed that the cricketers were noticeable by their absence when the rifle-club novices were on the range. A subsection of the rifle club was the Drill Squad, which performed their 'Swedish drill' in the Institute hall, adhering to the requirement of membership that rubber shoes should be worn to protect the floor. Enthusiasm was such that it was proposed to raise a Brentham platoon of 50 men among the Ealing Volunteers, a regiment formed to stimulate recruiting for the Territorials and the regular Army. It transpired, however, that residents could not be persuaded that joining the Brentham platoon might not commit them to active service at the Front, and, by February 1915, the idea of the platoon had been abandoned, although the drill section continued.

One feature of Brentham life that received a great stimulus from the war was allotment gardening. The Horticultural Society, which was subsidised by Ealing

ABOVE: *The Evans family outside their home, 4 Brentham Way, c. 1920. The children, Agnes, Kate and Richard (seen here with a toy car), are with their stepmother, Ellen. A contemporary of Richard Evans recalls how the absence of traffic in those early days meant that the street was a safe place in which to play.*

Tenants, could supply all garden requirements, including seeds for 26 kinds of vegetables, as well as the rose trees for which Brentham was renowned. There had been allotments in Brentham since 1909, but after incessant prodding from the Horticultural Society, Ealing Tenants Ltd made land available, including much that had been earmarked for building after the war, as temporary allotments. The first site offered, in 1916, was an area of 16 plots between Holyoake Walk and Pitshanger Lane, west of St Barnabas Church which was nearing completion. This land stretched as far west as the Methodist Church, because in April 1915 Ealing Tenants had demolished Pitshanger farmhouse and its outbuildings, thereby severing one of the last remaining links with the past.

Although the frontage of the farmhouse, the part visible in most surviving photographs, was less than a hundred years old, much of the building behind was much older and, as was known at the time, one of the barns was sixteenth-century. Given the Arts and Crafts creed of conservation, the decision to demolish seems extraordinary, but it appears to have been made with few qualms. There was a war on. The allotment gardeners turned up some interesting finds on the farmhouse site, including what was thought to be a Stone Age axe head. This prompted a poem in *The Brenthamite*, the magazine that replaced *The Brentham Magazine* in March 1916, about 'Prehistoric Ealing', and the observation that the 'ancient Brenthamite/Oftimes was spoiling for a fight'.

In 1917 Ealing Tenants gave up more land, this time at the north end of Fowlers Walk and Brentham Way, although this was so waterlogged that suggestions for aquatic gardening were invited. More attractive was

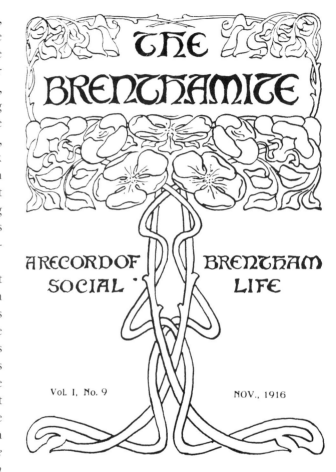

the site between Woodfield Avenue and Brunner Road, which had been used first for tennis courts and then as a bowling green: 'Where once the bowls so lively sped, the cabbage plant will raise its head', as *The Brenthamite*'s 'poet' put it.

Brentham residents were also the principal cultivators of the 'Dibdin House allotments' on land belonging to the Great Western Railway near what is now the Hanger Lane Gyratory System; the site had once been occupied by the home of Charles Dibdin, the nineteenth-century writer. Here the problem was not waterlogging, but rats and, on occasion, adders. Not all gardening, however, was done on allotments. In keeping with the spirit of looking after one's neighbours, a rota was organised to see that the gardens of men serving their country did not suffer. *The Brentham Magazine* issued a warning, however: 'Will the rota make quite sure, before entering a neglected-looking garden, that the occupier is really in the forces? Else there may be some slight mistakes.' And not all the cultivation in allotments and gardens involved plant life. During the war Ealing Tenants relaxed their rule about the keeping of hens, and many residents became self-sufficient in eggs.

Brentham residents also roused themselves in May 1916 to do something about the rise in the price of milk. The Brentham Protection Association had pledged itself to counter profiteering, and in May 1916 a meeting was called to protest at the rise from 5 pence to 6 pence a quart. The chairman was Fred Maddison, who had moved into 34 Brentham Way in 1915. He had been Liberal MP for, variously, Sheffield Brightside and Burnley, and was a long-time friend of Henry Vivian. After a rousing speech by Maddison, a milk strike was called and the BPA bought in boxes of condensed milk to keep the strikers supplied. By July 1916 the BPA was selling 300 tins a week. But the strikers lacked resolve or, according to *The Brenthamite*, the strength to operate a tin-opener. It was all over in a few weeks, and the price of fresh milk stayed up. But perhaps inspired by the spirit of self-help inherent in the milk strike, some enterprising Brenthamites produced Brentham-

brand toothpaste and Brentham-brand cigarettes, the latter on sale at the Institute.

With the introduction of conscription in 1916, the young men all but disappeared from the suburb. Until that summer, the tone of reports of the war had been generally light-hearted and optimistic. Sgt J.W. Small of Brunner Road and the Post Office Rifles, sent a cheery report from 'somewhere in France' about trench life, including the banter exchanged with the Germans in their front line 80 yards away, and the fact that signposts

ABOVE: *Protest against increased milk prices, London, October 1916. In May that year Brentham residents staged a milk strike to protest at the increase of one penny a quart. For several weeks they used tinned milk, bought in bulk by Ealing Tenants, to foil the 'profiteers', but resolve weakened and the strike collapsed.*

*BELOW: The Brentham Players in a production at the Brentham Institute, 1930s. The Players, who carried on into the 1960s, were founded by several members of the cast of the* Merrier England *pageant of 1912. As well as full-scale productions they performed readings, but their repertoire was more mainstream than the pageant, with a preponderance of Shakespeare, Shaw and Sheridan early on and Agatha Christie in later years. Hubert Brampton's daughter Elsie, a stalwart of the Brentham Players for many years, can be seen at far right.*

for Fleet Street, Victoria Street and Regent Street had been erected in the various trenches. By the spring of 1916 a trench had been named Woodfield Crescent in honour of Mr A.J.C. Edwards of 48 Woodfield Crescent, who had been sending parcels to the front.

But that summer the reality of the war's increasing brutality was finally brought home. Within a few days of each other, Gilbert Harris, Mortimer Downing and Arthur Sergeant, three young men who had been waved off in 1914 and 1915, were killed in France. In all, 19 Brentham residents died in action. The following year Julian Gould, the son of F.J. Gould of Woodfield Avenue, the writer on socialism, secularism and sociology, was killed in France; Arthur Turner and Percy Drover also died. But given the relatively high proportion of men of military age in the suburb, the losses could have been much greater.

Advances in technology also meant that the reality of the war became apparent in Brentham in a more general sense. Although bombing in the First World War was of minor importance compared to the Second, one of the memories that has stayed even with those who were very young at the time is of the 'daylight bombers', or Zeppelins, and the guns firing on them from Horsenden Hill. During one Saturday-morning air raid, one former resident remembered being sent with the other children into a field to lie beside a large Red Cross, in case 'the dreaded Hun' came over. It was because of the threat of these that a blackout was imposed, with 'Zepp paint' applied to most of the streetlights. Residents could also get a real sense of life at the front by attending film shows. Although these films were often of scenes contrived after the event, they created a sense of immediacy that had been missing in, for example, the Boer War only 15 years earlier. There were occasional 'kinema' presentations of these films in the Institute, as well as more regular showings in central Ealing. And not all technical advances related to the war. At this time residents in Brentham were offered the chance to try out a vacuum cleaner, when the Institute bought one and offered it for hire. This acquisition was very forward-looking, as vacuum cleaners had only been invented in 1901 and were still extremely rare.

On the home front, Brentham's social life had held up reasonably well right into 1917, with Saturday-night dances and regular performances and readings by the Brentham Players. But the last 18 months of the war were low-key in comparison with peacetime and the earlier part of the war. Hockey and cricket

ground to a halt, although children's sport continued, as did billiards and whist drives, but the liveliest occasions were probably the concerts given for wounded soldiers being treated at Montpelier Hospital. Even *The Brenthamite* ceased publication, temporarily as it happily turned out, in June 1918. The final blow to Brentham's social life was the requisitioning in September 1918 of the Institute building for the use of airmen. Nothing daunted, the Institute committee arranged for an empty house, 20 Neville Road, to be used as a clubhouse, and moved in one of the billiard tables, while the cricket pavilion was pressed into service for children's activities.

The disturbance was short-lived, in any case. At the eleventh hour of the eleventh day of the eleventh month, maroons were let off all over Ealing to signal the end of the war. Life – the influenza epidemic that blighted the peace notwithstanding – returned slowly to normal.

It took a little while for social and sporting activities to recover, but by 1921 membership of the Institute had risen to more than 550, from a wartime low of around 250. By the 1920s the way the club building was used had evolved. The 'ladies' room' had become a general common room, while one of the committee rooms was now the ladies' room. The reading room had become 'the small hall', and the lecture hall was no longer known by that name, presumably because it was more likely to be used for dances and plays than for lectures. A new development in the estate's sporting life took place in 1919 with the creation of a football section, which by 1921 was playing in the first division of the Dauntless League.

That year saw the first major separation between the Institute and Ealing Tenants, when the Brentham Club

and Institute was reconstituted as a co-partnership society, with its own committee. The independence was limited however, because the club was still heavily dependent on Ealing Tenants Ltd, both for direct financial support, and because the club and grounds were hired to the new society for a nominal fee. In 1922–4 the club spent £1,000, half of it given by Ealing Tenants Ltd, the rest subscribed by members, on improving the grounds. The money was used to build hard tennis courts, re-lay the bowling green, drain the cricket pitch, and rebuild the children's corner, with swings and baby swings, parallel bars or 'ladder', and an 'ocean wave'.

ABOVE: *The Brentham football team, 1920s. Although Brentham did not have its own club until 1919, it has been one of the most successful of Brentham's sporting clubs, with many cups to its credit.*

RIGHT: *C.R. Robinson plays chess with his brother-in-law, William Walls, at 28 Winscombe Crescent, 1920s.*

FAR RIGHT: *Brentham sports day, 1920s. The idea of this game was for the man in the wheelbarrow to pass his lance through a loop without tipping the bucket of water. Inevitably the participants got soaked.*

BELOW: *'Brentham Garden City'. The playground at the 'rec', 1920s.*

PUBLISHED BY   No. 196   BRENTHAM GARDEN CITY, EALING.   *Wakefields*   EALING. W. COPYRIGHT

These last facilities are remembered with fond affection by those people alive today who were children at the time. Living memory of Brentham stretches back to before the First World War, but memories are obviously more numerous of life in the period immediately after the war. The single most important aspect of Brentham for any child was clearly the recreation ground or 'rec', which is remembered as the focus for all the children's spare time, and was envied by school friends unfortunate enough not to live in Brentham. Recreation included taking part in 'official' sports, such as the Sports Days against Hampstead Garden Suburb (which had become an annual event in 1915), when children competed for the Godwin Cup; or playing beside, rafting on or falling into the River Brent. Eventually the Sports Days were discontinued. The reason, according to J.G. Taylor, a veteran resident looking back from the 1940s, was that 'Hampstead had nothing to offer in the way of a suitable venue . . . and had great difficulty in finding athletes to meet our fellows'. Among other developments, Douglas Dover (b. 1916) remembers the building of the Western Avenue over the Brent in 1924, and how the concrete supports were barely high enough when the Brent flooded, as water rose above the top of the arch. Doris Palmer (b. 1906), who lived in Fowlers Walk after the First World War, remembers the field to the east – ' a sea of buttercups' – before the Greystoke Estate was built in the 1930s.

All those with long memories remember the great variety of delivery carts that toured the estate, most of which came from businesses in Pitshanger Lane. There were milk deliveries twice a day, the dairyman pouring milk into the householder's jug, a baker, an oilman, a greengrocer, a knife grinder, and a man who repaired basket-weave chairs. The first shop locally was Kays, which was founded in 1903 and by the 1920s occupied four shops – a post office and newsagent, shoe shop, drapers and ironmongers – at 116–22 Pitshanger Lane. Until the 1930s shops were only on the north side, but these included an impressive variety such as the Pagoda sweet shop, Studds the greengrocers, several butchers, Sims the oilman and Benfields corn merchants. Then there was the Co-op, which started off at 50–2 Pitshanger Lane before the First World War, then moved to number 40 and ended up as a large shop on the south side of the Lane.

But the feature of Brentham life that remains most vivid in the minds of those who remember the years between the wars is, without doubt, the May Day processions, and because this is such an unusual survival, it is worth looking at in some detail. Until this time May Day in Brentham had been a sporadic occurrence, and restricted to occasional displays of maypole plaiting. The person who was responsible for developing this

and setting the pattern for May Day as it is celebrated in Brentham today was Molly Duncan. Miss Duncan had taught dance classes, especially ballets with fairy themes and 'acrobatic dancing', to local children during the First World War. In fact, the first postwar May Day, on 3 May 1919, bore little resemblance to the open-air procession and coronation. Miss Duncan's pupils assembled in the hall of the Institute where they crowned the May Queen and danced round an indoor maypole. The May Queen made a speech from her throne 'without preparation or prompting'. It was

ABOVE: *A snowy scene, Brentham Way looking towards Brunswick Road, 1920s. Delivery carts of all types – coal, fruit and vegetables, milk, meat, bread and fish, to name just the most common – were a fixture of street life in Brentham before the Second World War.*

RIGHT: *Atora delivery cart, Pitshanger Lane, 1920s. The choice of oxen to draw a cart advertising beef suet reflects the robust attitude to animals typical of the time.*

perhaps because so many children from the neighbourhood turned up to watch proceedings that it was decided the following year to expand the ceremony.

That year, 1920, saw the first Brentham May Day procession round the suburb, and although the exact route is not known, it was described as 'lengthy' and took in Pitshanger Lane. As well as the maypole dancers, the procession included Girl Guides and some adults in fancy-dress costume. One was a jester (perhaps reusing a costume from the *Merrier England* pageant), and another was described as a 'Glaxo baby'. For the first time in Brentham a Jack-in-the-green took part. In future years his identity would be a closely guarded secret, but on this occasion he was named as Mr L. Fielder. At the end of the procession were the May Queen-elect, Phyllis White, and her predecessor Audrey Mace. As in many future years, the procession ended at the football pitch of the recreation ground. (On other occasions the festivities took place between the Club and the Brent or on the cricket pitch.) The May Queen was crowned and she made a speech in which she hoped she would be worthy of the honour bestowed on her in her year of office. This has been the gist of May Queen speeches ever since. The dancing round the maypole began with the youngest children and was repeated by successively older age groups.

The 1920 festivities seem to have been almost an impromptu affair. Miss Duncan had prepared some of the dancers in only ten days. By 1921, however, reports suggested that the procession was beginning to be viewed as an annual event. New features that became standard in future processions were a cart (owned by Mr Pocknall, the greengrocer) decorated with flowers, carrying toddlers too young to walk with the procession, and drawn by members of the Brentham ex-servicemen's association; a crown bearer to carry the May Queen's crown of flowers; and the band of the Cuckoo schools in Hanwell, which headed the procession. Another new feature that became traditional was a tea for the children held afterwards in the Institute.

In 1921 the exact route was recorded. It resembles very closely the route of recent years. From the Institute the procession went east along Meadvale Road, then via Ludlow Road, Ruskin Gardens and Brunner Road to Pitshanger Lane. It is interesting that it then went off the estate along Pitshanger Lane as far as Harrow View Road, before returning to the Institute via Meadvale Road. Once again, the procession included a Jack-in-the-green, who amused the crowd with his antics. There was also, once again, a large selection of fancy-dress costumes, not necessarily 'old English' in character. For the first time the costumes were judged: 'Father Time', complete with hour glass and scythe (he sounds more like the grim reaper), and 'Early Victorian' both won prizes.

By this time Molly Duncan had bowed out of arranging the dancing, and the festivities were now in the hands of Connie Ephgrave and the children's committee of the Institute. The usual maypole dances were interspersed with Irish, Scottish and Welsh dances, stressing the British character of the occasion, as well a 'butterfly and flower dance' that suggests the influence of Molly Duncan's taste for whimsical fairy dances.

In 1922 a similar route was followed, although this year it took in Woodfield Crescent and Woodfield Avenue, and went along Pitshanger Lane only as far as Selby Road. Comic relief was provided by 'various male adults in grotesque costume' and by the Jack-in-the-green. The May Queen, Connie Taylor, made it clear in her speech that the children had been taught the *Golden Bough* line about May Day: 'Our May Day is held in the spring of the year, when we think of the return of life to all the plants, and the bright warm summer days to come. Our Keltic forefathers held a similar festival, and so did the Ancient Greeks and Romans'. The dances that year included a hornpipe.

The following year, 1923, saw two innovations that have now become standard features of Brentham May Day: the limitation of the route to the streets of Brentham, and the inclusion of boys among the maypole dancers. Most striking in the procession that year must have been the weird and wonderful array of fancy-dress costumes. These included old English favourites: St George and the Dragon, a Crusader, Robin Hood

and his Merry Men; but also some exotic and contemporary costumes, such as 'a posse of cow punchers' and a 'sports car' (a costume rather than a motor vehicle). Nothing dates the procession more surely than the presence of 'Tut-ankh-amen and his Queen'. Britain in the mid-1920s was in the grip of Egypt fever, brought on by the discovery in 1922 of Tutankhamen's tomb. Its influence led to fashionable Egyptian-style dresses, even Egyptian-style make-up, and it can still be seen in Egyptian details in buildings such as cinemas.

Tutankhamen is one of the more obvious examples of contemporary taste affecting Brentham's May Day:

ABOVE: *May Day, early 1920s. This is one of the first, possibly the first May Day parade. A suitable rustic note is struck by the baby in the straw-filled cart pushed by a 'yokel' (right), while the mother, dressed for the occasion (left), looks at the camera.*

RIGHT: *Programme for May Day, 1924. By this time many of the central features of Brentham May Days were in place – the procession led by a band, the crowning of the May Queen and an evening dance.*

BELOW: *Plaiting the maypole on the recreation ground, probably 1923. This was the first year boys (with dark stockings) took part in the plaiting. The third boy from the left is Fred Perry, the future tennis world champion.*

although the organisers, especially since the 1930s, have sought to preserve it unchanged, contemporary influences have always crept in. In 1923 it was Tutankhamen, but in any photograph of a May Day procession (even without the parked cars) it would be possible to date it to within a few years by the style of the participants' hair and costumes, even where they are dressed in the 'timeless' traditional white dresses.

These are, however, mainly questions of nuance and style. The core features of the festivities were already laid down by the early 1920s, but in 1924, two others were added: the procession was headed for the first time by a herald (now always played by a small boy), that year played by Dorothy, one of Hubert Brampton's

BRENTHAM CLUB & INSTITUTE, LTD.

PROGRAMME

Children's
May Day Festivities

ARRANGED BY THE CHILDREN'S COMMITTEE

Including the Crowning of the May Queen
MISS PEGGY WRIGHT

TO BE HELD ON THE

RECREATION GROUND

ON

Saturday, May 3rd, 1924

Procession starts from the Institute at 3 p.m. prompt

THE BAND OF THE CUCKOO SCHOOLS
will head the procession and play during the afternoon

ADMISSION TO THE GROUND — FREE

"MAY DAY" SPECIAL DANCE—LARGE HALL AT 8—1/-
"Shaftesbury" Orchestra

many daughters; and in the evening a May Day dance was held for the adults and older children (although this latter lapsed in the late 1980s and a 'family disco' would later replace it). Handing down the essential elements of May Day unchanged has been helped by continuity among the teachers. When Molly Duncan gave up, her place was taken by one of her pupils, Connie Ephgrave. In 1923 Miss Ephgrave shared the teaching with Doris Middleton, who took over on her own the following year. In 1924, for the last time, morris dancing was performed.

Despite the popularity of the May Day festivities, which, by 1924, were regarded as a set feature of Brentham social life, in 1925 there was no procession and no May Queen. (The new children's committee, it was said, had not had time to arrange the event.) That lack was made good the following year, but in the next four years there was no May Day, for reasons that are not explained. May Day as a children's ceremony had continued to be popular around the country into the 1920s. From 1907 a May Queen of London ceremony had been performed every year at Hayes Common, Bromley. The event's organiser, Joseph Deedy, had set up a 'Merrie England Society' in 1911 to encourage more such events, and by 1930 there were around a hundred. And new May festivities continued and were starting locally. Acton Wells School still had its May Day, and in 1923 Hobbayne School (originally Greenford Avenue School) in Hanwell had instituted a May Day ceremony that involved the selection of a May Queen by the children, a ceremonial presentation of a floral crown by a page to an honoured guest (usually a lady councillor) who would perform the coronation, and a maypole dance. As at Brentham it became customary over the years for May Queens from previous years to attend the ceremony.

However, the taste for Merrie England and for May games was on the wane by 1930. Many of the small local schools that had staged the events had closed, so the gap of four years after the 1926 ceremony might easily have

meant the end for Brentham May Day. But the event proved resilient, and was revived again in 1931, this time by E.J. Ephgrave, author of the 'Brentham Notes' column in the *Middlesex County Times* before the First World War, and a stalwart of Brentham social life for over 30 years. This time, apart from the interruption of the war years of 1940–5, the revival was for good, and continuity came from another of Molly Duncan's pupils, Peggy Cobbett, who taught the children the dances until well after the Second World War.

The May Day festivities from 1931 had almost all the essentials of Brentham May Days ever since. The herald was followed by the Jack-in-the-green, band (at that time the school band from St Mary's, North Hyde),

BELOW: *May Queen coronation, 1926. The queen was Margo Reading (b. 1910), daughter of the editor of* The Brenthamite. *Although May Day is often seen as 'timeless', the style of the costumes and the floral decoration would always date this picture to the 1920s.*

junior maypole dancers, senior maypole dancers, previous May Queens, the May Queen-elect, her crown bearer and attendants, and finally, children in costume. The route proceeded from the Institute via Meadvale, Neville and Brunner Roads, Woodfield Crescent and Avenue, Pitshanger Lane and Denison Road, back to the Institute. There the coronation of the May Queen took place, followed by the Queen's speech, and then the dancing. Successively older groups of children circled round the maypole, performing single and double plaiting of the ribbons and 'spider's web' plaiting. These dances are still performed by children participating in Brentham May Day today.

But other features of the early 1930s have disappeared. One is the cart full of babies, which only ceased to be in the procession in recent years. Another is the wide range of fancy costumes. In 1931 and 1934 there was a group of small children dressed to represent nursery rhymes. In 1932 'Long John Silver's pirates' seemed bizarre company for the May Queen, Connie Hammond. Perhaps because of the popularity of these non-traditional figures, 'pirates' became a regular part of the procession for several years in the late 1930s. The impact of popular culture on May Day should not be under-estimated. One reason for the persistence of pirates in the late 1930s' procession may have been the 1934 hit film *Treasure Island*; and the inclusion of Snow White and her dwarfs in 1938 is doubtless due to the enormously popular Disney film *Snow White* (the first feature-length cartoon) that was released that year.

These were to be ephemeral curiosities, but further new features have since become May Day fixtures. The most important was the character of Britannia with her attendants of soldiers and sailors, who first appeared in

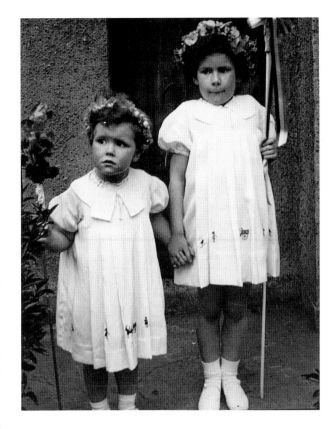

1934. was there perhaps a topical reason for this too? by the late 1930s the full repertory of maypole dances had been established – 'gipsies' tent' and 'amo amas' now augmented the circling, single and double plaiting, and 'spider's web'.

During these decades of the 1920s and 1930s, the social changes that had been under way from the earliest years of the suburb's development continued. By the time the First World War broke out, the typical tenant was more likely to be a civil servant or a teacher

than a bricklayer or a plasterer. More residents defined themselves as middle class than anything else, and at least half had paid help in the house for at least part of the week. Political radicalism persisted into the 1920s and 1930s, however. It is striking how, in what was, even then, predominantly a Conservative-voting borough, the great majority of those who were children then, irrespective of what their own politics are now, remember their parents defining themselves as Socialist or Liberal – although the mothers were more likely to be Conservative voters than the fathers. That lingering

radicalism is reflected in some of the lectures and debates at the Institute. While the majority were now on 'safe' subjects – 'Glimpses of Japan', 'The Romance of Wireless' and 'The Pageant of the English Novel' were just three of the talks on offer in 1921 – there was still an audience for debates, such as F.J. Gould supporting the motion 'Equal Pay for Equal Work' and Fred Maddison giving 'The Case against a State Church'.

It was perhaps this prevailing social and political awareness that explains the high number of MPs in the suburb. George Ridley, who from the 1920s to the 1940s

ABOVE LEFT: *May Day 1936: Pamela Hender on her tricycle in a splendid costume made by her mother entirely of crepe paper.*

ABOVE RIGHT: *Family at 44 Denison Road enjoying tubs of ice cream, 1930s. One of the party is clearly taking seriously the threat of melanoma.*

RIGHT: *George Ridley (right), prospective Labour candidate for Clay Cross, Derbyshire, talking to a voter, 1936. Ridley was one of several MPs who found the politically radical atmosphere of Brentham in the early days agreeable. In 1936 he was elected and he served until his death in 1944.*

BELOW: *Dudley Fairbridge Pope (1906–34). Pope, who grew up in Brentham, played cricket for Essex and Gloucestershire, before dying in a car crash in 1934.*

lived first at 48 Denison Road then at 6 Winscombe Crescent, was Labour MP in 1936–44 for Clay Cross in Derbyshire. Henry Vivian's friend Fred Maddison, who lived at 34 Brentham Way from 1915 to 1930, had been a Liberal MP in Sheffield and Burnley before the First World War. In the 1930s, just off the suburb in Barnfield Road lived George Hardie, a Glasgow MP, but better known as the brother of Keir Hardie, the founder of the Labour Party.

And then there was Sam Perry, who lived at 223 Pitshanger Lane from 1918 until his death in 1954. He was a Co-operative Party MP for Kettering in 1923–4 and 1929–31. He had a son, Frederick J. Perry, who is remembered by all his contemporaries. After he won the table-tennis championship in the 1920s, Perry Jnr told a friend he was going to win Wimbledon. Which he did, three times. It is the proud boast of many, now in their eighties and nineties, that they 'played tennis with Fred Perry'. Perry, like many of the children in Brentham, went to Ealing County School, on Ealing Green, and was in his own estimation 'pretty useful' at most sports. He only took up tennis at 15, and played for the first time at Wimbledon at 20, so his connection with Brentham was brief, although he always acknowledged the effect of the sports facilities at Brentham on his formative years as a player. The Brentham cricket club was also producing players of distinction. In the late 1920s one Brentham boy, Dudley Pope, played county cricket for Essex and Gloucestershire, while later, Frank Ahl was appearing for Worcestershire.

But what was happening, while Fred Perry was working his way to Wimbledon, to plans to complete the building of the estate? Work had ground to a halt

in 1915, and the economic effects of the war made building new houses less than attractive to Ealing Tenants Ltd. There had been a huge increase in the cost of building, and rent restrictions, which pegged rents at pre-war levels, had been introduced in 1915 and 1919. In 1920 the committee reported that government subsidies of £260 per house might make building viable, but nothing happened. By 1923 the subject of building had become a running joke in *The Brenthamite*. A rumour went round that 'They are going in for

Tenants immediately imposed a 50 per cent increase for new tenancies: it became apparent that they were planning a different strategy for the new houses.

They were going to build to sell. This was the final nail in the coffin of the co-partnership ideal of 'every tenant his neighbour's landlord'. Not only that, but the houses they built, from 1925, would be larger and more expensive, in real terms, than most of those they had built before the war, with prices between £1,075 and £1,200. That was partly the result of inflation, but their size was principally determined by their site: most were at the top of Brentham Way, an area that had been designated for 'a better class of house' as far back as 1906. G.L. Sutcliffe, the architect for Ealing

*LEFT: Fred Perry (1909–95). Fred Perry, three times Wimbledon tennis champion, arrived in Brentham in 1918 when his father, Sam Perry, moved into 223 Pitshanger Lane. Fred's first game of tennis was at the Brentham Club at the age of 15. He signed this photograph for Ramsay Hughes, long-time resident of Brentham, in 1931.*

*BELOW: Tennis party, c. 1935. In the 1930s the enjoyment of tobacco was seen as perfectly compatible with prowess at sport.*

skyscrapers' when a 50-ft radio mast was mistaken for high-rise scaffolding, but still there was no action. That year the rent restrictions were lifted to some degree when rents for new tenancies were decontrolled. Ealing

Tenants and Co-partnership Tenants, had died in 1915, so a new appointment was made. Co-partnership Tenants was now based in Hampstead Garden Suburb, and in 1923, with a view to starting building again in Hampstead, they had taken on Cecil George Butler as their architect. Butler, who had trained with the Shrewsbury architect Walter Richards and at the Architectural Association in London, was just 25 when he took the job. He was to spend 16 years at Hampstead, the first five as architect to Co-partnership Tenants. During his time there he produced numerous designs, including some very imposing detached houses in South Square, and the Lyttelton Court flats.

It seems likely that Butler never actually came to Brentham, but he supplied designs for two detached houses (7 and 8) and seven pairs of semi-detached houses (9–19 and 10–24) in Brentham Way in 1924–5, and a year later he completed the other end of Brentham Way (72–8). The larger houses are in a simplified Arts and Crafts style, with mainly rendered elevations and brick dressings, the doorways with some stripped-down classical detail. What is most striking about these is their large scale, compared with all the pre-war houses with the exception of a few houses in Brentham Way and Winscombe Crescent, and the fact that one of them – number 7 – was built with an attached garage (Butler added garages to 17 and 19 Brentham Way in 1926–7). Building was no longer contracted directly by Ealing Tenants Ltd, but was done by Garsubil (a contraction of 'Garden Suburb Builders') of Hampstead.

At the same time as building to sell, Ealing Tenants began selling off some of their existing rented houses to resident tenants. In the 1920s all the sales, including those of newly built houses, were of 99-year leases with a ground rent of around £6 to £9 per annum. Compared to the rate of sell-off from the late 1930s onwards, the number of sales was relatively modest, averaging fewer than five a year between 1925 and 1931. The prices for the existing houses were more modest: the first to be sold, 63 Fowlers Walk, went for £600 in March 1926, and the average was around £750 leasehold. From 1931, Ealing Tenants began selling the houses freehold, and selling the freeholds of the houses already sold to the leaseholders – for around 25 per cent of the price charged for the leasehold. It seems likely that Ealing Tenants did not actively promote the sale of the houses locally. When Doris Palmer and her husband decided to buy a house in 1934, they moved from their house in Fowlers Walk to the new Greystoke Estate: they were not aware that buying a house in Brentham was a possibility.

The sale of the houses was the most obvious symptom of the decline of co-partnership. By the 1920s, the broader concept of labour co-partnership had been largely eclipsed by profit-sharing schemes operated by private companies; even the Labour Co-partnership Association had reinvented itself as the Industrial Participation Association. Moreover, those who had played such an important role in the setting up of Ealing Tenants, and in co-partnership generally, were dying off: Frederick Litchfield in 1923, Aneurin Williams in 1924 and John Greenhalgh in 1928. Henry Vivian himself died in 1930. Although he had not been seen much in Brentham in the previous ten years, he remained a committee member to his death, and attended a meeting of the general committee in Bloomsbury Square in May 1929 when he was already seriously ill.

Housing co-partnership, meanwhile, was being squeezed on two sides. On the one hand there was a precipitate rise in private house ownership. On the other there was the great expansion in municipal housing, prompted by the 1919 Housing Act, based on the 1918 Tudor Walters report which was largely drafted by Raymond Unwin. Unwin's espousal of municipal housing did not endear him either to the co-partnership movement, which saw municipal housing as a solution only for housing the poorest in society, or to those who clung to Howard's original vision of a garden city, in that Unwin favoured satellite towns – effectively suburbs rather than new cities. It was left to Howard himself to set the ball rolling on the second garden city, Welwyn – like Letchworth, also in Hertfordshire – by buying the land for it in 1919 and later moving there.

The end came for Ealing Tenants as a co-partnership in the 1930s. In an attempt to protect the companies' positions it was agreed to merge Ealing Tenants with Stoke-on-Trent Tenants and Liverpool Garden Suburb Tenants, but the merger failed to take place. In April 1934 the £10 shares in Co-partnership Tenants were written down to £4, as it emerged that the company had a deficit on its capital account of more than £60,000. During 1935 Co-partnership Tenants acquired the bulk of Ealing Tenants' shares and then merged with the two Hampstead tenants' co-partnership societies. Ealing Tenants acquired shares in the new amalgamated society. But all this shifting back and forth of shares was merely 'rearranging the deck-chairs on the *Titanic*'.

Ealing Tenants was able to bolster its position somewhat by sales of various parcels of land between 1930

ABOVE: *Brentham Way, c. 1930. This is the same view as on the previous page. By this date Ealing Tenants had built several large houses at the top of Brentham Way. The architect was Cecil George Butler (1897–1947), a young Shrewsbury man who was taken on as Co-partnership Tenants' architect in Hampstead in 1923.*

# EALING.

## Ideal Labour-Saving Houses at Brentham Garden Suburb.

Semi - detached, containing 3 Bedrooms, 2 Reception Rooms, Tiled Kitchen and Bathroom.

Mortgages arranged at 5¼ per cent.

Easy Payments.

Price £1,075.    99 years lease.

A SMALL HOUSE WITH TWO BEDROOMS £575.

**EALING TENANTS, LTD., 7, Winscombe Crescent, Ealing, W.5**

Phone: EALING 0388.

ABOVE: *Advertisement for Ealing Tenants Ltd, 1927. When building resumed after the war, Ealing Tenants decided to build to sell, not rent. They also began to sell off existing houses.*

RIGHT: *Advertisement for the Greystoke Estate, 1936. This was built from 1931 on land east of Brentham, and the slogan – 'the rooms are larger than elsewhere' – may be a dig at Brentham.*

the rest of the suburb. Ealing Tenants, once so careful about the visual integrity of Brentham, were reduced to selling to the highest bidder: the land sales brought in more than £8,000.

It seems likely that by 1935 the committee knew that the society was going to be privatised. That year they were offered more than £20 a share for their holdings of £10 shares in Liverpool Garden Suburb Tenants Ltd, by a property company called the Bradford Property Trust. Shortly afterwards Ealing Tenants made shares available to their tenants, up to a maximum of £200 per investor. They did this, perhaps, because they knew that an offer, similar to the one they had been made for their Liverpool Garden Suburb Trust Ltd shares, was about to be made for Ealing Tenants Ltd's shares. Whether they knew or not, in May 1936 an offer was made to buy all the £10 Ealing Tenants Ltd's shares

and 1936. The largest was at the north end of Fowlers Walk, which was sold in 1930 to Ardsley Estates, who immediately resold it to the London and Provincial Building Company, who built the vast Greystoke Estate east of Brentham in the 1930s. There were also smaller sites at the corner of Winscombe Crescent and Brentham Way, on Pitshanger Lane next to St Barnabas and at the top of Holyoake Walk. These last three were all bought by two small developers who built blocks of flats in a watered-down 'moderne' style, with metal ribbon windows that jarred visually with

## We chose Greystoke!

BECAUSE THE ROOMS ARE LARGER THAN ELSEWHERE
(*Important—Look for the L & P sign on the houses*)

NO ROAD, LEGAL OR STAMP CHARGES

SEVERAL OTHER TYPES AT PRICES FROM £975 TO £1,875.

£955—£5 SECURES
Repayments 24/- Per Week

THREE LARGE BEDROOMS TILED BATHROOM, SEPARATE W.C. FITTED KITCHEN, DINING ROOM, LOUNGE, ATTRACTIVE PORCH, WIDE HALL, FINE GARDEN, AMPLE ROOM FOR GARAGE. HIGH HEALTHY ALTITUDE.

**LONDON & PROVINCIAL**
BUILDING COY. LTD · GREYSTOKE PARK ESTATE
LYNWOOD ROAD, Western Avenue, EALING W.5

at £24 a share. Although Co-partnership Tenants owned the great majority of shares – they had effectively had a controlling interest in any case since 1909 – shares were owned in considerable numbers, if in small quantities, by many tenants. The Fifth Earl Grey, the chairman of Ealing Tenants who had taken over when William Hutchings died in 1934, recommended the offer to the shareholders.

Grey was the son of the Fourth Earl, who had been a supporter of Ealing Tenants in the early days, and the Fifth Earl himself, when he was still Viscount Howick, had been at the opening of the Institute in 1911. His recommendation to sell, which would effectively confound the co-partnership aims of the founders, seems perverse. Yet he was right in that it would effectively make little difference. The tenants had never managed to buy out the outside shareholders; indeed the flow of shares and control of the society, had always been the other way. Many tenants held loan stock rather than shares; others held neither; and there were now 40 privately owned houses. Nevertheless one shareholder did refuse to sell. This was George Bernard Shaw, who, 30 years on, still had a substantial holding of Ealing Tenants' shares. These he declined to sell, on the grounds that if they were worth £24 to the Bradford Property Trust, they were worth that to him, and therefore worth hanging on to. Shaw remained a minority shareholder until his death in 1950.

The company making the offer for the shares was the Liverpool Trust, a wholly owned subsidiary of the Bradford Property Trust. Like Ealing Tenants it was registered as a co-partnership, but the company effectively belonged to a small group of men who

either owned or worked for the Bradford Property Trust. Chief among these were Fred Gresswell and Algernon Denham. Gresswell was the archetypal self-made man. He had only started in the property business in the early 1920s, when he bought a row of 16 back-to-back houses in Bradford at £95 each. He was able to buy them cheaply because the houses were tenanted, and with rent controls in place, owning rented property was seen as a poor investment.

ABOVE: *German planners visit Brentham, 1927. A quarter of a century after it was started, Brentham was still of interest to planners from abroad. The mayor of Ealing, William Hutchings, is seen here with the visitors, and behind him (with white moustache) is John Greenhalgh.*

RIGHT: *Rev. Richard Evans enjoys a cigarette while filling his birdbath at 4 Brentham Way, 1930s.*

BELOW: *Four generations of a Brentham family prepare for a flight, 1938. Leslie C. Davey of 22 Holyoake Walk, stands in front of his plane with his grandmother, daughter and father.*

However, the move towards owner-occupation, and the increasing availability of mortgages, meant Gresswell was able to sell them either to the sitting tenants at a modest profit, or to new buyers at a much greater profit as they came empty. The breakthrough in his business came in 1928 when he formed the Bradford Property Trust with Algernon Denham, who was a bank manager and board member of the Halifax Building Society. Denham's financial links were crucial

to the Bradford Property Trust's business, and by the mid-1930s, when they made the offer for Ealing Tenants' shares, they had bought thousands of houses in London and the north, including the whole of Saltaire. This was the industrial village near Bradford, a forerunner of Brentham and home of the Brentham architect F. Cavendish Pearson.

When the Liverpool Trust acquired Ealing Tenants in 1936, only 40 houses in the suburb had been sold, out of more than 600. However in the three years 1937–9 inclusive, 132 houses were sold in Brentham, all but a handful freehold, and almost invariably to the sitting tenants. And, in keeping with the business principle of buying in bulk and selling cheap, the prices were no higher than those the co-partnership had charged.

In fact, apart from the great increase in sales, the take-over by the Bradford Property Trust made very little difference to life on the estate. In 1935 the Brentham Club – the tenants' club that ran the Institute (which was now routinely just called 'the Club') – had acquired a drinks' licence for the first time, and although Ealing Tenants still owned the Institute building and the 'rec', the Club had separated from Ealing Tenants. Liverpool Trust continued to assist the Club financially and to pay a £5 subsidy for every house that was wired for electricity. But events were about to take a turn over which neither the Trust nor the tenants living on the estate had any control.

LEFT: *Members of the Brentham Horticultural Society about to set off on an outing, Denison Road, 1920s. Buses like these had been requisitioned during the war and sent to the front. This photograph shows the original pattern of the pavements, with a grass strip, and setts between kerb and road surface.*

# 8

# Brentham in war and peace 2:
# 1939–1968

*Small and medium sized houses of unusually attractive designs situate on a mature
Garden Village Estate . . . the houses offered for sale have been thoroughly overhauled
internally and externally. Prices from £625–£975 freehold.*

Ealing Tenants Ltd sales brochure, *c.* 1939

 VEN BEFORE the ill-fated Munich agree-
ment of September 1938 that was supposed
to deliver 'peace for our time', preparations
for war had begun in Britain. Air Raid
Precaution (ARP) committees had been set up, gas-
mask production had been started and plans had been
mooted for the evacuation of 3½ million Londoners. In
Ealing, by the end of 1938, trenches had been dug in
public parks, and more than 120,000 gas masks had
been distributed. Even before Chamberlain's grave
announcement on 3 September 1939 that war had been
declared, 50,000 children had been dispatched to the
West Country from Ealing Broadway station. Within
minutes of Chamberlain's broadcast, the wail of the air-
raid sirens was heard all over London.

On that occasion the siren was a false alarm. Rather,
as in the First World War, life in Britain settled down,
and by the end of the year many evacuees had returned.
The sense of relief was short-lived, however. The

RIGHT: *News announcing conscription
for 20-year-olds, May 1939. When
war broke out on 3 September 1939,
Brentham felt the effects almost
immediately. Even before the outbreak
of war, the lives of many Brenthamites
had been affected with the introduction,
in May, of military training for 20- and
21-year-old men. On the day war broke
out conscription was extended to all
men aged between 18 and 41.*

evacuees returned just in time to see the Germans over-run the whole of northwest Europe, British troops retreat from Dunkirk, the Battle of Britain and the beginning of the Blitz, all by the autumn of 1940. The 'phoney war' was well and truly over.

Because the war was not unexpected, Brentham felt its effects more immediately than had been the case in 1914. Whereas during the First World War conscription had not been brought in until 18 months after the outbreak of war, in the Second, all men aged between 18 and 41 became liable to call-up from the day war broke out. By the end of September 1939, the Brentham Institute, which had operated throughout the First World War, was requisitioned by the Army for the use of a unit in charge of four anti-aircraft guns on Ealing Golf Course, just the other side of the River Brent. The mounds for the guns, and several of the buildings used by the soldiers, survive to this day in the shadow of the Western Avenue. To compensate for the loss of the Institute, Ealing Tenants offered the Brentham Club the use of 2 Winscombe Crescent, William Hutchings's old home. In the event, the Institute still provided some social facilities to Brentham residents, such as the popular dances held on Saturday nights.

Those anti-aircraft guns were soon pressed into service with the coming of the Blitz. Although Ealing and west London in general did not suffer to the same extent as the East End, the first raids on Ealing took place only one day after the Blitz proper began on 7 September 1940. Brentham escaped damage throughout the bombing of 1940–1, except for one bomb that fell nearby in Mount Park. By the time the Blitz ended in May 1941, 190 people had been killed in Ealing.

Against this background, certain aspects of life seem remarkably little affected by the war. Since the buyout of the shares in 1936, Ealing Tenants Ltd – Bradford Property Trust always kept the name – had continued to be run as a co-partnership, but in 1940 it was turned into a private company. This seems to have had little effect on the tenants. Even as a private concern, Ealing Tenants still paid a rent dividend in the early years of the war – albeit of just sixpence in the £1 – to tenants who held loan stock. And people still took up the offer to buy their own houses, war or

BELOW: *Police and railwaymen help with the evacuation of children from Ealing Broadway station, 1 September 1939. Although war did not break out until two days later, 800 children left on this day – a small proportion of the 50,000 who had been evacuated from Ealing to the West Country by the time war broke out. The children, all labelled with name and address, are carrying their gas masks in a cardboard box hung around their necks.*

no war. In the six years of war, 1940–45 inclusive, 52 more houses were sold to tenants. The prices of these remained steady until the last year of the war, when they went up by a figure of around 30 per cent.

Memories of life in Brentham during the Second World War are of course much more varied than for the First, which is now remembered only by those who were children then. Among those who were already adults during the Second World War, such as Frank Turner (b. 1912) and Douglas Dover (b. 1916), the principal recollections are, unsurprisingly, not of Brentham at all, but of service overseas, in Egypt, North Africa and Italy. And of those unmarried women who joined up, many were active on the home front. Betty Black (b. 1924), whose father was the MP George Ridley, joined the ATS and was employed as a firewatcher. Others worked at local factories such as Hoover, which had opened on the Western Avenue in the early 1930s, switching to war work during the period of the conflict.

Another difference from the First World War was the blackout, which was enforced much more rigorously. Jean George (b. 1923) remembers going for an evening out to the Brentham Club in the pitch dark, feeling her way along the hedge. She also has memories of one of the last of the Brentham pioneers, her grandfather Hubert Brampton, then in his late eighties, on one of his regular outings to the Club. 'You had to keep out of the road because of falling shrapnel, but my granddad, stubborn character that he was, insisted on walking in the middle of the road, where he would pause and gaze at the sky, watching the searchlights and pointing out the tracer fire from the anti-aircraft guns with his walking stick.'

The children seem to have found the war a time of great excitement. Several recall roaming the streets of Brentham, collecting the shrapnel from the anti-aircraft guns. All, whether adults or children, remember the incessant noise from the anti-aircraft guns, the increasing privation as rationing took effect, and, of course, the air raids. A few houses had Anderson shelters in the garden, but most people's memories, in the early part of the war, are of sheltering under the stairs when the sirens went off. Many houses were later

supplied with Morrison shelters, a mesh cage with steel legs and top that doubled as a table.

Until 1944, Brentham had largely escaped damage from bombing. A stick of incendiaries had fallen in Brentham Way, and another bomb fell on the cricket pitch. But the hope that the suburb might emerge unscathed was dashed in the early morning of Sunday 20 August 1944. That June the D-Day landings in Normandy had offered hope that the war was being won, but almost immediately the Germans countered with their secret weapon, the V1 or 'doodlebug', a pilot-less bomb that could be launched from the ground or from an aircraft, and which delivered a tonne of explosive at a speed of 400 mph. In the ten-week V1 campaign, 58 people were killed in Ealing.

Four of them died in Brentham that Sunday morning in one house in Meadvale Road. The tenant was Freddy Watts, who had worked for Ealing Tenants since 1904 and had gone to Sevenoaks to help with the building of the second co-partnership estate there.

During the war Watts had become an ARP warden; he had also come out of semi-retirement to collect rents while another member of staff was away on active service. He had just returned from visiting another flying-bomb site, when the back of his house, 45

FAR LEFT: *Morrison shelter, c. 1941. This photograph demonstrates the dual function of these steel indoor shelters that doubled as a table. They were introduced in 1941 by the new Minister of Home Security, Herbert Morrison, and were much in use in Brentham, where some of the gardens were too small for an outdoor Anderson shelter.*

LEFT: *The devastation caused by the flying bomb that hit Brentham on 20 August 1944. The bomb hit the back of 45 Meadvale Road killing the Watts family who lived there and a Canadian soldier billeted with them. The structure in the foreground is the remains of a Morrison shelter.*

Meadvale Road, took a direct hit. Watts, his wife, his daughter Rosemary, and a Canadian serviceman billeted with them, were all killed. The only survivor in the Watts family was their son Ivor, who was injured. Others were more fortunate that night. Two women who remained in their Morrison shelter survived unscathed when their house collapsed on top of them.

The devastation from the Meadvale Road bomb was considerable, quite apart from the loss of life. A total of 26 houses were totally demolished – eight in Holyoake Walk, eight in North View and ten in Meadvale Road; a further 29 of Ealing Tenants' houses were very seriously damaged, to the extent that the residents had to move out. But all over the suburb there

was minor damage, cracked windows mainly, as far away as Winscombe Crescent and Brunner Road.

By the time the V1 fell on Meadvale Road, the worst of the Ealing bombing was over. Nine months later came VE Day, and Ealing, like the rest of the country, celebrated. Huge bonfires were lit on Horsenden Hill and Walpole Park, and Hitler was burned in effigy all over the borough. Brenda Brant (b. 1925) remembers: 'We danced all night on Ealing Green. It was wonderful: no more air raid warnings. We could sleep in peace at last.' In Brentham there was a street party for the children in Meadvale Road.

What the peace meant initially for Brentham was reconstruction. The devastated houses around Meadvale

RIGHT: *A street party in Pitshanger Lane, late 1940s. Similar events were held in other parts of Brentham to celebrate the end of the war, although rationing probably meant the treats on offer were rather modest.*

Road were repaired or rebuilt in 1946–7, paid for by the government under the War Damage Act of 1943. Generally they were rebuilt as replicas of their prewar selves, but some owners took the opportunity to improve the layout. Mr Harrison at 11 North View opted for a larger kitchen and a smaller dining room, and the owners of 47 and 49 Meadvale Road added small extensions to the backs of their houses, the first of many such alterations made in Brentham over the years.

This reconstruction aimed to restore Brentham to its prewar appearance, but another development mooted at the same time would have completely destroyed the suburb's greatest amenity. In 1946 plans were prepared for Ealing Tenants Ltd to build over the recreation ground. Two schemes were proposed, one of which would have seen 137 houses built on three roads, leaving only a small plot about 200 ft square around the Institute. The surveyor's report that accompanied the plan seems rather over-optimistic: 'There would appear to be little risk of flooding from the River Brent'. Clearly the surveyor did not live in Brentham.

In fact, there seems to have been little chance that the houses would be built: no private companies were building houses in 1946. The scheme was, in effect, a scam. Ealing Tenants Ltd was at the time in negotiation with the Brentham Club, which since 1935 had been separated from the company, to sell them the recreation ground and Institute building. The company knew that the recreation ground was likely to be scheduled as public open space, as had been recommended by the Borough of Ealing Draft Town Planning Scheme and also in Patrick Abercrombie's *Greater London Plan* of 1942. And if that happened, the company knew that the land would lose value. The company would then be able to sell the land to the Brentham Club at a price the Club could afford, and would also qualify for compensation for loss of the building value of the land. That way the Club and Ealing Tenants would benefit; only the taxpayer would lose out. In fact, Ealing Tenants decided against submitting the plan because of the ill

LEFT: *Advertisement for the Brentham Horticultural Society, 1948. Having urged its members to 'Dig for Victory' during the war, the Horticultural Society was on hand to encourage residents to continue growing their own produce during the years of reconstruction. During this period a plan to build more than 130 houses on the Club sports ground was considered, although it is unlikely that it was a serious proposition.*

feeling the prospect of the 'rec' being built over would generate in Brentham – even if, as is clear, the company had no intention of building the houses. In the event the land was, indeed, designated as public open space. As a result, the Brentham Club and Institute was able to buy the Institute and the grounds in 1947 at a much lower price, as it now had no value, even theoretically, as building land. In the wider world of planning, Abercrombie's plan was part of a postwar revival of Howard's ideas about garden cities; it saw the founding of New Towns, such as Milton Keynes, Stevenage and Peterborough, which often developed around the nucleus of an existing town or village.

Once the Brentham Club came to own the Institute and grounds, its range of activities was somewhat reduced compared with the period between the wars.

Nevertheless, although the days of improving lectures were over and Brenthamites no longer gathered to debate the merits and demerits of vegetarianism or communism, other social activities flourished. The Brentham Players were still going strong, even if they were more likely to be putting on an Agatha Christie than a Merrie England Pageant. The late 1940s also saw Brentham, albeit briefly, with its own magazine once again, for the first time since the demise of *The Brenthamite* in 1925: *The Brentham Bulletin* ran in 1948–9 for 24 issues before folding, while *The Brentham Club Magazine* managed a further eight issues in 1950–1.

And even if the Brentham Club never produced another sportsman of the calibre of Fred Perry, the sports sections of the Brentham Club were as vibrant as they had ever been. The Brentham football club won the Amateur Football Association Cup, and several players went on to join league sides. Someone who remembers Brentham's sporting life in the 1950s and 1960s is the former England cricket captain Mike Brearley, who lived at 62 Brentham Way from 1945 to 1968. Brearley played for England from 1976 to 1981, and was captain 31 times; during his captaincy England won 18, drew 9 and lost only 4 test matches – the most successful postwar record for an England team. Brearley's father, Horace, was also an active sportsman, a stalwart of both the football and cricket teams. Mike Brearley remembers 'the thrill of getting him and his fellow-players to bowl at me, or allow me to field for their pre-match knock-ups'.

One aspect of life in Brentham that survived the war was the May Day procession. The arrival of war had meant that 1939 was the last May Day for six years, but on 18 May 1946, the festivities were revived yet again.

BELOW: *The Evans family relax at their home, 4 Brentham Way, c. 1940. After the war, although the rate of sell-off of the houses picked up, many long-established residents continued to rent: two generations of the Evans family rented this house for 88 years.*

dressed as foresters, sailors, soldiers and airmen – although there have from time to time been cowboys and what the *Middlesex County Times* described one year as 'costumes that defied quick analysis'. During the 1950s the route was adapted to take in Brentham Way, when one of Brentham's elderly residents, Mrs Dudeney of 11 Winscombe Crescent, wanted to be able to watch the procession from her front door. The country dances which in the 1930s ran to up to a dozen items, dwindled to three or, occasionally, just two.

The 1950s is usually seen as a rather grey decade, as rationing dragged on year after year. Many

*LEFT: Brentham May Day procession about to set off from the Brentham Club, 1948 or 1949. Fancy-dress costumes that year included two drummer boys, a cowboy and a sweep. This last costume was especially appropriate because the Jack-in-the-green, one of the main characters in the Brentham procession, was associated with sweeps' parades throughout the nineteenth century.*

After the war certain features of the procession continued to evolve. By 1952 the traditional babies' decorated cart had become a babies' lorry, and by 1973 it had become a babies' Range Rover. But further aspects of the day were becoming fixed as part of the tradition. The free-for-all in fancy costumes ended with the war, and since then the children who followed the May Queen at the end of the procession have tended to be

Brenthamites remember this period as little better than the war years. Although it was now possible to get a good night's sleep, the sense of comradeship, the Blitz spirit, was necessarily less pronounced. But the good times were just around the corner. In a few years the British population would, in the words of Harold Macmillan, realise that 'we had never had it so good'.

Signs of improving prosperity were evident by 1954, when building began again in Brentham. There were still a few odd plots of land that had never been built on, and with the end of restrictions on building materials in 1953, Ealing Tenants were keen to capitalise on these. The first was the site on Brunner Road that had served as tennis courts and then a bowling green before the First World War. In 1954 a dull but inoffensive house, bizarrely called Rookery Nook, was built here. Equally dull were the two houses, 186 and 188 Pitshanger Lane, built at the same time between Pitshanger Court and St Barnabas Church.

The final site sold off was at the corner of Brentham Way and Woodfield Crescent, opposite the site that had been the Ealing Tenants works until the mid-1930s. This plot had always been intended for building. Unwin had intended it for shops in his 1906 plan, and F.C. Pearson had produced a design for houses in 1910, but somehow it had remained undeveloped. For years it was cultivated as allotments by P.J. McCarthy, the demon rose-grower of Brentham. Although it was originally intended for two houses, economies of scale meant that when Ealing Tenants sold the land in 1955, four terraced houses were built – hence the numbering 21, 21a, 23, 23a. The design, if lacking in dynamism, was unobtrusive compared with the infill blocks of flats that had been built in the 1930s, such as Pitshanger Court.

An unfortunate loss of a piece of old Brentham was the accidental burning down in 1958 of the old cricket pavilion. Although it was replaced, the new building could not match F.C. Pearson's charmingly quirky design.

But the most powerful indication of returning prosperity was the sell-off of houses by Ealing Tenants Ltd. Between 1945 and 1968 more than 200 more houses were sold off, as tenancies ended, so that by 1968 around two thirds of the suburb was privately owned. The majority of these were sold in the 1960s, as general prosperity and the tendency to private home ownership both accelerated. Two aspects of this prosperity had a considerable impact on the appearance of Brentham. One was the great increase in car ownership, which saw the streets of Brentham that appear largely empty in old photographs, lined with cars. To cope with this, in the 1950s and 1960s Ealing Tenants built blocks of garages on allotments, notably behind Fowlers Walk, or on some of the back land that had been open space for the 'common enjoyment of all residents'. In the same decades,

was made connecting the kitchen to the hall. But there were two types of alteration that more than any other threatened to destroy the aesthetic coherence of the suburb as it had been established by Unwin, Pearson and Sutcliffe half a century earlier. One was the removal of hedges, sometimes in conjunction with the provision of hard standing for car parking in the front garden. The other, a trend which really only began in the 1960s, was the replacement of the original small-pane wooden windows with plate-glass windows, a development that threatened to destroy what made Brentham architecturally distinctive. That this did not happen was due to a series of events in the late 1960s, the first of which was the passing of a piece of legislation, the Civic Amenities Act, in 1967.

LEFT: *Rookery Nook, Brunner Road. In the mid-1950s, at the same time as house sales accelerated, the Bradford Property Trust sold off the remaining small plots of land in Brentham to speculative builders. This house, built in 1954, occupies the site that, in Brentham's early days, was successively a tennis court and a bowling green.*

there was also a sharp increase in the number of owner-occupiers who built garages beside their houses. This happened in all areas of the suburb where there was space; and it marked a change from the prewar period when, with one or two exceptions, only the owners of larger houses in Brentham Way had built garages.

But the most tangible sign of prosperity and increased private ownership was in alterations that were made to the houses. In the 1960s, as the records of Ealing Borough Council's Building Control department reveal, the commonest alterations made were single-storey extensions to the rear (usually to extend kitchen space), the removal of chimney breasts (and therefore original fireplaces) to increase room sizes and, in the smaller houses, the moving of a bathroom from downstairs to the smallest upstairs bedroom. In many houses the doorway from the living room into the kitchen was closed off, and a new one

## 9

# The battle for Brentham:
# the Brentham Society and the
# conservation of the suburb, 1969–2000

*This bill aims . . . to preserve beauty, to create beauty and to remove ugliness.*
Duncan Sandys MP, 1967

FACING PAGE: *Pearson's 'butterfly' houses at the corner where Neville, Brunner and Brunswick Roads meet, 1968. By this time, cars were beginning to line Brentham's streets and alterations to Brentham houses could be carried out without planning permission – the centre house has lost its original small-pane windows. Brentham would soon become one of the first conservation areas in the country, and new legislation would be introduced to curb such alterations.*

NCE THE 1967 Civic Amenities Act became law, the preservation of many of the features that make Brentham distinctive received a considerable boost. It was this legislation that saw Brentham, in 1969, become one of the first conservation areas in Britain. Until this time, householders had not been entirely free to alter their houses as they liked, as planning permission was often required. But the difference was that until 1969, the Building Control department at Ealing Council concentrated on alterations that would not degrade the structural integrity of buildings. As long as an alteration would not make the house unsafe, or, for example, block light to another house, it was likely to be passed. Applications were considered on a case-by-case basis; the character of the suburb as a whole was not a focus for concern.

But conservation did not begin with the 1967 Act. Since the middle of the nineteenth century there had been a small but growing band, largely inspired by John Ruskin's architectural writings, who resisted the destruction of historically and architecturally important buildings. Local archaeological societies also salvaged parts of old buildings that were being demolished. But the best known pressure group was the Society for the Protection of Ancient Buildings (SPAB), founded in 1877 by, among others, William Morris. SPAB popularised the so-called 'anti-scrape' approach, whereby ancient stonework should not be routinely replaced just because it was weathered; they favoured preservation and conservation over wholesale restoration. In the twentieth century, statutory listing of architecturally and historically significant buildings was introduced, at first only for pre-1714 buildings, then later extended to those dating from up to 1830. In time more specialised pressure groups were set up, such as the Georgian Group in the 1930s and the Victorian Society in the 1950s.

So far, such groups had advisory rather than statutory powers. Statutory protection was restricted to individual

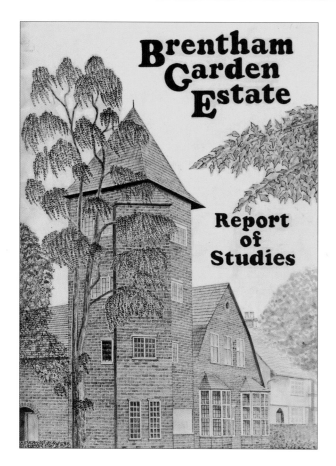

groups of buildings that were important not for the architectural or historic interest of any particular building, but taken as a whole. In fact, while the legislation encouraged local authorities to 'preserve or enhance . . . the character or appearance . . . of areas of special architectural or historic interest' it did not give them much in the way of new powers, although it enabled them to make recommendations and raise public awareness of the built environment.

Most early designations reflected the prevailing view that what mattered most were medieval street patterns, such as York, or Georgian terraces, like those in Bath, and many conservation-area designations were concerned with improving the settings of individual buildings already acknowledged to be architecturally or historically important. In 1969 in Ealing, however, a new approach was taken to further the principles of conservation. In that year Ealing Borough Council designated seven conservation areas. Four of these (Northolt Village Green, Norwood Green, Ealing Green and Churchfields in Hanwell) were typical conservation-area designations of the time, in that they were self-evidently 'historic' – old village centres with notable survivals of pre-nineteenth-century buildings.

But the three others – the Hanger Hill Garden Estate, Bedford Park in Chiswick, and Brentham – were unusual choices for the time. Bedford Park dates from the mid-1870s onwards, and, despite the foundation of the Victorian Society in 1958, Victorian buildings were still routinely dismissed in the 1960s as 'monstrosities'. Equally unusual was the official recognition of the twentieth-century buildings of Brentham and the Hanger Hill Garden Estate, especially since the 'architectural and environmental qualities' of the latter were

LEFT: *'Report of Studies' on Brentham by Town Planning Department, London Borough of Ealing, 1979. Over the years the borough council has produced a number of reports and design guidelines to explain why Brentham is a conservation area and how best to maintain it. The name 'Brentham Estate' or 'Brentham Garden Estate' supplanted 'Brentham Garden Suburb', which fell out of use in the 1930s, although it has enjoyed a revival in recent years.*

buildings, and the principal factor in determining what made a building valuable was its antiquity. What was different about the Civic Amenities Act of 1967, brought in by Harold Wilson's government of 1966 – 70, was that it recognised and sought to protect the wider environment of buildings. Firstly it sought to preserve the setting of listed buildings, but also, and more significantly for Brentham, it recognised that there were singled out. Brentham and Bedford Park, on the other hand, were chosen principally for their 'historic value'.

Whatever the council's reasons for selecting Brentham, the creation of the conservation area had immediate local repercussions. Inspired by the official recognition of what was then known as the Brentham Garden Estate, on 10 March 1970 a group of enthusiastic residents called a meeting to form a society that would 'encourage the preservation and improvement of the character of the estate, and to promote such activities as may be desired by residents'. All this struck a chord with the residents: the Brentham Society was set up and within four months of its first meeting it had attracted a membership of 150.

The Society was not then, and never has been, a pressure group. The aims outlined showed that while the Society hoped to improve life in Brentham in a wide variety of ways, conservation of the suburb's character was, as it still is, the principal aim. That character can perhaps be summed up in three words: windows, trees and hedges. The character of Brentham is made up of many other factors, both tangible and intangible, but it has been the loss of and alterations to these three characteristic features that has always posed the biggest conservation threat. In the case of windows, that threat was perhaps at its greatest in the late 1960s and early 1970s. By the end of the 1960s around two-thirds of the houses in the suburb were privately owned. With private ownership came diverse treatment within groups of houses that were designed to be painted and maintained in a consistent manner; individual owners painted the woodwork and roughcast as they pleased, usually without any consideration for the overall appearance of the block.

But more worrying was the tendency to remove the traditional small-pane casement windows, and replace them with picture windows, in aluminium or uPVC frames. This was partly motivated by the mistaken belief that these materials were longer-lasting than wood – even 'maintenance-free' – and partly by the contemporary taste for simple modern design, where the small-pane windows were perceived as unappealingly old-fashioned. The Society did its best to discourage this vandalism, by finding suppliers who could manufacture windows of the original pattern in properly treated wood, and more generally by a steady drip-drip of talks, leaflets and newsletters about the estate's history and design.

Their efforts were not, however, universally appreciated or understood. Early in the Society's history the *Middlesex County Times* carried letters from 'Worried Resident' and others, deploring the 'increasing interference by small bodies of people sitting round committee-room tables and deciding what we should or should not be allowed to do within the confines of our own homes and private property'. This ignored the fact that the Society had no power to decide anything; even the council at this time could not prevent the replacement of windows and doors because they counted as 'permitted developments'.

But the resentment reflected how far Brentham had moved from its original collectivist aims. In the past, Ealing Tenants Ltd had aimed at a harmonious balance between individual freedom and expression, and communal responsibility and collective action. With the sale of the houses, individual interest had so come to dominate that the Brentham Society's mild entreaties for a more communal approach to design could be presented as 'the restriction of the freedom of each of us'. But the message did slowly percolate through, and by the mid-1970s some previously 'modernised' windows had been replaced with small-pane reproductions.

Hedges were in some ways a more difficult, in others an easier, problem to solve than windows. Since 1908, low privet hedges had been the customary garden-

boundary marker in Brentham, but over the years, the time involved in maintaining these had led a significant proportion of residents to dig them up and replace them, usually with a dwarf brick wall. As traffic increased, and parking became more difficult, a number of front gardens were also paved over to provide hard standing for a car. Although replacing a hedge once it has been removed is more time-consuming, if not more expensive, than replacing windows, the Society encouraged residents to keep the remaining hedges in good shape. By the late 1970s two men had been found who were regularly employed at cutting hedges. And this problem of hedge-loss has been as severe at the back of the houses as at the front. An open aspect to the rear, with

ABOVE: *The Hanger Hill Garden Estate, Ealing. This estate, just half a mile east of Brentham, was another unusual choice as a conservation area in 1969, a time when architecture of the 1920s and 1930s was not widely appreciated.*

pioneers broke down. No one seems to have anticipated that the pollarding that is necessary to keep these trees to a manageable height would one day no longer be carried out on a regular basis. This failure to control the height of trees has happened partly because of the expense involved, and partly because pollarding is perceived in some quarters as 'unnatural'. Lime trees also tend to drip a sticky substance, which is not appreciated by the owners of cars parked beneath them.

Then there is the problem of tree roots that are traditionally blamed for structural damage. In fact, the root ball of the lime tree is relatively compact, and cracking to walls is more likely to be a sign of subsidence caused by the drying out of the soggy London Clay soil in hot summers. All these factors saw a number of lime trees removed, before the Town and Country Amenities Act of 1974 was brought in to provide protection. To minimise the chances of trees being lost, the Brentham Society worked with Ealing

*ABOVE: The Brentham Society 'go walkabout', c. 1970. Founders of the society present include Brian Fallon (in front, with pipe), Tony Oliver (with beard, next to car) Margaret Tims (with handbag) and Tony Scanlan (at the back, in light suit). The Ford Corsair appears in need of some urgent conservation.*

*RIGHT: Corner of Pitshanger Lane and Ludlow Road. Such replacement picture windows are damaging to the visual cohesiveness of the suburb.*

garden boundaries formed by low chestnut paling in the early days, and by low hedges from 1908, was as important an aim to Unwin and the pioneers, as the street-front appearance of the houses. High fences in back gardens have had as serious an impact on the environment of the suburb as the loss of hedges to the front.

The other defining characteristic of the Brentham scene, which forms a foil to the hedges, is the street trees. Of the varied street trees planted by Ealing Tenants before the First World War, only the lime trees, along with some birch trees in Ludlow Road and plane trees in Meadvale Road, survived by the 1970s. By this time the lime trees were creating something of a problem: trees were one way in which forward planning of the

THE BRENTHAM SOCIETY

NEWSLETTER

1

APRIL 1970

A Newsletter will be produced at intervals and distributed to all members
of the Brentham Society.  The first copies are being distributed to all
residents of the Brentham Garden Estate, whether or not they have chosen
to join the Society.

The Brentham Society was formed at a public meeting on 10th March, 1970,
at which the following Steering Committee was elected:

    Mr. Clive Hicks,      72 Brentham Way
    Miss M. Tims,        137 Fowlers Walk
    Mr. C. Higgins,       18 Ludlow Road
    Mrs. M. Aarens,        8 Winscombe Crescent
    Mrs. J. Irvine,       38 Meadvale Road
    Mr. A. Scanlan,        3 Winscombe Crescent
    Mr. A. Oliver,        48 Denison Road
    Mr. B. Fallon,        12 Winscombe Crescent

ABOUT THE SOCIETY

The Brentham Society is an independent body and membership is open to all
residents (whether house-owners or tenants) of the Brentham Garden Estate,
the boundaries of which are as specified in the Ealing Council's Report on
Conservation Areas.

Council to identify trees for pruning, and to suggest
replacements when trees died.

As well as hedges and trees, some of Brentham's
characteristic open spaces were showing signs of age-
ing by the early 1970s. In 1970 the small green in
Meadvale Road opposite the Brentham Club was badly
overgrown, and was being used as an impromptu rub-
bish dump. Within the year the Society had raised a
band of volunteers to clear the undergrowth, plant new
grass and bedding plants, and replace the high palings
with a chain fence of the style used in the early days
when the hedges were first planted. Paving, waste bins
and benches re-established the area as a public open
space, the maintenance was taken over by the council, and it was unofficially rechristened Brentham Green.

FAR LEFT: *The Brentham Society newsletter, issue number 1, April 1970. The Brentham Society was established a month earlier by a group of residents who wished to 'encourage the preservation and improvement of the character of the estate'.*

LEFT: *39–51 Holyoake Walk. Green and golden privet hedges are a characteristic feature of Brentham Garden Suburb. Here they create an especially attractive vista, the varying hedge height providing added visual interest.*

RIGHT: *13–15 Brentham Way. Before Brentham was designated a conservation area, a number of front gardens were replaced by hard standing for cars, following the great increase in car ownership that began in the late 1950s. This photograph also features a Brentham Society notice board, which was intro-duced in 1999 to publicise Society events after a council ruling had made it illegal to attach posters to street trees.*

The work at Brentham Green saw the Society putting into practice conservation at what might be called the micro-level. But there was also activity at the macro-level: within its first five years the Society had to deal with three major planning proposals that threat-ened the suburb. The first of these came in 1970, only

have had a major impact on Brentham. And while the Society recognised that the school would be a welcome amenity in itself, the proposal as it was presented would also have involved the demolition of houses within Brentham – in Neville Road – for access, which clearly breached the spirit of the council-designated conservation area. In the end it was politics, not persuasion, that decided this case. Control of the council changed, and the plan for a school was dropped in June 1971.

But the allotment site had clearly caught the council's eye. By 1972, despite the fact that the site was designated as open space in its own Plan for Ealing, the council had come up with another proposal, this time for housing. There was ample justification in principle for this as there was a chronic housing shortage, but many in Brentham were not convinced that this site, on open land by the River Brent, was the best place for it. The proposal dragged on for years, gathering momentum, and by 1975 nearly 60 houses on 3½ acres were projected. In the end, the Brentham Society enlisted the help of an unexpected source to thwart the plan. The then-chairman, Martin Jiggens, was a town planner, familiar with some arcane legislation that could be turned to the suburb's good. He invited the allotments' surveyor for the Ministry of Agriculture to look at the site, the surveyor reported to the Department of the Environment which, in turn, refused permission for building to take place over the allotments. In all, it had taken six years to save the site.

But the council was more usually an ally in protecting Brentham's amenity, as became apparent when two other planning applications threatened the suburb in the early seventies. The first, in 1970, was for a block of 13 flats in the grounds of Mount View, at the top of

*LEFT: The reclaiming of Brentham Green, 1970. One of the Brentham Society's first acts was to organise volunteers to renovate the small green (sometimes referred to, in Brentham's early years, as Meadvale Square) opposite the Brentham Club in Meadvale Road. Undergrowth was cleared, new grass and bedding plants put in, and low post-and-chain fencing was used to replace high palings. Paving, waste bins and benches re-established the area as public open space.*

a few months after the Society was founded. That year Ealing Borough Council proposed building a school on the allotment land behind Neville Road known as Brentham Fields. This land, which had been allotments for more than 90 years, firstly owned by the Great Western Railway and later by the council, was outside the conservation area, but any development there would

RIGHT: *Allotments, Brentham Fields. Over the past 30 years the Brentham Society has had to fight two major planning applications – one for a school, the other for housing – to build over this land just outside the Brentham conservation area beside the Western Avenue, which has been allotments for more than 90 years. At the time of writing the Brentham Allotments and Gardens Society (BAGS – the renamed Brentham Horticultural Society) is under threat of closure after 96 years, during which time it has dispensed seeds, equipment and advice, mostly from a hut on Brentham Fields.*

Brentham Way, just outside the conservation area. Because of its elevated site, the development would have blighted the southeast corner of the estate. The second application, in 1974, was for further flats to be built behind Holyoake Walk, in the heart of Brentham. In the event the Society did not have to mobilise resistance because the council rejected both applications out of hand.

One of the most protracted planning battles of the 1970s was also fought in the heart of the suburb, at the even more sensitive site of the sports fields of the Brentham Club. In 1968, before the conservation area designation, the Brentham Club had applied to build a four-lane indoor bowling green, only a few feet from the back gardens of the houses in Meadvale Road. As

well as building over several hundred square yards of open land, the proposed structure was architecturally undistinguished and out of character with the Club and other nearby buildings. It also spoiled the rear view of several houses in Meadvale Road. This was another case that dragged on for years, as the Club appealed against the council's refusal to grant permission. In the end it went to the Environment Secretary, Geoffrey Rippon, who finally rejected it in September 1973.

The case provoked considerable ill feeling between the Brentham Society and the Brentham Club, and relations between the two have not always been friendly since. Perhaps this is inevitable. The Brentham Institute was for the first 35 years of its life an integral part of the Brentham estate, with residents enjoying its

exclusive use at nominal fees. As such, it had to be heavily subsidised by Ealing Tenants Ltd. When the Institute separated from Ealing Tenants in 1935, and especially when the building and grounds were bought from the Bradford Property Trust in 1947, wider sources of income were needed than could be found in a suburb of fewer than 700 houses. The result has been that an increasing proportion of the Club's membership is from outside Brentham, and it is the membership that is, of necessity, the Club's first priority. The main priority of the Brentham Society, however, is Brentham's residents and the conservation of Brentham Garden Suburb, and inevitably the different groups will have clashing priorities on occasion.

But the old co-partnership spirit had not entirely died out. In the early 1970s, 40 years after Ealing Tenants Ltd issued its last co-partnership shares, the Club, which is still collectively owned by its members, was still issuing its own shares. And the Club and the Society have co-operated in a co-partnerly way. One example of this was in the setting up of a luncheon club for pensioners, the Club providing the accommodation, the Society the organisation. 'A neighbourly concern for the interests of elderly or retired residents' was one of the aims of the Society from early on, and by June 1971 a hot midday meal was being provided on weekdays for any pensioners who wanted it, at the modest charge of 7½ pence. By 1973 more than a hundred residents were taking advantage of the scheme, and for a while priority had to be given to the over-80s until further accommodation could be found. It is perhaps a reflection of increasing cosmopolitanism and health consciousness that over the 20 years or so that the luncheon club was in operation, the menu on offer

LEFT: *Garden of 64 Meadvale Road. This front garden is one of the longest in Brentham, and its owner for 20 years, Brian Vaughan, has made the most of the space by cultivating it as an especially attractive and appropriate cottage garden. It has won Mr Vaughan the Rose Bowl on two occasions.*

ABOVE: *Brentham Rose Bowl. This bowl has been awarded annually since 1972 to the best front garden in Brentham. The origins of the trophy go back to before the First World War, when it was known as the Vivian Trophy and awarded at the annual Brentham Rose Show; Brentham growers were renowned for their roses.*

diversified from the ever-popular 'English' to include diabetic, vegetarian and Indian meals.

The Society's social activities also diversified over the years. They included talks such as one on William Morris by Sir Nikolaus Pevsner, whose research assistant, Margaret Tims, was a founder of the Society; slide shows, many raising awareness of the suburb's history; a chess club and a choir; and trips, including what was, for a while, a regular annual visit to the country's second oldest nature reserve, Perivale Wood, run by the Selborne Society. There was also contact and co-operation with like-minded bodies, such as the Ealing Civic Society, the Bedford Park Society and the Hampstead Garden Suburb Residents' Association.

One of the Brentham Society's most successful ventures was the revival in 1972 of the garden competitions that had run for many years from 1903. In its revived form an award was made for the neatest front garden. It was judged by the Brentham Horticultural Society, who presented the Rose Bowl (at one time known as the Vivian Trophy), that had in the past been presented to the winner of the Rose Show. In 1979 the criteria for choosing the winning garden changed when Pam Turner, an architect and landscape designer, took over the judging, sometimes with additional assistance. She felt that 'neat' was too restrictive a criterion, and instead looked for 'interest throughout the seasons, good foliage contrasts, layout in scale with the garden size and with the house'. All did not run smoothly, however, when the judges one year ventured to offer some gentle criticisms of some otherwise commended gardens. Offence was taken, apologies had to be tendered, and the decision was taken to 'restrict our notes to those of a general nature or purely favourable comments on the winning

garden'. But the annual judging was generally welcomed, and it was felt by the early 1980s that there had been a 'general improvement in the gardens in the suburb since the Society began the competition in its present form'. By the 1990s the judging became wider still in its scope, with prizes given for the best garden in each season, as well as an overall award.

The garden awards are a prime example of the Society's founding aim to improve the suburb, but the other aim, to preserve it from unnecessary alterations, still needed to be pursued with vigour. This was especially difficult in the early years when the conservation area status was little more than a statement of intent. Listing had come to be the main legislative tool used in conservation. If a building is listed, whatever the grade of listing (Grade I, Grade II* or Grade II), Building Consent from the local authority is required for any alterations, inside or out, irrespective of whether or not a feature has been singled out on the list description. In Brentham, only the Club and St Barnabas church have so far been listed, but there did exist another mechanism that could give teeth to the conservation-area designation, and which had been available at the time Brentham had become a conservation area. In its initial report in 1969, the council had recommended that all seven of the new conservation areas should be subject to an 'Article 4 direction'.

This refers to Town and Country planning legislation rather than the Civic Amenities Act. To make planning procedures easier for councils, the Town and Country Planning Acts of 1963 and 1971 specified that certain 'permitted developments' would not require planning permission. Unfortunately these developments included almost everything that had eroded Brentham's character since the 1960s, such as alterations to windows, doors and porches, small extensions, garages, car standing spaces, and walls and fences. As a result these changes carried on unimpeded, except for the Society's protests, until well into the 1970s. But as part of the Town and Country Planning legislation there was scope for an Article 4 direction which, if imposed, would withdraw the right to these 'permitted developments'.

The problem was that whereas the conservation area designation cost councils very little, an Article 4 direction would necessarily involve them in a lot more work assessing planning applications, and many councils continued to allow 'permitted developments'. However, Ealing Borough Council had originally indicated that it favoured making the Article 4 direction, and every year, sometimes several times a year, the Brentham Society would write to the council asking them to make the direction. This finally bore fruit in 1975, when Brentham, and also the Hanger Hill Garden Estate, were awarded Article 4 conservation-area status.

The wider effects of this action took a while to make themselves felt, but the Article 4 direction meant that the Brentham Society's involvement in planning matters immediately intensified. Since the founding of the Society it had had a member on the three-person advisory panel set up by the council when the suburb was made a conservation area. With the Article 4 direction, although the panel still acted purely as advisers, it was necessarily much more closely involved in planning decisions and the council committees that made them.

The council took its responsibilities seriously. It has drawn up and published in booklet form a set of conservation guidelines for Brentham, and over the years a number of residents have been prosecuted for making unauthorised alterations, such as replacing the plain red tiles used in most of the suburb with concrete pantiles. One especially intractable case arose in 1985–6, when, despite warnings from the Society, doors and windows in a house in Holyoake Walk were replaced without planning consent. This case went, via a council enforcement order, all the way to the Department of the Environment, which upheld the council's order requiring the replacement of the windows and doors. The ultimate sanction for anyone contravening the legislation – imprisonment – has never been applied. At least, not so far . . .

Unfortunately, but understandably, the council has not always been as stringent with itself as it is with residents. 'Understandably', because the council has responsibility for public safety in Brentham, which is why streets and their fittings are exempt from the Article 4 direction. This safety aspect, along with the need for pavements to be better lit, accounts for the replacement, begun in the 1970s, of many of the old street lamps with a new slimline design. The Society protested, but the council pointed out that although cost was a consideration – it could not afford to reproduce the Edwardian lamp standards – safety was more so. The old street lights in Brentham are a hybrid: their standards are an Edwardian relic, some dating back to before any houses were built, but the lamps are a later electric replacement, probably from the 1920s, of the original gas mantles and square lamps. These swan-neck lamp-brackets are fragile and prone to break when rusty, endangering the hapless passing Brenthamite, and even where they are still structurally sound, the electric fittings do not comply with modern safety standards. The new slimline lights are safer and

RIGHT: *Old (left) and new (right) Brentham streetlights. Lamp standards were put up in Brentham even before the houses were built. These originally had a box-shaped lamp housing a gas mantle. In the 1920s these were replaced by electric lights on a swan neck, attached to the original standards. Unfortunately the swan necks are thin and prone to rust, and the electrics outdated, so new slimline electric lights have gradually been introduced.*

cheaper to maintain and, while they are not stylistically in keeping with the suburb, they are designed to be as unobtrusive as possible.

But the streets contain a range of other environmentally and architecturally sensitive features whose alteration it is less easy to justify. These include the pavements, which traditionally had a paved footpath edged on the roadside by a narrow strip of grass, or sometimes gravel, where the street trees were also planted (page 198). Next to this strip were kerbstones, and at the edge of the roadway itself, were cobblestones or 'setts'. Most of these, with the exception of the paving and kerbstones, were lost, or obscured by further paving or tarmac, many years ago, but it is especially regrettable that even now paving is still being replaced with tarmac or 'bitmac', and wide kerbstones with narrow concrete strips, when repairs are undertaken. The council has

not been the only culprit. In the 1970s and early 1980s, Brentham saw its traditional red telephone boxes replaced by glass boxes: this was introduced as part of a country-wide trend, but the new design is particularly jarring to Brentham's rustic aesthetic.

A more sensitive and considered approach has, however, usually been applied to the street trees. The council began in the 1970s by pruning the large limes, and in 1981 they undertook, in conjunction with the Society, a survey of all street trees, which resulted in a schedule of works for the whole suburb, and a list of acceptable replacement varieties. These included silver birch, Raywood ash, white flowering cherry, crab-apple and pear. The Society, while accepting the need for trees of a manageable size, was not entirely happy with some of the smaller flowering trees, such as the cherries. These cause pavement damage and are prone to unsightly suckering and distortion to their bark and trunks. It is now generally accepted that they are unsuitable street trees, and cause damage to paving, as has happened in Fowlers Walk. The Society's preference for traditional old English forest trees was therefore a matter of practicality as well as of taste. In this they were more rigorously discriminating than the builders of the estate, whose choices included acacia, plum, apple and even laburnum.

Much of this steady improvement of the trees came to a sad and abrupt end in the early hours of 16 October 1987. That morning a vast weather front swept in from the Atlantic, leaving a trail of destruction that stretched all along the south coast of England. Although the southern counties were worst hit by what became known as the 'Great Storm', Brentham, along with the rest of London, suffered major damage. The suburb's residents awoke to find nearly 70 trees destroyed or damaged beyond saving, including a number of 80-year-old limes, some of which had fallen, damaging houses and blocking streets. The Society immediately set up a tree fund to replace the lost trees, and within a month, more than £1,200 had been raised. For this the council agreed to replace all the lost street trees, and a new list of tree species that would be planted was drawn up.

This list appears to be evidence of the Society's influence, as it includes a greater proportion than in the 1981 selection, of traditional English trees such as hornbeam, apple, ash, various types of beech, as well as more evolved species such as 'elm (disease-resistant)' and 'lime (drip-reduced)'. Some reservations were expressed about the choice of rowan, or mountain ash, a species that tends not to thrive in London clay soil. However, its berries are a favourite with many species of bird, and

the desire to encourage wildlife was generally agreed to accord with the 'Green' agenda of the garden city movement, even if the choice of tree did not match the original planting. In all, the council planted 89 new trees, and the Society did its best to ensure a good survival rate for these by its Adopt-a-tree scheme that encouraged residents to nurture the tree nearest to their houses. In fact the survival rate for the replacement trees was much better than average, at least until the council had an accident with a weedkiller in 1993, which resulted in the loss of a number of young trees.

ABOVE: *Uprooted tree, Brentham Way, 1987. The 'Great Storm' of 16 October 1987 destroyed nearly 70 trees in Brentham, including some of the 80-year-old lime trees planted by Ealing Tenants Ltd when the suburb was new.*

RIGHT: *The mayor of Ealing, Councillor Rabindaran Pathak, and the mayoress, accepting a cheque towards replacing Brentham's lost trees, 13 February 1988. Following the storm, Audrey Jones, who is presenting the cheque, was elected to the Brentham Society committee and set up a tree fund. Within a month more than £1,200 had been raised and, after the mayor took a personal interest in the project, the council agreed to replace all the lost street trees for this sum. Here, on a wet and windy day at the corner of Fowlers Walk and Brentham Way, the mayor is about to plant an oak to commemorate the storm.*

In the 1990s the worst threats to the character of the suburb appeared to be past. The Society's efforts at education, the Article 4 direction and a widespread change in taste that saw Arts and Crafts architecture much more widely valued, meant that fewer people were inclined to replace windows and doors, or gates and hedges. Indeed, an increasing number of residents were replacing aluminium and uPVC-frame picture windows with small-pane windows to the original pattern. This appreciation applied increasingly to the interiors as well as the exteriors, as people came to enjoy the original doors, fireplaces and other features.

But new technology has also brought problems. The laying of cables for cable television has scarred pavement tarmac, while relay boxes for the same purpose have not always been sensitively sited by the cable companies. Satellite dishes are also a potential problem, as many householders do not realise that dishes require planning consent, even for those situated at the rear of houses. Compromises can be reached, however. In one case in Brentham Way, a large, unsightly dish positioned high up on a wall was changed for a smaller piece of equipment, which was located inconspicuously with no loss of reception. Other threats were natural rather than technological. In the early 1990s a number of privet hedges were destroyed by honey fungus, or *Armillaria*, although the Society quickly did its homework and came up with a list of plants, including box, hawthorn, blackthorn and yew, all of which are resistant to the disease. And the problem of subsidence, a perennial affliction in Brentham and elsewhere in London, is still with us, made worse by hot summers such as those of 1976, 1983 and 1998. The effects of this are sometimes highly visible: for some time the wall of a house in Brunswick Road was supported by wooden struts.

While conservation continues as a principal aim of the Society, it has also maintained its efforts to foster friendly relations among residents in the suburb, in the old co-partnership spirit of brotherhood. New 'traditions' have become established with this aim in mind. One example is the annual Strawberry Tea held every June since 1981 in the garden of 2 Winscombe Crescent, the home of Mrs Barbara Murray. Another event, that took place three times in the late 1990s, was the Family Picnic and Sports Day, held on the green between Ludlow and Denison Roads. This seems an appropriate activity here, as this was one of the open spaces intended by Raymond Unwin as a safe play areas for children,

LEFT: *Pushchair race, Brentham Family Picnic and Sports Day, 1997. This event on Ludlow–Denison Green seems an especially appropriate use of this space, one of several designated by Raymond Unwin as safe play areas for children 'within sight of their own homes'. The pushchair race also has an historical resonance as Brentham sports days before the First World War included 'baby carriage' races.*

BELOW: *Brentham Family Cycle, 1999.*

RIGHT: *Garden of 28 Holyoake Walk, Brentham Garden Day, 1999. This was a new event in 1999, but has proved so popular that it promises to become a permanent fixture. Visitors follow a map and see a selection of Brentham gardens. This garden is unusually large and oddly shaped because it includes a section of ground that originally formed separate allotments behind the gardens.*

BELOW: *Strawberry Tea, June 2000. Sue van Raat hands out strawberries and cream at this popular annual event. The Strawberry Tea, first held in 1981, brings residents together in Barbara Murray's delightful back garden in Winscombe Crescent.*

'within sight of their own homes'. The races included a pushchair race, an echo of the pram races that were included in the sports days before the First World War – although it must be considerably easier to steer a modern buggy than an Edwardian baby carriage. In recent years a family cycle trip, reminiscent of the old Brentham cycle club outings, has become a regular event. Another recent event, held for the first time in 1999, and one that promises to become a regular part of the Brentham calendar, is Brentham Garden Day, when visitors may follow a map and see a selection of Brentham's many and varied gardens. Brentham also takes part in the Civic Trust's London Open House scheme every autumn.

Alongside these new activities, Brentham May Day has survived now for more than 90 years. That survival is not something that can be taken for granted, however. Less than 30 years ago, in 1973, 'black clouds of cancellation' threatened. As in 1925, the problem was the May Day committee, which by that time had been organising the festivities for many years. In the words of one less-than-tactful commentator at the time, they were 'elderly and tired', and in March they announced that they could not organise that year's May Day. Sympathetic to tradition, two local residents, Tony and Mary Scanlan, set up a temporary committee; the old committee lent costumes, and the festivities went ahead without a hitch.

The new committee proved to be rather more permanent than anticipated, as the Scanlans were still arranging May Day eight years later in 1981 when, bizarrely, the Brentham May Day procession was banned. The day before the procession was due to take place the committee received a letter from Scotland Yard instructing them to observe the 28-day ban on all marches in London imposed by the then Home Secretary, Willie Whitelaw, on 25 April. This was ordered in anticipation of trouble between National Front and Anti-Nazi-League groups in the lead up to Greater London Council elections, but religious and traditional marches were supposed to be excluded. Perhaps the name 'May Day procession' suggested an extreme left-wing intent on the part of the Brentham children. In the event the organisers had to arrange a High Court hearing, where, when shown a portfolio of pictures of past May Day

FAR LEFT: *Wounded soldier helps plait the maypole, May Day, 1980s.*

LEFT: *Brentham May Day, 1969. In the early days of Brentham May Day 'a babies' cart' – a decorated greengrocers' cart for conveying toddlers – was a regular part of the procession. By 1969 it had become a babies' Land Rover.*

RIGHT: *Brentham May Day, 1975. The dress style of the 1974 May Queen, Clare Clements (in front), and the long hair of the boy bandsmen, date this to the 1970s. The 1975 May Queen, Lindsey German (behind Clare, her train carried by attendants), has yet to be crowned. The sound of the band has, from the early days, been a popular way of drawing residents to their garden gates to watch the procession. In the background, the babies' Land Rover has become a babies' Range Rover.*

LEFT: *May Day procession, 1977. The May Queen from accession year, Marianne Aldridge (née Bruce), returns after 25 years to join in the celebrations for May Day in Silver Jubilee year.*

RIGHT: *The march they couldn't ban: May Day, 1981. The May Day procession nearly did not take place in Brentham in 1981, as the police interpreted a London-wide ban on marches (leading up to elections to the Greater London Council) as including Brentham's May Day. The organisers, led by Tony Miller (left) and Tony Scanlan, had to go to the High Court before the police agreed that the march could be exempted from the ban – bizarrely, on the grounds of its 'religious' character.*

processions, Mr Justice Comyn observed that they 'did not look like a very subversive lot'. In any case the police had already agreed that the procession could go ahead. Oddly, the grounds the police accepted were that the procession was 'religious' in character, rather than 'traditional', and prayers were said at the beginning and end of the festivities.

Since then May Day has proceeded without incident. In the past decade, the evening dance at the Club has disappeared (although a children's disco has been a feature of recent years), but the procession is now larger than ever, with 100 to 150 children taking part each year. The popularity that this represents means that Brentham May Day seems safe for the time being.

But the survival of May Day in Brentham has been the exception rather than the rule in May Day festivities generally. All the other May Day festivals in Ealing, such as those at Drayton, Hobbayne and Acton Wells schools, as well as the old May Day horse parade, died out before the Second World War, as did the Letchworth and Hampstead Garden Suburb events. Compared to the heyday of the May Day revival between 1880 and 1930, there are just a handful of these festivals left in the country. Some, such as Knutsford, are survivals from the first period of revival in the nineteenth century. Other revels, such as at Milford in Derbyshire, are of much more recent date, and are part of the second folk revival of the 1960s and 1970s (although this time morris dancing was the form of expression that found most favour).

Whether long-established or of more recent origin, there are differences between festivals in terms of how much they have been allowed to evolve. Rochester in Kent has a May Bank Holiday festival which only began

in 1980 (although a sweeps' procession, described by Dickens, was held until the early twentieth century). As in Brentham, the organisers try to preserve the features of the revels from one year to the next. The festivities include the 'waking' of the Jack-in-the-green at dawn, and culminate in a procession with sweeps, morris dancers and many other characters. By contrast, Powell Corderoy Primary School in Dorking, Surrey, which has held a summer festival with a May Queen and maypole dancing every year since 1896, has added to its repertoire – in 1999 dances were performed to songs by Abba and Andrew Lloyd Webber.

But Brentham's May Day is significant for two reasons. First, it is one of only two long-standing May

229

Days in London. Only the May Queen of All London Festival at Hayes Common, Bromley, has a longer unbroken history, and since that began in 1907, it is a year younger than Brentham's May revels, which date from those first maypole dances on 9 June 1906. The second reason is not immediately obvious because of popular assumptions about May revels as a rural or village activity. Brentham's May Day might appear, on the face of it, as the nostalgic revivalists' twentieth-century suburban pastiche of an 'authentic' ancient rural custom. In fact, many of the features associated with May revels ancient and modern, such as morris dancing, maypole plaiting and the Jack-in-the-green, began not in the heart of the country, but in London. Brentham's May Day can therefore lay claim to this hidden metropolitan tradition in a way that no other May revels can. Of such paradoxes are customs and traditions made.

As the twentieth century drew to a close the survival of May Day appeared secure, but the same could not be said for the architectural character of the suburb. Once again the Brentham Society's principal energies were caught up with conservation issues, as two major planning applications loomed. Both were significant cases, and each threatened the suburb in different ways: one involved the largest building operation to take place in the suburb for 40 years, while the other affected the wider environment of Brentham. Just after the Second World War, St Barnabas Church had built a temporary church hall to the west of the church. It was not a prepossessing structure, still less so because although only intended to have a life span of ten years, it stayed in place for nearly half a century. By 1998 it was dilapidated and too small for the parish's needs. The problem

the church faced was to find a building that met the needs at an affordable cost; the Society's aim was ensuring that what replaced the old church hall would be in keeping with the rest of the church architecture. After fraught discussions among the three principal interested parties – the church, the council's conservation officer, and the Society – the award of a Millennium grant meant that a new hall could be built that met the parish's needs yet was in keeping with the church's details, materials and architectural manner.

Such a happy outcome has, unfortunately, not been forthcoming in the other case, which is still ongoing at the time of writing. This is the application for developments at the Brentham Club. The plans include building hard tennis courts, an artificial hockey pitch and athletics track, a pavilion, and an extension to the Grade II-listed Clubhouse. The pitch would cover the field that was first used in the 1920s as a site of the Brentham May Day dancing, and would come within a few metres of 20 houses in Meadvale Road, while the courts would reach to within 13 metres of the River Brent, cutting across the green swathe of the Brent River Park. The Club's financial situation may explain their desire to develop their facilities, but it would be less understandable if Ealing Council were to pass a scheme that would not only contravene its own Unitary Development Plan, but which would also affect the building and environment of a listed building in an Article 4 conservation area. To pass the plan would be all the more inexplicable, given the council's declaration in 1991, when the Club was granted planning permission to build more hard tennis courts, that this was 'the limit to the acceptable expansion of the Brentham Club and no further intensification of use

ABOVE: *Jack-in-the-green, May Day procession, 1998. Jack, whose identity is traditionally kept secret, decides to go barefoot this year.*

RIGHT: *Brentham Way. The streets of Brentham are now typically entirely lined with parked cars. The contrast in Brentham Way can be appreciated by comparing this photograph with those on pages 193 and 194.*

would be permitted'. The present scheme involves both 'expansion' and 'intensification of use'.

Another piece of historic Brentham is also under threat as this book goes to press. This is the Brentham Allotments and Gardens Society – or BAGS for short. BAGS is the renamed Brentham Horticultural Society, which has been in continuous existence since 1904, dispensing seeds, equipment and advice from a hut by the allotments on Brentham Fields. But membership has dwindled to such an extent that the Society's viability after 96 years is now in question.

The decline in allotment gardening is perhaps a symptom of wider changes in Brentham in recent years. Partly because the architecture and general environment of the suburb are now more widely appreciated, and partly because of the high place enjoyed in school 'league tables' by several local schools, Brentham is now more desirable than ever as a place in which to live. This has brought in many new families with young children, but also increasing gentrification. House prices are now high enough to preclude all but the wealthiest single-income households. Few Brentham residents now have the time, energy or inclination for allotment gardening. The gentrification has had other ramifications. There has, in recent years, been an upsurge in the number of loft conversions, as residents attempt to squeeze the maximum space out of the small Brentham houses. Planning guidelines direct that windows for these must be located to the rear of the houses. Other symptoms of gentrification are the congestion of the streets with parked cars, while free access to some of the pathways between the houses is now barred with locked gates erected by house owners understandably

fearful of burglars. Such attitudes, combined with an increased preoccupation with private space, account for the less open outlook to the rear of the houses, over what was once communal space.

But not every development represents a step away from the pioneers' intentions. A small victory was recently secured just off the suburb, in a small development on Pitshanger Lane, where the developer, Laing Homes, proposed building six town houses. Here local residents, unhappy with both the design and the location of the houses very close to the road, were successful in persuading the developer to reconsider their plans. A new architect, Robert Rigby, was engaged, and at the request of the residents, made an inspection of

Brentham Garden Suburb. Impressed by the houses at the corner of Winscombe Crescent and Woodfield Crescent, he produced a design that features some roughcast and F.C. Pearson's square corner bays, set at 45 degrees to the wall, that both 'turn' the corner and provide angled views along the streets. It is only a minor matter, but it is gratifying for those who have worked so hard to protect Brentham that it still has something to offer architects a century after it was built. With this in mind, in 1999 the Brentham Heritage Society was set up as a charitable arm of the Brentham Society, with the specific aim of promoting an appreciation of Brentham's architectural amenity and an interest in its history; in keeping with this aim, one of its first acts has been the publication of this book.

So Brentham is 100 years old, and its residents are now, as Henry Vivian and the pioneers were on that night in February 1901, looking to the future and wondering what the new century – and for us, the new millennium – will bring. The changes in store cannot possibly match those early times, when the fields of Pitshanger Farm were transformed in 15 years into the pioneer garden suburb. But change is not now the priority in Brentham Garden Suburb. The rest of the twentieth century may have seen Howard's dream of a garden city, and Vivian's equally passionate belief in co-partnership housing, swamped by the capitalist forces they sought to harness. But their legacy, and the legacy of Unwin and Parker, Pearson, Sutcliffe and the pioneers, is a very real one – the suburb itself. The spirit of co-partnership that built Brentham has not disappeared. It is now harnessed to protect the suburb, and cultivate a wider appreciation of it – and may it continue to do so for another 100 years.

ABOVE LEFT: *The new church hall, St Barnabas, 1998. Consultation between the Brentham Society, the church and the council's conservation officer resulted in a satisfactory solution on this sensitive site.*

ABOVE RIGHT: *Football field, Brentham Club, 1999. This site is under threat at the time of writing, by a planning application to build an artificial hockey pitch and athletics track here and new tennis courts on land beside the Brent, and to extend the Club – all this despite the fact that the grounds are part of the 'green corridor' along the Brent, and the Club is a listed building in an Article 4 conservation area.*

# APPENDIX

# Around the streets of Brentham

JUST WHAT IS typically Brentham? Ask anyone who knows the suburb and they will usually talk about its rural qualities – hedges and street trees, cottage gardens and allotments, small greens and the wide acres of the sports ground along the River Brent. Certainly all these help to create a verdant environment rarely found in Greater London. But they would also surely mention the charming Arts and Crafts cottages. These display a vast array of features which all contribute to the suburb's unique appeal. There is the characteristic palette of colours, the soft red brick and tiles, contrasting with the pale, colour-washed roughcast and occasional accents of dark timber-framing. Then there are the typical Brentham small-pane windows, the tiled dormers, steep tiled roofs, half-hip gables and timber gates. They might mention the arrangement of the houses into groups of two, four or six, each block unified by shared gables or porches, and the way these build up along the informal, curving plan to produce an endless variety and visual delight of 'street pictures'. This grouping of houses is more than a visual trick: it was a deliberate move to foster the sense of community that was an essential aim of the co-partnership pioneers in 1901.

These are the defining qualities of what makes Brentham as a whole a special place, and although they are typical of most of the sixteen streets that make up the suburb, each of these streets has its own character, points of visual interest, and some curiosities that lend variety and interest to any walk around Brentham. This is true even of those 'Cinderella' streets, Woodfield Road and Woodfield Avenue. **Woodfield Road** provides a fine view down Denison Road to the Brentham Club, and shows how the later architects and planners tied Woodfield Road into their scheme to provide vistas

RIGHT: *79 Woodfield Road. This house was part of Vivian Terrace, the first nine houses built by Ealing Tenants Ltd. It is especially well preserved, and retains the original door, stained glass, Art Nouveau letterbox, and porch and path tiling.*

towards points of interest. The houses in these streets are more like conventional Edwardian terraced houses than most of the other streets, but they are not without architectural interest. For example, the stretch of Woodfield Road between Pitshanger Lane and Woodfield Crescent appears to be a terrace of identical houses, yet numbers 49–69 have lots of features that the Ealing Tenants Ltd houses at 71–95 lack, that show they were built by a different builder. Notice, for example, all the little decorative details in numbers 49–69 – the Edwardian porch of number 49, with its fretwork and turned decoration, the carved bargeboards to many of the gable eaves, the moulded stone capital between the windows, even the fancy ridge tiles; the Ealing Tenants houses at 71–95 are much plainer. But even these have some delightful period features: 77 and 79 are particularly well preserved. There is an oddity in the numbering of Woodfield Road here. The first house past number 41, to the south of Woodfield Crescent (outside the conservation area) is not, as might be expected 39, but 35. This is a consequence of the different periods of building on Woodfield Road. When numbers 41–95 were being built in 1901–6, the road down towards Eaton Rise between here and 3 Woodfield Road (now demolished) was not built up; those who had to give the houses numbers had to estimate how many houses would be built in between, so that when the road was finished there would be an unbroken sequence of numbers. In fact they seriously overestimated the number of houses they expected on that side of the road, and as a result, 5, 7, 9 and 11 Woodfield Road, as well as 31, 37 and 39, never existed. There are other more minor oddities of numbering – usually numbers missing – elsewhere in Brentham for the same reason.

LEFT: *Armorel, Woodfield Avenue. This house, which has never had a street number, was the home for many years of the secularist and socialist writer, F.J. Gould. The houses at either end on both sides of Woodfield Avenue ended in these bays with pointed roofs, which are an example of Ealing Tenants designing for overall coherence, even before an architect was employed. The house displays a moulded brick panel on the bay that reads 'ETL' (Ealing Tenants Ltd) '1904'. The roughcast panels were not painted originally.*

Back in **Woodfield Avenue**, the houses follow the lead of 71–95 Woodfield Road in their design. Again there is a slight oddity in the numbering: the house next to number 1 is not number 3, as might be expected, but 1a, which sounds like the number of a flat. Equally, across the road, Armorel has no number at all. The reason for this is that these larger corner houses were built before the rest of the terraces, and in this case the number of houses that would be built in between was slightly underestimated.

Woodfield Road, and especially Woodfield Avenue, have suffered more over the years than most of Brentham from alterations, although Woodfield Avenue retains a reasonable number of street trees, two or three of which, on the west side, appear to be from the original planting. But because these streets are architecturally more conventional, conservation restrictions have perhaps been less rigorously applied than in the rest of Brentham. Alterations and additions that compromise the overall visual integrity of the terraces include replacement doors (mainly of glass), aluminium windows, the concreting over of front gardens and the addition of doors to create porches. Some of the timber-framing in the gables has been painted over or picked out in darker paint. These latter cosmetic changes would not matter so much if the whole street were treated in this way; it is the variations between houses that were designed as part of a coherent street scene that degrade the overall visual amenity of the suburb. It is probably safe to say that such changes would not have been sanctioned to the same extent in the Arts and Crafts cottages. This is a pity. Brentham was made a conservation area initially because of its historical rather than its architectural interest, and Woodfield Road and Woodfield Avenue are the streets that most fully reflect the co-partnership history of the estate, in that they were designed and built by the pioneers. One of the better-preserved houses is number 1, at the corner, which has its original black-and-white path, porch tiles, and rope-pattern edging tiles.

Woodfield Avenue was the home of one of Brentham's most distinguished residents. Frederick James Gould, the prominent secularist and socialist, lived at Armorel on the corner, from 1910 to his death in 1938. Gould's son, Julian, died in action in France in 1917, a loss from which, it is said, F.J. Gould never fully recovered. This perhaps accounts for the active part F.J. played in the League of Nations after the War. Gould's daughter, Romola, ran the children's library at the

Institute for many years, and took over the house after her father's death. Two doors away, at 4 Woodfield Avenue, a very different sort of writer lived, from his birth in 1906 until he was 17. He was born René Lodge Brabazon Raymond, but understandably he changed his name. As James Hadley Chase he wrote more than 50 detective novels of the 'hard-boiled' American school – a sort of sub-Raymond Chandler – the best known of which was perhaps *No Orchids for Miss Blandish*.

**Woodfield Crescent** has a much greater variety of houses than the other Woodfields. It gains its name from the curve in the street, which follows the original southern boundary of the old Wood Field. The first few houses (1–7) are really part of the development in Woodfield Road. Woodfield Crescent is especially

RIGHT: *Road sign for Woodfield Crescent. A number of older street signs in Brentham have one end chopped off. The reason (although it might sound like an 'urban myth') is that during the war it was thought that removing the part of the sign displaying the postcode – W5 – might disorientate and so foil any Nazi spies who were parachuted into Brentham.*

235

interesting because here one can see the first signs of Arts and Crafts influence in the design of the houses. For example, the long terrace at numbers 16–32 has roughcast first floors, no gables, and red-tiled canopies that tie together the bay windows and the porches, so that it is almost like a series of semi-detached pairs of houses. Between numbers 16 and 17, and again 24 and 25, are passages that provided access for the delivery of coal to the rear of the houses.

An especially attractive feature of Woodfield Crescent is the terrace of houses on the north side, at numbers 41–51; variety is provided by the decorative treatments of the big shared gables and the end houses, which have their own gables. This is probably the earliest terrace that features the plain red roof tiles that are such a pleasing feature of the estate; although red tiles had been used on porches and gables, until then the houses had been roofed with slates from the Bethesda co-partnership slate mine in Wales.

Historically, the most interesting houses in this part of Woodfield Crescent are number 32, which was the office of Ealing Tenants Ltd in 1905–9, number 33, which served as the temporary institute in 1906–11, and number 15, which was the home of the architect F. Cavendish Pearson in 1907–12. Beyond Brunner Road, the houses in Woodfield Crescent are later. The houses in Woodfield Crescent beyond Winscombe Crescent are examples of some of the early houses built in pairs and short terraces after Unwin had provided his plan for extending the estate. Numbers 37 and 38 have angled bays at the corners that give wide-ranging views along Woodfield and Winscombe Crescents.

Woodfield Crescent was originally intended to stop at Brunner Road, into which it turned sharply as a road

RIGHT: *5, 6, 7 and 8 Brunner Road. These four houses are the first in Brentham to have small-pane windows. Although the tenants generally preferred the sashes seen here, the later casements were cheaper and thought to be healthier in admitting more fresh air.*

BELOW RIGHT: *Kitchen of 11 Winscombe Crescent. All of Pearson's houses, from Brunner Road onwards, had kitchens similar to this, which is unusually well preserved: the copper is gone, a gas cooker has been added, but the original sink and shelves remain, and the decoration has changed little in 90 years.*

LEFT: *41–51 Woodfield Crescent. This terrace, the only one in Brentham that steps back along the line of the road in this way, has been well maintained in a way the founders intended: the houses are all painted the same colour, and the hedges are roughly the same height, so that the visual coherence of the whole terrace is maintained.*

called Woodfield Crescent East. The view from Woodfield Crescent into **Brunner Road**, named after the businessman Sir John Brunner who lent Ealing Tenants money to extend the estate, provides one of the suburb's many attractive vistas typical of garden suburb planning. The terrace at numbers 1–12 is the earliest example of a block designed as a symmetrical whole, with the centre four houses rendered to break up the monotony of the terrace. Brunner Road, unlike most of the streets in Brentham, has sequential numbering, the reason for this being that the land on the west side of the road (now occupied by the house called Rookery Nook) was used as tennis courts, so that the terrace at numbers 1–12 might have been the only houses in the street. Number 6 was briefly, in 1912, Pearson's home. The houses that were built later, on the curved part of Brunner Road, especially numbers 17–22, which were

the first 'cheap cottages', feature lots of typical F.C. Pearson Arts and Crafts details, such as the mansard roof, tiled dormers and gables, and hipped-roof porch. Number 18 was the home of Thomas Brampton, eldest son of the pioneer Hubert Brampton, and it was this house that John Burns looked round on Whit Monday, 1908, when he opened the recreation ground. Another example of numbering miscalculation: there is no number 38 Brunner Road.

Brunner Road leads into **Neville Road**, named after the barrister Ralph Neville, who was both a co-partnership supporter from the 1890s, and an early promoter of the garden city ideal that led him to found Letchworth with Ebenezer Howard. Neville Road, which is all F.C. Pearson's work, ends at the recreation ground, to which it was deliberately left open at the end

towards this, to provide a delightful open vista across the sports ground and the Brent to Harrow far beyond. Fringing the Brent here is a row of poplars, which were planted as a memorial to Brentham residents who died in the First World War. The pair of houses at numbers 21–3 is slightly set back behind the line of the road, and the pavement here curves in towards the houses; the explanation for both these features is that this pair form an endpoint to the long straight stretch of Meadvale Road. The block at numbers 12–18 is unusual for Brentham in that it is faced in Flettons, pink bricks that were cheaper than the usual red facing bricks, or even than pale brown London stocks, and which were usually only used where they would be out of sight, such as beneath roughcast. Opposite this terrace is number

11 Neville Road, originally called 'Cornwood' after Henry Vivian's birthplace on Dartmoor, the house that was visited by the Duke and Duchess of Connaught on 27 May 1911, the day the Institute was opened.

Neville Road leads into **Meadvale Road**, a long street that forms an east–west counterpoint to the north–south avenue of Brentham Way. In some ways it supplanted Brentham Way as the principal road, notably because the Institute was built here instead. Meadvale Road is a good illustration of the varying ways the two architects F.C. Pearson and G.L. Sutcliffe responded to Unwin's planning ideas: the east half (on the south side up to number 15 and on the north side up to number 30) is by Pearson, the rest up to the end of the suburb at numbers 71 (on the south side) and 90 (on the north) by

*BELOW FAR LEFT: The Brentham Club, Meadvale Road. The three windows on the first floor were originally those of the 'ladies' clubroom' (now the bar), while those on the ground floor were the reading room. The tower, once used for committee rooms and, for a while, a photographic studio, is now used mainly for storage. It is a prominent feature in this part of Brentham, and forms the focal point of vistas down both Denison Road and Holyoake Walk.*

*LEFT: 18 Meadvale Road. A slanting tree happily echoes the lines of a house designed by Pearson. The irregular design of the chimney brickwork, which runs from ground level, set against the contrasting roughcast, was intended to provide visual interest in this block.*

ABOVE: *56–64 Meadvale Road. These houses show the architect G.L. Sutcliffe at his most restrained. The simplicity of the design, with one material for the walls (red brick), one angle for the roofs (45 degrees) and regular 12-, 20- and 24-pane windows, contrasts with the riotous variety of some Pearson houses.*

front gardens up to numbers 70–2, when they gradually step forward again. The effect of this is to break up the vanishing perspective of the houses on this long straight road, creating, with the two more sharply angled blocks opposite (numbers 37–53) a sense of informal green space that contrasts with the treatment of the public green at the end of Denison Road. This green is the centre of a semi-enclosed *place*: numbers 25–9 Meadvale Road form the south side, the angled blocks at the ends of Denison Road and Holyoake Walk the east and west sides, and the Club the north side. Originally the effect was designed with the first plan for the Institute in mind; this featured an arcade and balancing hostel building. Even in its incomplete form it is a delightful area of the suburb, and provides an arresting spectacle not only on Meadvale Road, but from Denison Road and Holyoake Walk which converge here. It also represents a fusion of Pearson's and Sutcliffe's work, as Pearson designed the layout of roads and Sutcliffe the arrangement of houses around them.

There is also an architectural contrast between the houses of Pearson and those of Sutcliffe that is especially notable in Meadvale Road. Pearson's blocks of houses tend to be riotously complicated in terms of roofs, gables, porches, windows and so on, but are all symmetrical within the block. He also reuses designs on a number of occasions; for example, the pair at 4 and 6 Meadvale Road is the same as the pair at 2 Neville/42 Brunner Road; and the block of six houses at 8–18 Meadvale Road is almost identical to 5–15 Ludlow Road. Sutcliffe's houses in Meadvale Road, by contrast, are much simpler in design, with fewer chimneys and fewer types of windows, gables and roofs; neither are they usually symmetrical, and he does not repeat designs.

Sutcliffe. The Pearson houses are picturesquely arranged with blocks angled at 45 degrees across the junctions with Neville and Ludlow Roads, but on the straight stretch of road the blocks are aligned with each other. Sutcliffe, on the other hand, designed his blocks so that they work in relation to each other. The five blocks on the north side of the road between the Brentham Club and the end of the suburb, numbers 40–90, are set back gradually from the road, with longer and longer

LEFT: *12–18 Ludlow Road. Many of the houses in Brentham were built in symmetrical blocks of four or six houses – the many designs add constant variety and visual interest to the street scene, and the use of blocks was also intended to encourage a sense of community among the residents. The combination of these varied designs with the curving streets created what Unwin termed 'street pictures'. The block illustrated is one of two in Ludlow Road that have strange rhombus-plan houses at either end. The novelty of this design has led to some planning infelicities – for example, because of the way the roof meets the angled front walls, rainwater from the roof is thrown straight down the front of the building. This photograph also shows the discordant effect that a mix of painted and unpainted roughcast can have to the visual cohesion of the whole block.*

Two of the most charming and typical streets in Brentham are **Ludlow Road** and **Ruskin Gardens**. Ludlow Road sees Pearson at his most exuberant, especially in the two blocks at 12–18 and 28–34. But the combination of Ruskin Gardens and Ludlow Road provides a limitless supply of interesting views from whichever angle or end they are viewed. The postbox at the corner of the two roads is an original piece of Edwardian street furniture.

The only occasion when Sutcliffe reuses designs is when he plans a block to be a mirror image of the block opposite, for example in **Denison Road**. Denison Road, named after the co-partnership pioneer Frederick Denison Maurice (1805–72), is generally a very simply treated road, designed as a continuation from Woodfield Road to form a long vista towards the tower of the Brentham Club. In the straight section three blocks of simple roughcast, similar to the cottages in Fowlers Walk, are arranged opposite one another; the centre block is set back slightly and linked to the other two by a round-headed archway that leads through to open ground behind the houses. These houses have canopies over the front doors, apparently supported by chains – however, the fact that some have broken chains or are missing them altogether, shows that they are just decorative. The south end of Denison Road comes as something of a shock: instead of a row of houses that would have been numbers 1–7 there rises, sheer and vast, the east end of St Barnabas Church. The purple brick, stone dressing and exuberant

RIGHT: *Houses at the corner of Ruskin Gardens and Ludlow Road. The square oriel supported on wooden struts is a favourite F.C. Pearson device. The four pairs of semi-detached houses in Ruskin Gardens are of the same design, a necessary architectural restraint in this, Brentham's shortest street. The postbox is an original Edwardian street feature – it was set up on this spot before any of the houses round about had been built.*

FAR RIGHT: *East end of St Barnabas Church, Denison Road. While its scale and materials are out of keeping with the rest of Brentham, St Barnabas is a fine and unusual example of twentieth-century Gothic architecture.*

RIGHT: *9 Denison Road. These canopies on chains are a particular feature of Denison Road. Although the canopies appear to hang from the chains, they are in fact cantilevered out of the wall – when the chains break, as they do from time to time, the canopies stay where they are.*

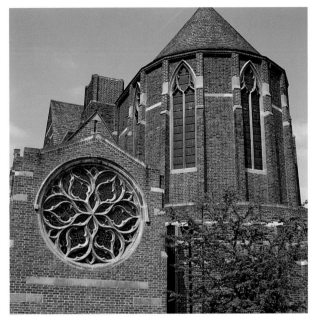

window tracery make this a fine late Gothic Revival church, but it is out of step in both scale and materials with the rest of Brentham. The small rustic war memorial cross, at the junction with Pitshanger Lane, is much more in keeping.

The block of houses opposite the church is one of only three in Brentham to feature decorative timber framing. One of the others is at the corner of Meadvale Road and **North View**. North View, in spite of its name, was never going to provide much of a view once the houses on the north side of Meadvale Road were built, as the road rises only gently from north to south. This is a deceptive street, as most of what we see now was only built in the late 1940s: the bomb that fell on 45 Meadvale Road in 1944 meant that the east side of North View, the centre

FAR LEFT: *Holyoake House, Holyoake Walk. This block of 24 small flats features open arcading and walkways that were favourite architectural devices of the architect G.L. Sutcliffe. Holyoake House is one of just a handful of Brentham houses and flats that still belong at the time of writing to the Bradford Property Trust, which bought out the Ealing Tenants co-partnership in 1936. The building is now all but obscured by creepers and trees, although just visible here on the doors is the bright blue paint that was once a Bradford Property Trust 'livery' and that was at one time seen all over Brentham.*

of the north section of Holyoake Walk, and 37–61 Meadvale Road, all had to be rebuilt. The rebuilding follows Sutcliffe's designs very closely, however. An attractive feature in North View, not found elsewhere, are the three-sided windows at first-floor level in numbers 1 and 2. But there is a reason that these windows were introduced here. The junction of North View and **Holyoake Walk** is another example, like the area in front of the Club, of a semi-formal space created by grouping buildings together round a junction and a small area of green space. Numbers 1 and 2 North View relate to the mirror-image blocks that flank the end of North View – 30–6 and 38–44 Holyoake Walk – and across the road to Holyoake House, with its front square of lawn, which in turn makes an endpoint to North View.

The effect would be even more striking if the trees in front of Holyoake House were not so overgrown.

Holyoake Walk is another street, like Denison Road, that leads to the visual endpoint of the Brentham Club tower. At the other end it peters out into **Pitshanger Lane**, at the 1930s' blocks of flats, Pitshanger Court and Holyoake Court. The latter, although it has metal-ribbon windows, makes some attempt in the mix of red brick and roughcast and the visible tiled roof, to fit in with the rest of Holyoake Walk. Most of the rest of Pitshanger Lane, heading east, is either off the suburb, or taken up with the ends of Woodfield Road and Woodfield Avenue, which are good examples of the visible back extensions that Unwin abhorred. From Pitshanger Lane, between numbers 204 and 206, one gains a glimpse of

NEAR LEFT: *51 Holyoake Walk. These triangular windows, which form a square bay across the corner, were another favourite device of G.L. Sutcliffe. This house is an example of an attempt by owners to reverse the effects of earlier unsympathetic additions. The single-storey extension to the side was once a garage, built on as a 'permitted development' before the conservation area received its Article 4 designation. It was later incorporated into the house, and given a 'Brentham-style' window that goes some way to helping the addition blend in with the original design.*

RIGHT: *Ludlow–Denison Green. This area, originally designated by Unwin as an open space, was cultivated for many years as allotments. It has since reverted to open space, shared by the houses that back on to it. The tree is one of the old field oaks, shown on Unwin's plans, that preceded the estate. As recently as the 1980s druids used this tree as a focus for their ceremonies.*

the open green between Denison Road and Ludlow Road. This is one area that was for a long time cultivated as allotments, but has reverted to its original intended use as a green space, still dominated by one of the old field oaks visible on Unwin's plan. At the other end of Pitshanger Lane where it joins Brunner Road, is number 223, which currently rejoices in the name 'Pooh Corner'. This was the home from 1918 of the Co-operative Party MP Sam Perry and his son Fred Perry, the Wimbledon champion. Fred Perry recalled in his autobiography 'I spent hours practising at home because our house had a big wall facing south and a greenhouse in front of it. I specialized in learning to volley over the greenhouse and onto the wall. My volley prospered better than the greenhouse.' However, that greenhouse, or its successor, looks none the worse for it today.

Almost opposite Pooh Corner, between numbers 16 and 17 Brunner Road, is one of a network of pathways, the equivalent of the 'twittens' at Hampstead Garden Suburb, that lead between the houses to back land that was intended for public open space or allotments. Most of these narrow access paths are for the use of allotment holders and residents of the adjoining houses, but this one, between Brunner Road and Brentham Way, is public property. To stand here and look through the hedges to the allotments and old oaks is to experience Brentham at its most rural, and areas like this contribute to the habitat that has made Brentham home to an extraordinary variety of plant and animal life.

A former resident, Dr Mike Silverman, found that more than 50 species of bird had been seen or heard in Brentham, attracted variously by low density of housing, many trees and the River Brent. These included oddities such as a gannet, which had been blown off course, and, even more bizarrely, a cockatiel and some rose-ringed parakeets, part of a colony of birds that had 'gone native' after being released into the wild'. More typical native species include blackcaps, various types of woodpeckers and tits, and bullfinches. A species found especially in the road closest to the River Brent, Meadvale Road, is the house martin, which has been known to make its mud-formed nests beneath the eaves. Mammals that have been seen regularly include the usual hedgehogs and urban foxes, as well as bats, ferrets and, to the dismay of householders, brown rats from the Brent. There have also been unexplained appearances by a donkey and a sheep.

The allotments in the area between Brunner Road and Brentham Way are dominated by perhaps the largest of the surviving old oaks, which towers over the houses. But there are other floral relics from the days when Brentham was open pastureland. Anyone who leaves their lawn unmown for any length of time will find dandelions growing, but may also be rewarded with spring bluebells, cuckoo pint, garlic mustard, buttercups, betony and an especially rampant creeping perennial, nightshade.

The path behind Brunner Road also provides one of the few publicly available views of the backs of the houses; this reveals the success the architects enjoyed in making the backs of the houses, and the views to and from them, as attractive as the fronts. This path leads through to the middle of **Brentham Way**, which was intended originally as the main street of Brentham, complete with public buildings and shops. None of these was built, but Brentham Way displays a number of features that mark it out from the rest of Brentham. One is the greater width of the street, and the greater

RIGHT: *50–4 Brentham Way. The bands of alternate red brick and render on these houses are found only in this central part of Brentham Way. They give the area, once intended as the main social centre, a more formal character than the rest of Brentham. The side window, which provides views up the street, and the circular bull's-eye window are favourite Sutcliffe features.*

number of large trees. In the section of the road below Fowlers Walk, Brentham Way retains the strip of grass behind the kerb that was once a feature of most of Brentham's pavements.

But the best place from which to experience Brentham Way is at the top, before it turns sharply into Winscombe Crescent. From here the road drops away to the north and still provides a fine distant vista towards Harrow. This corner at the top of the Way is an example of one of Unwin's 'enclosed spaces', with the houses set back round an arc. The brick pair at the top, numbers 4 and 6, are linked by an arch that is in line with the centre axis of the street, and provides a striking endpoint from the lower part of the street. The houses at this top part of Brentham Way are examples of the larger houses Vivian favoured at what was considered the entrance to the estate. It is here that the few detached houses in the suburb are found. The earliest of these, number 2, was designed by Parker and Unwin in 1909 for William Hutchings, who was chairman of Ealing Tenants from 1911 until his death in 1934. Its name 'Widecombe' recalls Hutchings's native Devon. The others, numbers 7 and 8, although they were built in the 1920s, pay homage to Unwin and Parker's work in their design: note the simple white-painted roughcast and brick dressings around the windows. The semi-detached houses at 14/16 and 18/20, which are mirror images of each other, are unusual because they are asymmetrical; they appear at first glance to be single houses. C.G. Butler, the architect, was careful to fit the designs to the rest of the suburb. Note the tiled gables and the half-hip gabled dormers that Pearson also used; but some features like the brick door-surrounds are more typical of the

numbers 72–8, that was built by C.G. Butler in the 1920s, opposite a block built by Sutcliffe before the First World War. Although this follows the form of the earlier block, there are subtle differences that give it away, such as the use of stock brick and the brick porch to number 76.

At the end here, in the later houses of the Greystoke Estate, one can see a relic of Brentham planning. The land on which the Greystoke houses at 7–13 **Brunswick Road** are built was originally Ealing Tenants' land. By the time it was sold in 1930, the road and pavement opposite the end of Brentham Way, including the curved indent in the pavement, was already built. This explains why that terrace is set further back than the

*LEFT: Houses at the corner of Brunswick and Brunner Roads. The 'butterfly' design of these F.C. Pearson houses makes for some very oddly shaped rooms.*

*BELOW: 123–5 Fowlers Walk. This pair of houses is built to form a visual 'endpoint' to Woodfield Crescent, and with its neighbours to the right, forms part of a semi-enclosed space, with Fowlers Walk running through it. The trees have obscured some of the intended effects of the planning.*

stripped classical manner of the 1920s. There are later houses also at the corner with Woodfield Crescent: numbers 21–23a built in the 1950s; and the flats opposite built on the Ealing Tenants works site. These flats combine small suburb-style windows with simple round-topped doorways more typical of the 1930s.

This junction, with Fowlers Walk opposite, provides another semi-enclosed space, with numbers 123–5 Fowlers Walk, but the lower part of Brentham Way is more formal in design, a relic of the original plan for what was proposed as the 'main avenue'. The design of the houses in this middle section reflects this in the way that they are arranged in blocks, exactly parallel to the road; this is very different from the informal grouping along another long straight street, Meadvale Road. The formality is emphasised by horizontal bands of red brick, a feature of many grand public buildings in London from the 1880s onwards. A local example of this treatment are the municipal buildings in Acton. The bottom end of Brentham Way includes one block,

ABOVE: *1–7 Winscombe Crescent. These four imposing houses and 2 Brentham Way – at the 'entrance' to the suburb – were the only houses in Brentham designed by Parker and Unwin.*

path, known locally as China Alley and visible in maps going back to the eighteenth century; it was used for access to Brentham Halt station from 1912. The junction of Brunswick Road with Neville and Brunner Roads features F.C. Pearson's most unusual houses: the 'butterfly'-plan triples at numbers 2/4 Brunswick and 33 Brunner Roads, and 1/3 Brunswick and 1 Neville Road. These create striking endpoints to vistas from all three roads, as well as a diversity of views from the many-angled windows of the houses, a classic piece of Unwin-manner planning.

Before Brunswick Road was built, **Fowlers Walk** was intended to curve around and join up with this junction (numbers 1 and 3 Brunswick Road were originally numbers 74 and 76 Fowlers Walk), which explains why the numbering in Fowlers Walk is so odd – at the beginning of the First World War Fowlers Walk, as we know it, was built, but it was intended to extend the building round to meet Brunner/Neville. This never happened, as the land in Brunswick Road and at the bottom of Fowlers Walk was sold off, so that number 53 is the lowest odd-numbered house, and 22 the lowest even-numbered. Fowlers Walk as a whole is remarkably consistent in design, with small rough-cast cottages. Any alterations are particularly jarring in a streetscape such as this where the design is so simple and so consistent. This is why number 81, which was built as the Ealing Tenants office in the mid-1930s, stands out so much; it is of brown stock brick with a typical 1930s' feature, the bolection-moulded door surround. The most striking feature in Fowlers Walk, and one of the most charming areas of the entire suburb, is the cul-de-sac near the south end. This is a classic Unwin-manner enclosed space, with the houses grouped

other houses on that side of the road. Between numbers 5 and 7 Brunswick Road is a path providing access to Brentham Fields, and the allotments that form part of the Brent River Park. The path alongside the allotments, which leads to Lynwood Road, is an old field as round a village green, an effect enhanced by the hedges, most of which survive. The rural aspect of this would have been enhanced by the allotments that were planned for the back land, but this was sold off to the Greystoke Estate in the 1930s, and built over.

There are today rather fewer areas of green in Brentham than Unwin and the pioneers intended, mainly because much more of the back land was turned into allotments than originally projected, and most of this back land, whether it has reverted to green space – as at Ludlow/Denison Green – or is still cultivated as allotments, is no longer available to be enjoyed by the public, or even by the residents of Brentham. This is a pity, although perhaps understandable, given fears about security. One such small area was in **Winscombe Crescent**, where numbers 6, 8, 10 and 12 were grouped around to form another informal enclosed village green. In time part of this green was sold to the owners of number 6 and incorporated into their front garden. The other half belongs to number 12, whose owner, Brian Fallon, a founder member of the Brentham Society, has kept it as a small, separate green, in keeping with the social and planning spirit of the Brentham pioneers. The rest of Winscombe Crescent includes, on its west side, some curious, rather Art Nouveau front walls, designed by F.C. Pearson in the manner of C.F.A. Voysey, and it also features his largest houses in the suburb, the semi-detached pairs at numbers 9–23.

One of these, number 11, which is angled across the sharp bend in the Crescent, stands out from the rest of the estate, indeed from the rest of Brentham. The house's owner, Mrs Ramsay Hughes, came to live in the house in 1912, when her father, Leonard Dudeney, journalist and friend of Ramsay MacDonald (hence

Mrs Hughes's unusual first name), moved in. Her house is the last one left in the suburb that features Ealing Tenants' original colour scheme of unpainted rough-cast and dark-green woodwork. It is perhaps therefore fitting, as we begin the twenty-first century, to end with Mrs Hughes's house, a rare survival and living link with those hopeful pioneers at the beginning of the twentieth century, without whose hard work and vision Brentham Garden Suburb would never have been built.

ABOVE: *11 Winscombe Crescent, one of the larger semi-detached houses designed by F.C. Pearson in 1908, and the last in Brentham to retain the original Ealing Tenants Ltd colour scheme of unpainted roughcast and dark-green woodwork. It has been in the same family since 1912.*

# ACKNOWLEDGEMENTS

## AUTHOR'S ACKNOWLEDGEMENTS

This book would not have appeared without the hard work, dedication and enthusiasm of a great many people, all of them volunteers. My greatest debt of gratitude is to Wendy Sender who has over the past two years shown enormous patience and tenacity, not just in encouraging a dilatory author and editing the text, but in organising oral history interviews, interviewers and interviewees, finding pictures, commissioning photography, helping with fundraising and publicity – in fact, every aspect of the book's production. Without Wendy, this book would never have been published, and my debt to her is immeasurable, as it is to her family, Peter, Kate and Sam Sender, for tolerating a house full of papers and photographs (and the author, on numerous occasions) for so long. I would also like to thank Professor Sir Peter Hall for kindly agreeing to write an Introduction to the book long before a word was written; and Roz Archer for her encouragement and generous sharing of her research on G.L. Sutcliffe and Hampstead Garden Suburb, and for several most enjoyable and enlightening trips in connection with this book.

In Brentham, Alan Henderson, curator of the Brentham Archive, has given very generous access to the archive and tolerated extended loans from it. Many past and present officers of the Brentham Society have greatly assisted me by answering questions and commenting on aspects of the text, so I would like to thank Pat Baxendale, Brian and Thelma Fallon, Clive Hicks, Martin Jiggens, Heather Moore, Tony Oliver, Tony and Mary Scanlan, and Pam Turner for their help. Eleanor Cowie and Gill Silvester provided timely and diligent assistance with last-minute research. Around the suburb, many residents have allowed me in to look at and photograph their houses and gardens, and lent photographs and drawings, and I would like to thank Margaret and Norman Conroy, Delphine Nunn and Robert Staines, Vicky Dale, Ramsay Hughes, Teresa Sawicka, Jonathan and Renáta Pearce and Hugh and Josephine Watkins.

I would also like to thank Professor Eric Fernie, Dr R.C. Gurd, Professor Sir Peter Hall, John Newman, Ray Rogers and Sarah Harper for writing letters commending the project to potential supporters. Several Ealing Borough employees have helped in various ways, and I would like to thank Mike Beadle, Noel Johnston, Ray Rogers and Ian Williams.

The descendants of Brentham's founders and architects have been uniformly positive about being hunted down and plagued for information and photographs. I would particularly like to thank Barbara Norrice (Henry Vivian's daughter); Michael Sutcliffe (G.L. Sutcliffe's grandson); Hazel Grattan (F.C. Pearson's daughter); Richard Whatton (F.C. Pearson's grandson), John Butler (C.G. Butler's nephew) and David Perry (Harry Perry's great-nephew). A most enjoyable part of the research for this book has been talking to them all, and also present and former residents of the suburb. I would particularly like to thank Mrs Doris Palmer (and her daughter Mrs Gillian Howell) for sharing with me vivid memories of Brentham in the days when it was still being built and the Duke of Connaught came to visit.

I would also like to thank the following men and women who have either been interviewed or completed the lengthy questionnaire: Mr Arthur Allport (E.W. Roe's grandson), Mrs Margaret Arnison-West, Mrs Gladys Bailey, Mrs Margaret Baldwin, Mrs Diana Barlow (S.B. Hocking's daughter), Mr John and Mrs Mary Bartlett, Mrs Audrey Beacham, Mrs Betty Black (George Ridley's daughter), Miss Stella Bloxam, Mrs Brenda Brant, Mr Ivor Bush, Mr Douglas Dover, Mrs Margo Fuggle (W.E. Reading's daughter), Mrs Jean George (Hubert Brampton's grand-daughter), Mrs Anne Gilronan, Mr Guy Hawtin, Miss Margaret Hewett, Dr Kaspar Hocking (S.B. Hocking's son), Mr Brian Hughes (Hubert Brampton's grandson), Mrs Ramsay Hughes, Mrs Madeline Jones, Mrs Ann Kendrick, Miss Dorothy Lawrence, Mrs Madeline Marshall, Miss Joy Meldrum, Miss Madge Mitcham, Mrs Betty Moorcroft, Mrs Barbara Murray, Mrs Doris Palmer, Mrs Lois Preston, Miss Judy Sharman, Mr Frank and Mrs Joan Turner, and Mrs Pamela Wood (F.J. Milner's granddaughter). Many thanks also to the interviewers, George Barnes, Brian Fallon, Mandy Fodrio, Alan Henderson, Krystyna Niedenthal, Delphine Nunn, Marion Oliver, Teresa Sawicka and Wendy Sender.

I would like to thank the members of the Brentham Club for sharing their memories, and especially Alwyn Roberts for showing me around the Club and grounds, and for lending archive material. David Baker and Simon Halls of the Bradford Property Trust in Epsom spared me a lot of time and gave me valuable insights into BPT's involvement at Brentham over the past 35 years, as well as access to their remaining papers and photographs of Brentham, which they have since generously deposited in the Brentham Archive. I would also like to thank another David Baker – formerly of David Baker Architects in Pitshanger Lane – for an interesting discussion about Brentham's architecture and for lending his copies of a number of Brentham architectural drawings; and Ann Thomas of Rothermel Thomas for information about Sutton Garden Suburb, on which her firm produced the conservation report.

The range of subjects that a book like this necessarily covers has meant that I have had to bone up on subjects with which I was only passingly familiar at the outset. In this I have had assistance from a number of people. Malcolm Taylor and his deputy at the Vaughan Williams Library confirmed my suspicions about May Day, while my *Telegraph* colleague Gerald Hill was most helpful with research on cricketers, of which Brentham has produced a good few. Paul Fitzmaurice kindly helped me with tracking down Ealing field names, and Steve Smith (great-grandson of Hubert Brampton) was very generous in sharing his photographs of the other co-partnership estates, which he has toured. Professor Michael Hebbert and Professor Andrew Saint pointed me in the right direction at an early stage with some useful suggestions. Dr Gavin Stamp provided some illuminating observations, especially about Ernest Shearman and St Barnabas. All errors and omissions are of course my responsibility.

Finally, I would also like to thank the staff of Camden Local Studies Library, London; Ealing Local History Centre and Ealing Borough Records (Jonathon Oates); First Garden City Heritage Museum (Elizabeth Cummings, Robert Lancaster); Hampstead Garden Suburb Archive and London Metropolitan Archives (Dr Ann Saunders, Emma Bashforth); Kantarowich Library, University of Manchester (Valerie Gildea); Modern Records Centre, University of Warwick (Richard Temple and Christine Woodland); National Co-operative Archive (Gillian Lonergan); Rothschild Archive (Melanie Aspey); Drawings Collection and Archives, Royal Institute of British Architects (Eleanor Gawne); Sutton Library; Town and Country Planning Association; and the English Folk Dance and Song Society.

## Editor's acknowledgements

This book would never have been published without the help of many generous people. The many 'shareholders' who felt this was a project worth supporting, and more Brentham residents than I can mention here, gave us enormous encouragement, especially during the early, uncertain days. I wish to thank them all, as well as all the sponsors and organisations who gave us their generous backing. Heather Moore, Chair of the Brentham Society, and all the committee members, had the difficult task of continuing the usual busy programme of the Society's calendar, and supporting a project that was bigger than any of us had envisaged. Mark Greenwood, with a characteristic touch of genius, dreamt up the Co-partnership Share Scheme, and designed all the publicity material that was an essential element of the scheme's success. Sue van Raat kept on top of the stream of share applications that landed on her doormat and, as treasurer, brought good-humoured efficiency to our finances. Ewa Krygier soon found that her hobby of calligraphy had taken on a life of its own – she painstakingly inscribed all 375 share certificates. Armies of volunteers folded newsletters, posted flyers through letterboxes, put up notices in notice boards, and helped with many other small but important tasks.

Several residents helped organise fundraising events. Pat Baxendale, a constant source of ideas and enthusiasm, transformed her home one weekend into an intimate and surprisingly profitable art gallery; and Elizabeth Atkinson helped launch the popular Brentham Garden Day, when residents are treated to a tour of some of Brentham's delightfully varied back gardens. Others helped with the book itself. Norman Silvester proofread and copyedited the manuscript with great attention to detail, a sense of humour, and incisive use of the red pen. Eleanor Cowie became an energetic and skilful picture researcher, with a knack for beating deadlines and bureaucracy, and she helped with much else besides. The Brentham archivist, Alan Henderson, and the launch co-ordinator, Rosanna Henderson, generously converted their dining room into an archive office during the course of Aileen's research. As newsletter editor Alan cheerfully accommodated the extra copy generated by the project. Others interviewed older residents and filled out questionnaires.

Right from the start Professor Sir Peter Hall felt that he wanted to support our efforts to publish this book – even if that meant being dragged to photo opportunities in bitter weather. During the uncertain, early days Peter's involvement and encouragement was a lifeline. My special thanks go to Peter, and also to Sue Elliott for her enormous contribution to the project – fundraising, copywriting, dealing with the press – and making things happen! Producing this book has required imagination, energy, unflagging commitment and a good sense of humour to counter the repeated setbacks we have faced. Sue has all these qualities and more. I am also grateful to Mrs Ramsay Hughes, who first came to Brentham in 1913, and whose vivid memories were often shared at the weekly coffee mornings she still holds at her home. It isn't usual to thank an author, but Aileen Reid is no ordinary author. She has repeatedly taken on far more than her role as writer: she has been public speaker, fundraiser, courier and an entertaining source of titbits from Brentham's past. My thanks go, too, to Martin Bristow, who designed this book with flair, care and a great deal of good humour; and to Robin Oliver of BAS Printers, for his time, patience and readiness to embrace yet another change to the specifications for this book. And last but not least, to my husband, Peter, and to my children, Kate and Sam, who have had to live with this book for as long as I have – the phone calls, visitors, meetings, and most especially, the huge amount of my time given to the book – a very big thank you! The project has not been without uncertain moments, and Peter has been there throughout, to coax me through the bumpy times, to turn the PC into an indispensable ally and to encourage me to set the alarm for 5 a.m. to meet the next deadline.

The lives of many of the families of those drawn in to the project have been disrupted. As well as to all those named above, my thanks go to all the families and partners of those who have given up so much of their spare time, to all those who contributed their memories and their photographs, and to those listed below:

John Aarons, Joyce Adefarasin, Arthur Allport, Tony Arnell, David Baker, Margaret Baldwin, George and Anne Barnes, John Benson, Geoff Baxendale, Peter Bigwood, Anna Black, Stella Bloxam, Brenda Brant, Ivor Bush, Paul Cater, Peter Cattermole, Sue Chandler, Brenda Clements, Judy Collins, Nigel and Catherine Dodd, Lucienne Donnelly, Douglas Dover, Mrs N. Fagan, Brian and Thelma Fallon, Paul and Mandy Fodrio, Anita Fookes, Vanda Foster, Graham and Pauline Fox, Tonia and Simeon Gann, Jean George, Julie and Colin Gibson, Alan Gillett, Mandy Greenwood, Bob Gurd, Deborah Hall, Lawrence and Debbie Hamilton, Nigel Harvey, Clive Hicks, Chris Hill, Simon and Penny Hoets, Gillian Howell, Robert Holmes, Ellen Jackson, Martin Jiggens, Bevan Jones, Madeline Jones, Kirsten Kaluzynski, Sally Kelly, Dorothy Lawrence, Dorothy Lawson, David Lunts, Krys Mackersie, Michael McCarthy, Mrs V. Marchant, Paula Middlehurst, Maureen Monaghan, Jackie and James Moss, Barbara Murray, Krystyna Niedenthal, Delphine Nunn, Tony and Marion Oliver, Ann and Robert Perkins, Sandra Phillimore, Councillor Philip Portwood, Steve Pound MP, Ray Rogers, John Rolfe, Teresa Sawicka, Mary and Tony Scanlan, Eva Seidner, Gill Silvester, Chris Snodin, Susan Stephenson, Philip and Melanie Sutcliffe, Frank and Joan Turner, Pam Turner, Brian Vaughan, Richard Wakefield, Adam Watrobski, David Webster, Pamela Wood and Bea and Walter Wyeth.

## Picture credits

The editor and publisher are grateful to the individuals, archives and organisations listed below for their kind permission to reproduce illustrations in this book. Special thanks to Simon Halls and the Bradford Property Trust for their generous donation of archival material to the Brentham Archive; to Derek Pratt for finding the sun (and dodging the cars) in his photos of Brentham; to Stuart Freeman, for rigging cameras on ceilings (and himself on a van) to help illustrate this book; and, for their kind help, to Emma Bashforth and Rhys Griffith (LMA), Elizabeth Cummings and Robert Lancaster (FGCHM), Gillian Lonergan (NCA), Nick Matthews (TCPA), Jonathan Oates (ELHC), Dr Ann Saunders (HGSA Trust), and Christine Woodland (MRC).

Abbreviations: t (top), b (bottom), l (left), r (right), BA (Brentham Archive), CH (Clive Hicks), DP (Derek Pratt), *EG* (*Ealing Gazette*), ELHC (Ealing Local History Centre), *MCT* (*Middlesex County Times*), MS (Mary Scanlan), SF (Stuart Freeman).

Arthur Allport 60r, 78, 113, 197l; Roz Archer 165; Mary Barrett (née Fuller) 105, 185; Beamish Open Air Museum 17l; Betty Black 191r; Bournville Village Trust 37r; Brentham Archive 1 (CH), 4 (DP), 6 (Mark Greenwood), 7 (Michael McCarthy), 8, 65 (ELHC), 69, 70, 72, 84, 86, 87, 88l, 95 (CH), 97, 98, 99b, 101, 102, 103, 105r, 106, 107b (CH), 108, 110, 111 (ELHC), 112 (CH), 115, 116, 123, 125, 127l, 130b (Pamela Wood), 130t, 134, 135, 136, 137, 139, 143, 148 (SF), 149, 150r (SF), 151t (CH), 152 (SF), 154l (DP), 155r (SF), 155 (SF), 159, 167 (both SF), 168l, 169, 170 (SF), 171 (SF), 172, 182 (Pamela Wood), 183tl (Jean Johnson), 183tr (CH), 183b, 192l (Ramsay Hughes), 192r, 198, 202r (CH), 203, 204, 208l (DP), 213l (CH), 213r (DP), 214l, 214r (DP), 215 (DP), 216 (CH), 218 (DP), 219, 221l&r (DP), 224t (Julie Gibson), 224b (Alan Henderson), 225t (Sue Elliott), 225b (Alan Henderson), 229 (CH), 231–48 (DP); British Architectural Library, RIBA, London 163; British Library 49l, 49r (*Co-partnership Tenants Ltd, Prospectus*, 1907), 50, 66 (C. Lloyd *Henry Demarest Lloyd, 1847–1903*, 1912), 82l (*Garden Suburbs, Villages and Homes*, No. 2, 1912), 140, 179; British Library (Newspapers), Colindale 56l, 62 (*EG* 10/3/23), 85 (*Co-partnership* Dec 1910), 88r (*EG* 20/1/12), 89r (*EG* 3/5/13), 94r, 114 (*EG* 18/5/07), 158 (*Building World* 2/10/09), 195l (*MCT* 1/10/27), 195r (*MCT* 8/8/36), 196 (*MCT* 4/6/27); British Library of Political and Economic Science 60l, 77, 80, 94l, 151b; Cadbury Ltd 37l; Dave Collins 206l; Devon Library Service 21; *Ealing Gazette* 206r (MS), 207 (Jean George), 217 (ELHC), 226l (MS), 226r (BA), 227 (MS), 228 (MS); Ealing Local History Centre 58 (both), 61, 76, 83, 122, 153l, 157, 208r; Reg Eden 57; Richard Evans courtesy Teresa Sawicka 178, 193, 194, 197r, 205; First Garden City Heritage Museum 41, 48; Stuart Freeman 10; Margo Fuggle (née Reading) 187l, 188; Tonia & Simeon Gann 190r; Anne K. Gilronan 189; Hampstead Garden Suburb Archive at the London Metropolitan Archives 43, 44, 45, 52, 53, 55, 56r, 59, 82r, 90r, 92, 96, 109, 124, 127r, 129l, 132, 153r, 166, 168r, 173, 174, 175; Clive Hicks 170r, 184, 186, 187r; 230; Hounslow Library Services (Chiswick Library) 31; Brian Hughes 131t, 181; Maureen Hughes 100, 138, 141; Hulton Getty Picture Collection 18l, 19, 25, 28, 30, 32, 33l, 34, 36, 39, 42, 51r, 81, 89l, 90l, 104l, 118, 119, 120, 128, 180, 199, 200, 201, 202l; Audrey Jones 222, 223; London Borough of Ealing (Planning) 210; London Borough of Ealing (Tourism) 211, 212; Helen Long 156; Modern Records Centre, University of Warwick: from *Labour Copartnership* (ref. MSS. 310) 24, 26, 68, 71, 73, 75, 99t, 129r; from *Co-partnership* (ref. MSS.310) 22, 27, 67, 107t; National Co-operative Archive, Co-operative College 17r, 18r, 20, 23; National Portrait Gallery, London 79; Barbara Norrice 15; The Robert Opie Collection 150l; Ordnance Survey © Crown Copyright (Ref. nc/00/1170) 14; Doris Palmer 191l; Private collections 33r, 35, 47, 51l, 54, 142, 144, 145, 146, 160, 161, 162; Rochdale Pioneers Museum 16; Mary Scanlan 131b; Steve Smith 64, 74, 91; Michael Sutcliffe 164, 176; Town and Country Planning Association 29, 40; David Webster 14 (line drawings); Richard Whatton 147 (both); Pamela Wood 90l.

# BIBLIOGRAPHY

## Archives

**Brentham Archive**
c/o Alan Henderson, 47 Meadvale Road, London W5 1NT. *Extensive archive of architects' drawings, maps, plans, photographs, press cuttings, rent books, magazines and other material relating to Brentham, as well as the Brentham Society's own records.*

**British Library**
Dept of Manuscripts, 96 Euston Road, London NW1 2DB. *Diaries and letters of John Burns; letters and papers of George Bernard Shaw.*

**Ealing Central Library**
Ealing Local History Centre, 103 Ealing Broadway Centre, London W5 5JY. *Records of Ealing Tenants Ltd, 1901–74: minute books, share and loan stock ledgers, rent books, etc. – the most important source for Brentham's early history.*

**First Garden City Heritage Museum**
296 Norton Way, Letchworth Garden City, Hertfordshire SG6 1SU. *Papers of Richard Barry Parker.*

**London Borough of Ealing**
Building Control Department, Perceval House, 14–16 Uxbridge Road, London W5 2HL. *Microfiches of architectural drawings submitted to Ealing Borough Council and its predecessors, 1870s–1980s.*

**London Borough of Ealing Archives**
Town Hall, New Broadway, London W5 2YX. *Records of Ealing Urban District and Borough Councils (apply to Local History Librarian, Ealing Central Library for access; catalogue in Ealing Central Library).*

**London Metropolitan Archives**
40 Northampton Road, London EC1R 0HB. *Extensive Hampstead Garden Suburb Archive, including c. 60 lantern slides of Brentham.*

**London School of Economics & Political Science**
Archives Division, British Library of Political and Economic Science, 10 Portugal Street, London WC2A 2HD. *Financial records of George Bernard Shaw; papers of Fabian Society.*

**National Co-operative Archive**
Co-operative College, Stamford Hall, Loughborough, Leicester LE12 5QR. *Papers of Edward Owen Greening, George Jacob Holyoake, Robert Owen, etc.*

**RIBA Archives and Library**
66 Portland Place, London W1B 1AD. *Papers of Sir Edwin Lutyens and of Sir Raymond Unwin. Biography files and membership records for C.G. Butler, A. Lancelot Lang, Richard Barry Parker, Ernest Shearman, G.L. Sutcliffe and Sir Raymond Unwin.*

**Sutton Central Library**
Archive and Local Studies Department, St Nicholas Way, London SM1 1EA. *Papers of Frederic Cavendish Pearson and records of Sutton Garden Suburb.*

**University of Manchester**
Kantarowich Library, Dept of Planning and Landscape, Oxford Road, Manchester M13 9PL. *Papers, books, lantern slides, etc. of Sir Raymond Unwin.*

**University of Warwick**
Modern Records Centre, Coventry CV4 7AL. *Records of the Labour Association (listed under Involvement and Participation Association), and the Amalgamated Society of Carpenters and Joiners.*

**Victoria and Albert Museum**
RIBA Drawings Collection, Department of Prints and Drawings, Cromwell Road, London SW7 2RL. *G.L. Sutcliffe's drawings for Brentham Club and Institute.*

## Annotated select bibliography

Place of publication is London, unless stated otherwise.

### London (including Ealing and Brentham)

The essential source for Brentham history is Margaret Tims's excellent 1966 history of Ealing Tenants Ltd, which was, however, written before all the Ealing Tenants papers now held in Ealing Library were available. Contemporary published sources include *The Brentham Magazine* (copies in the Brentham Archive) and *The Brenthamite* (in the Brentham Archive and the British Library), and the regular reports on events in Brentham in *Labour Copartnership*. The local newspapers, the *Middlesex County Times and West London Gazette* and the *Ealing Gazette and West Middlesex Observer* (which ceased publication in September 1923), contain much useful information, especially in the period after 1910 when both had weekly news columns on Brentham; there is a basic index to the *Middlesex County Times* in Ealing Central Library. The Brentham Society has produced leaflets on Brentham Garden Suburb, the Brentham Club and Institute and St Barnabas Church. There are few detailed modern histories of Ealing, the most authoritative being the volume of the *Victoria County History of Middlesex* that covers Acton, Ealing, Chiswick and Brentford.

#### PUBLISHED BEFORE 1914

Booth, C., ed. *Life and Labour of the People in London* (1892).

Brown, W.H. *The Pioneer Co-partnership Suburb* (1912; facsimile reprint by the Brentham Society, 1990).

'A co-operative garden party', *Labour Copartnership*, 10: 99 (July 1904).

*Ealing Yearbook: Local Guide and Almanack for 1905 etc.* (1904 etc.).

Falkner, T. *The History and Antiquities of Brentford, Ealing and Chiswick* (1845).

'From Ealing to Hampstead', *Co-partnership*, 17 supplement: 4–5 (April 1911).

George, W.L. *Engines of Social Progress* (1907) [rare view of co-partnership, and Brentham, by a disinterested observer].

'Haven slate club', *Ealing Gazette*: 2 (11 May 1901).

'House at Cowden, Kent', *The Studio*, 51 (211): 54–5 (15 Oct 1910) [work by G.L. Sutcliffe].

Hutchings, W. 'The pioneer co-partnership suburb: Ealing Tenants Ltd', *Co-partnership*, 15: 57–8 (April 1909).

Jackson, E. *Annals of Ealing* (1898).

Jones, C. *Ealing: From Village to Corporate Town, or Forty Years of Municipal Life* (n.d. [1902]).

London County Council, *Housing of the Working Classes in London* (1913).

Marshall, A. 'The housing of the London poor. I: Where to house them', *Contemporary Review*, 45: 224–31 (1884).

Mearns, A. *The Bitter Cry of Outcast London: An Inquiry into the Condition of the Abject Poor* (1883).

'Mr. Vivian and the Ealing Tenants Ltd', *Co-partnership*, 18: 2 (Jan 1912).

'The pioneer co-partnership suburb', *Co-partnership*, 17: 89 (June 1911).

'Recent designs in domestic architecture', *The Studio*, 42: 195–200 (14 Dec 1907) [work by G.L. Sutcliffe].

'A £650 house erected by Ealing Tenants Ltd', *Building World*, 729: 11 (2 Oct 1909) [perspective, plans, sections and elevations of 2 Brentham Way].

'The social side of the Ealing Tenants', *Co-partnership*, 15: 123 (Aug 1910).

Sutcliffe, G.L. *Concrete, its Nature and Uses* (1893; rev. edn, 1905).

— *The Disposal of Refuse from the City of London* (1898).

— *The Principles and Practice of Modern House Construction*, 6 vols. (1898–9; rev. edn, 1909).

— ed. *The Modern Carpenter, Joiner and Cabinet-maker: A Complete Guide to Current Practice*, 8 vols. (London, 1902–4).

— ed. *The Modern Plumber and Sanitary Engineer*, 6 vols. (1907, rev. edn, ed. R.H. Bew, 1927).

— ed. *Sanitary Fittings and Plumbing* (1901).

Sykes, D.F.E. *Ealing and its Vicinity* (n.d. [c.1895]).

Vivian, H. 'Ealing Tenants Ltd: its past, present and future, from a paper by its chairman', *Labour Copartnership*, 11: 52–5 (April 1905).

— *The Pioneer Co-partnership Village* (1908).

Walter, W. 'The Arts & Crafts movement on co-partnership estates', *Co-partnership*, 16: 39–40 (March 1910).

— 'Arts & crafts . . .', *Co-partnership*, 17: 121–2 (Aug 1911), cont. 131 (Sept 1911).

Willifield Way [pseud] 'Conference at Ealing', *Co-partnership*, 16: 93 (June 1910).

### PUBLISHED IN OR AFTER 1914

Abercrombie, P. *Greater London Plan 1944* (1945).

Baker, T.F.T., ed. *Victoria History of the County of Middlesex. Vol. 7: Acton, Chiswick, Ealing and Brentford . . .* (1982).

Beattie, S. *A Revolution in London Housing: LCC Housing Architects and their Work, 1893–1914* (1980).

Cherry, B. and Pevsner, N. *Buildings of England. London 3: North West* (1991; repr. with corrections, 1999).

Delafons, J. 'Brentham estate – a new community, 1901', *Town and Country Planning* 61 (11/12): 317–19 (Nov/Dec 1992).

Essen, R. *Ealing and Northfields* (Stroud, 1996).

— *Ealing, Hanwell, Perivale and Greenford* (Stroud, 1997).

Grosch, A. *St Pancras Pavements: An Autobiography* (1947) [useful if somewhat fanciful book by E.W. Roe's son-in-law].

Hall, P. 'Brentham – London's forgotten garden suburb', *Town and Country Planning*, 68 (6): 180–1 (June 1999).

Hankinson, C.F.E. *A Political History of Ealing, 1832–1970* (n.d. [1971]).

Hebbert, M. *London: More by Fortune than Design* (Chichester, 1998).

Hounsell, P. *Ealing and Hanwell Past* (1991).

Jackson, A. *Semi-detached London: Suburban Development, Life and Transport, 1900–39* (1979).

Jahn, M.A. *Railways and Suburban Development: Outer West London, 1850–1900 (Acton Chiswick, Ealing, Hanwell)* (M.A. thesis, University College London, 1971).

— 'Suburban Development in outer west London, 1850–1900'. In F.M.L. Thompson, *The Rise of Suburbia* (Leicester, 1982).

Johnson, B., ed. *Brentham: Ealing's Garden Suburb* (1977).

Kilmister, C.A.A., ed. *St Barnabas Church, Ealing: Golden Jubilee Souvenir* (1966).

Neaves, C.M. *A History of Greater Ealing* (1930).

'Notabilities, no. 19: Mr. F.J. Gould', *Middlesex County Times*: 8 (12 May 1928).

'Notabilities, no. 25: Mr. Fred Maddison, JP', *Middlesex County Times*: 8. (30 June 1928).

Peake, H.D. *Conservation in Ealing: Draft Report* (1969).

Perry, F. *Fred Perry: An Autobiography* (1984).

'The pioneer garden suburb coming-of-age', *Co-partnership*, 29: 44 (March 1923).

Porter, R. *London: A Social History* (1994).

Reeder, D.A. 'A theatre of suburbs: some patterns of development in west London, 1801–1911', in Dyos, H.J., ed. *The Study of Urban History* (Leicester, 1966).

Saint, A. intro. *London Suburbs* (1999).

— ed. *Politics and the People of London: The London County Council, 1889–1965* (1989).

Schneer, J. *London 1900: The Imperial Metropolis* (1999).

Scouse, F.W., ed. *Ealing 1901–1951* (n.d. [1951]).

Thomas, D. *London's Green Belt* (1970).

Tims, M. *Ealing Tenants Ltd: Pioneers of Co-partnership* (Ealing Local History Society, 1966).

Upton, D. *The Dangerous Years: Life in Ealing, Acton and Southall in the Second World War 1939–45* (1993).

## Co-operation, co-partnership and Christian Socialism

The modern literature on the co-partnership movement is very sparse compared to the garden city movement, the various writings of Johnston Birchall being the exception. A comprehensive bibliography of labour co-partnership can be found in the entry on Edward Owen Greening in the *Dictionary of Labour Biography* (*see* below). By far the richest primary source is *Labour Copartnership* (1894–1906; known as *Co-partnership* from 1907), the journal of the Labour Association, which had reports and features virtually every month on Brentham and the other co-partnership estates before the First World War; there are complete runs at the British Newspaper Library at Colindale, London, the Modern Records Centre at the University of Warwick and the National Co-operative Archive in Loughborough. (*See also* the annual reports of the Labour Association at the Modern Records Centre, Warwick.) The primary periodicals of the wider co-operative movement are *Co-op News*, *Co-op Official*, *Millgate Monthly* and *Wheatsheaf*. Bibliography of co-operation in Birchall's *Co-op: The People's Business*.

### PUBLISHED BEFORE 1914

Bonar, J. *Labour Co-partnership* (Labour Association pamphlet, 1899).

Borissow, Miss [K.], 'Women and labour co-partnership', *Co-partnership*, 14: 59 (April 1908).

'Co-operative building', *Labour Copartnership*, 10: 5 (Jan 1904).

'Co-operators and the Garden City', *Labour Copartnership*, 10: 146–7 (Sept 1904).

'Co-operators and the housing question', *Labour Copartnership*, 8: 166–7 (Nov 1902).

*Co-partnership in Housing . . . Being an Account of the Two Hampstead Tenants' Societies* (1910).

'Co-partnership in housing: present position of the movement', *Co-partnership*, 15: 169–70 (Nov 1909).

'Co-partnership Tenants Housing Council', *Labour Copartnership*, 11: 61 (April 1905).

Co-partnership Tenants Housing Council, *Garden Suburbs, Villages and Homes: All About Co-partnership Houses* (1906).

'Earl Grey and co-partnership', *Co-partnership*, 17: 179–80 (Dec 1911).

Edwards, J. *Liberalism and Socialism: A Reply to Recent Speeches of Mr. H. Vivian, MP, and Mr. W.H. Lever, MP* (Liverpool Fabian Society, Liverpool, 1906).

Ensor, L.R. *Notes on the Management of a Co-partnership Society* (Labour Association pamphlet, n.d.).

Fay, C.R. *Co-partnership in Industry* (Cambridge, 1913).

*Garden Suburbs, Villages and Homes*, issue 2 (Summer 1912).

George, H. *The Complete Works of Henry George* (New York, 1898).

Goss, G.W.F. *A Descriptive Bibliography of the Writings of George Jacob Holyoake, with a Brief Sketch of his Life* (1908).

Grey, Earl, *What Co-operation will do for the People* (Labour Association pamphlet, n.d. [<1902]).

Gurney, S. *Sixty Years of Co-operation* (Labour Co-partnership Association pamphlet, n.d.[c.1904]).

— 'Co-operative housing', *Labour Co-partnership*, 11: 104–7 (July 1905).

— 'Co-partnership in housing: as it affects the home', *Co-partnership*, 15: 7 (Jan 1909).

*Harborne Tenants Ltd* (Birmingham, 1909).

Holyoake, G.J. *Bygones Worth Remembering*, 2 vols. (1905).
— *Essentials of Co-operative Education* (Labour Co-partnership Association pamphlet, n.d. [*c*.1901–5]).
— *The History of Co-operation in England*, 2 vols. (1875, 1879).
— *Self-help by the People: History of Co-operation in Rochdale*, 2 vols. (1858, 1878).
— *Sixty Years of an Agitator's Life*, 2 vols. (1893).
'The late Mr. George Jacob Holyoake', *Labour Copartnership*, 12: 17–19 (Feb 1906)
Lloyd, C. *Henry Demarest Lloyd, 1847–1903: A Biography*, 2 vols. (1912).
Lloyd, H.D. *Labor Co-partnership: Notes of a Visit to Co-operative Workshops, Factories and Farms in Great Britain and Ireland* (1898).
McCabe, J. *Life and Letters of G.J. Holyoake* (1908).
McInnes, D. *How Co-operative Societies Can Supply Their Members with Dwelling Houses* (Manchester, 1899).
Maddison, F. 'The Labour Co-partnership Association', *Economic Review*, 20: 314–17 (July 1910)
— *Should Workmen be Partners?* (Labour Association pamphlet, 1901).
Neville, R. *Co-operation: The Place of Co-operation in Political Economy* (Labour Association pamphlet, 1901).
Pitman, H., ed. *Memorial of Edward Vansittart Neale: His Co-operative Life and Work* (1908).
Potter, B. [i.e. Beatrice Webb], *The Co-operative Movement in Great Britain* (1891).
'A practical solution of the housing problem: the co-partnership tenant scheme and what it is accomplishing', *The Sphere* supplement, 1–3 (23 May 1908).
Owen, R. *The Book of the New Moral World* (1836).
— *A New View of Society* (1813).
Pratt, H. 'An annual pilgrimage to Godin's industrial commonwealth', *Labour Copartnership*, 7: 149–51 (Oct 1901).
Vivian, H. *For all works by Henry Vivian see list below.*

Williams, A. 'Co-operation in housing and town building', *Co-operative Congress Report* (1907), 379–98.
— 'Co-operative societies and co-operative towns', *Labour Copartnership*, 8: 5–6. (Jan 1902).
— *History and Present Position of Labour Co-partnership* (Labour Association pamphlet, 1901).
— *Labour Co-partnership and Labour Unrest* (Labour Co-partnership Association pamphlet, 1912).
— trans. *Twenty-eight Years of Co-partnership at Guise* (1908).
Wolff, H.W. 'Co-operative housing', *Municipal Affairs*, 6 (3): 462–72, (1902).
'Women in peace and war', *Co-partnership*, 18: 39 (March 1912), [on Mabel Stobart Greenhalgh].
Yerbury, J.E. *The Story of Co-operative Housing* (1913).

PUBLISHED IN OR AFTER 1914

Backstrom, P.N. *Christian Socialism and Co-operation in Victorian England* (1974).
Bellamy, J.M. and Saville, J., eds. *Dictionary of Labour Biography*, 9 vols. to date (1972–1993) [an invaluable source for the lives of most of the prominent people who feature in this book].
Birchall, J. *Building Communities: the Co-operative Way* (1988).
— *Co-op: The People's Business* (Manchester, 1994).
— 'Co-partnership housing and the garden city movement', *Planning Perspectives*, 10: 329–58 (1995).
— 'Managing the co-partnership way', *Town and Country Planning*, 64 (12): 333–5. (Dec 1995).
Bonner, A. *British Co-operation* (Manchester, 1970).
Carpenter, C. *Co-partnership in Industry . . . 1829–1914* (1914).
Chitty, M. *Discovering Historic Wavertree* (Liverpool, 1999) [on the estate of Liverpool Garden Suburb Tenants Ltd].

Cole, G.D.H. *A Century of Co-operation* (Manchester, n.d. [*c.* 1945]; repr. 1994).
Crimes, T. *Edward Owen Greening: A Maker of Co-operation* (1923).
Culpin, E.G. 'Mr. Litchfield's work for housing', *Co-partnership*, 29: 35 (March 1923).
Destler, C.McA. *Henry Demarest Lloyd and the Empire of Reform* (Philadelphia, 1963).
Jernigan, E.J. *Henry Demarest Lloyd* (Boston, 1976).
Masterman, N.C. *John Malcolm Ludlow: The Builder of Christian Socialism* (Cambridge, 1963).
Raven, C.E. *Christian Socialism, 1848–54* (1920).
Skilleter, K.J. 'The role of public utility societies in early British town planning and housing reform, 1901–36', *Planning Perspectives* 8: 125–65 (1993).
Sparrow, P. and Marchington, M. *Human Resource Management: The New Agenda* (1998) [includes material on the evolution of the Labour Association into the Involvement and Participation Association].
Stobart, M.A. St Clair *Miracles and Adventures: An Autobiography* (1935) [autobiography of J.H. Greenhalgh's widow].
Taylor, A. 'The garden cities movement in a local context: the development of the Penkhull Garden Village', *Local Historian*, 27 (1): 30–47 (Feb. 1997).

HENRY VIVIAN'S WRITINGS, 1893–1927
(in chronological order)

Evidence before the Royal Commission on Labour, 1893–4, XXXXIX Pt I Qs 7523–688.
*with* Williams, A. *The Co-partnership of Labour* (Labour Association pamphlet, 1894); also in *Economic Review*, 4: 297–317 (July 1894).
*The True Position of Employees in the Co-operative Movement* (1894).
*What Co-operative Production is Doing* (Labour Association pamphlet, 1894).
*The Objects and Methods of the Co-operative Movement* (Labour Association pamphlet, 1895).

*Some Aspects of the Co-operative Movement* (Labour Association pamphlet, 1895).
'A novel attempt at co-operative production in the building trades', *Economic Journal*, 6: 270–2 (June 1896).
*How Co-operative Production May be Successfully Applied to the Building Trades* (Labour Association pamphlet, 1897).
*Co-operators and the Thorough Cultivation of the Land* (Newcastle, 1898).
*Partnership of Capital and Labour as a Solution to the Conflict Between Them* (Labour Association pamphlet, 1898).
*Co-operative Stores and Co-operative Partnership* (Labour Association pamphlet, 1899).
*Co-operative Production* (Labour Association pamphlet, 1900).
*The Efficient Organisation of Industry* (Labour Association pamphlet, 1901).
*with* Williams, A. 'Recent progress of labour co-partnership', *Economic Review*, 12: 472–6 (Oct 1902).
'An interesting co-operative housing experiment', *Co-operators' Year Book 1902*: 119.
*Co-operation and Trade Unionism* (Labour Co-partnership Association pamphlet, 1903).
*Industrial Democracy* (Labour Co-partnership Association pamphlet, 1903).
*The Labour Co-partnership Movement* (Labour Co-partnership Association pamphlet, 1904).
'Ealing Tenants Ltd: its past present and future, from a paper by its chairman', *Labour Copartnership*, 11: 52–5 (April 1905).
'Co-partnership in Housing', *Economic Journal*, 15: 254–7 (June 1905).
'Co-partnership in Housing', *Economic Review*, 16: 76–81 (Jan 1906).
*A New Chapter in the History of Co-operation and Labour: The North Wales Quarries Ltd* (Co-operative Union pamphlet, Manchester, 1906).
'Co-partnership in Housing', *Westminster Review*, 168: 615–21 (Dec 1907).
*The Pioneer Co-partnership Village* (1908).
'The journal: its past and future', *Co-partnership*, 15: 2 (Jan 1909).

*Notes on the Problem of Unemployment* (Liverpool, n.d. [1909]).

*Co-partnership in Housing* (Labour Association pamphlet, n.d. [1910]).

*Fact v Fiction in Two Open Letters to Mr. F.E. Smith, MP* (Cobden Club pamphlet; 1910).

'Welcome home to the chairman . . .', *Co-partnership*, 16: 185–6 (Dec 1910), cont. as 'Mr. Vivian on Canada and co-partnership', *Co-partnership*, 17: 3 (Jan 1911), [includes text of Vivian speech].

*Labour Co-partnership . . . an Address to the Employees of Messrs Lever Bros Ltd* (n.d. [1911]).

*Problems of Finance, with Special Reference to the Co-partnership Movement* (Labour Co-partnership Association pamphlet, n.d. [1912]).

'The co-partnership tenants' movement', *Garden Suburbs, Villages and Homes*, issue 2 (Summer 1912), 29–36.

'Garden cities, housing and town planning', *Quarterly Review*, 216: 493–515 (1912).

Intro. to Wood, A. *Co-partnership Housing* (1913).

*Housing and Health* (Co-partnership Tenants Ltd pamphlet, 1913).

*Co-partnership in Practice* (Labour Co-partnership Association pamphlet, 1914).

'Tidy towns', *Co-partnership*, 24(9): 69 (Sept 1918).

'Mr. Frederick Litchfield', *Co-partnership*, 29 (338): 34–5 (March 1923), [obituary].

*A Plea for Freedom* (Individualist pamphlet 3, 1927) [text of an address given at the third Individualist luncheon, 26 Jan 1927].

**Garden cities, housing and town planning**

The literature on garden cities and town planning is extensive. Relevant journals include *The Garden City* (continued as *Garden Cities and Town Planning*), *Planning History*, *Planning Perspectives*, *Town Planning Review*, *Town and Country Planning* and *Urban History*. Extensive general bibliographies in Hall's *Cities of Tomorrow* and Sutcliffe's *History of Urban and Regional Planning*; bibliographies for Hampstead Garden Suburb and Letchworth in Mervyn Miller's monographs on each; bibliographies for Raymond Unwin in Frank Jackson's and Mervyn Miller's monographs on Unwin.

PUBLISHED BEFORE 1914

Abercrombie, P. 'Modern town planning in England: A comparative review of "garden city" schemes in England', *Town Planning Review*, 1: 18–38 (1910).

Allen, J.G. *The Cheap Cottage and Small House* (Letchworth, 1912).

Ashbee, C.R. *A Book of Cottages and Little Houses for Landlords, Architects, Builders and others* (1906).

Baillie Scott, M.H. *Houses and Gardens: Arts and Crafts Interiors* (1906; facsimile edition, Woodbridge, 1995).

*Book of the Cheap Cottages Exhibition* (1905).

Burns, J. *The House of the People is the Homestead of the Nation* (1909) [foreword to the 1909 Housing and Town Planning Act].

Culpin, E.G. *The Garden City Movement Up-to-date* (1913).

'The garden city', *Labour Copartnership*, 8: 133–4 (Sept 1902).

*Garden Suburbs, Town Planning and Modern Architecture . . . With Contributions by M.H. Baillie Scott [and Others]* (1910).

Greenhalgh, J. H. 'A housing tour in Germany', *Co-partnership*, 17: 102 (July 1911).

— J.H.G. [i.e. J.H. Greenhalgh] 'German town planning', *Co-partnership*, 18: 10 (Jan 1912).

Harvey, W.A. *The Model Village and its Cottages: Bournville* (1906).

Howard, E. 'Garden City Association', *Labour Copartnership*, 7: 170–1 (Nov 1901).

— *Tomorrow: A Peaceful Path to Real Reform* (1898); republ. as *Garden Cities of Tomorrow* (1902).

Muthesius, H. *The English House* (Oxford, 1979; abr. trans. by J. Seligman, ed. by D. Sharp, of *Das Englische Haus*, 3 vols. [Berlin, 1904–5]).

Neville, R. 'The extension of co-operation: garden cities', *Labour Copartnership*, 7: 33–4 (March 1901).

Parker, B. and Unwin, R. *The Art of Building a Home: A Collection of Lectures and Illustrations* (1901).

Purdom, C.B. *The Garden City: A Study in the Development of a Modern Town* (1913).

Sennett, A.R. *Garden Cities in Theory and Practice*, 2 vols. (1905).

Sutcliffe, G.L. 'Streets: straight and otherwise', in *Garden Suburbs, Villages and Homes*, issue 2: 78–81 (Summer 1912).

Unwin, R. *Cottage Plans and Common Sense* (Fabian tract 109, 1902).

— *Nothing Gained by Overcrowding* (1912).

— *Town Planning: Preparation of the Plans* (1908).

— *Town Planning in Practice* (1909; rev. edn, 1920).

PUBLISHED IN OR AFTER 1914

Archer, R. *The Listing of George Lister Sutcliffe* (Conservation Diploma diss., Architectural Association, 1999).

Armytage, W.H.G. *Heavens Below: Utopian Experiments in England, 1560–1960* (1961).

Beevers, R. *The Garden City Utopia: A Critical Biography of Ebenezer Howard* (1987).

Brunt, A.W. *Pageant of Letchworth, 1903–14* (Letchworth, 1942).

Buder, S. *Visionaries and Planners: The Garden City Movement and the Modern Community* (Oxford, 1990).

Cherry, G. 'Bournville, England, 1895–1995', *Journal of Urban History*, 22 (4): 493–588 (May 1996).

— ed. *Pioneers in British Planning* (1981).

Creese, W. *The Legacy of Raymond Unwin: A Human Pattern for Planning* (1967).

— ' Parker and Unwin: architects of totality', *Journal of the Society of Architectural Historians*, 22: 161–70 (1963).

— *The Search for Environment: The Garden City Before and After* (rev. edn 1992).

Darley, G. *Villages of Vision* (1975).

Daunton, M.J. *House and Home in the Victorian City: Working-class Housing 1850–1914* (1983).

Davey, P. *Arts and Crafts Architecture* (1995).

Edwards, A. *The Design of Suburbia: A Critical Study in Environmental History* (1981).

Englander, D. *Landlord and Tenant in Urban Britain, 1838–1918* (Oxford, 1983).

Fishman, R. *Bourgeois Utopias: The Rise and Fall of Suburbia* (New York, 1987).

*Garden City Houses and Domestic Interior Details* (1924).

Geddes, P. *Cities in Evolution* (1915).

Girouard, M. *Sweetness and Light: The 'Queen Anne' Movement 1860–1900* (1977).

Gray, A.S. *Edwardian Architecture* (1985) [biographical entries on James Ransome, G.L. Sutcliffe, Raymond Unwin, etc.].

Hall, P. *Cities of Tomorrow: An Intellectual History of Urban Planning and Design in the Twentieth Century* (Oxford, updated edn 1996).

Hardy, D. *From Garden Cities to New Towns: Campaigning for Town and Country Planning, 1899–1946* (1991).

— *Utopian England: Community Experiments 1900–1945* (2000).

Hawkes, D. 'The architectural partnership of Barry Parker and Raymond Unwin', *Architectural Review*, 163: 327–32 (1978).

— ed. and intro. *Modern Country Homes in England: The Arts and Crafts Architecture of Barry Parker* (Cambridge, 1986).

— and Taylor, N., eds. *Barry Parker and Raymond Unwin, Architects* [exhibn. cat.], Architectural Association (1980).

Ikin, C.W. *Hampstead Garden Suburb: Dreams and Realities* (1990).

Jackson, F. *Sir Raymond Unwin: Architect, Planner and Visionary* (1985).

Layton, E. 'How was the Suburb built?' In Abbott, S., ed. *Hampstead Garden Suburb, 1907–1982: A Seventy-fifth Anniversary Celebration* (1982).

Lewis, J.P. *Building Cycles and Britain's Growth* (1965).

Long, H. *The Edwardian House: The Middle-class Home in Britain, 1880–1914* (Manchester, 1993) [an excellent survey with a useful bibliography].

Meacham, S. *Regaining Paradise: Englishness and the Early Garden City Movement* (1999).

Miller, M. *Letchworth: The First Garden City* (Chichester, 1989).

— 'Letchworth revisited: cheap cottages from 1905', *Housing Outlook*, 4: 10–14. (Autumn 1978).

— 'Homesgarth: Howard's model for co-operative living', *Town and Country Planning*, 60: 119–20: (April 1991).

— *Raymond Unwin: Garden Cities and Town Planning* (1992).

— and Gray, A.S. *Hampstead Garden Suburb* (Chichester, 1992).

Muthesius, S. *The English Terraced House* (1982) [the standard work on the subject].

Nettlefold, J.S. *Practical Town Planning* (1914).

*One Man's Vision: The Story of the Joseph Rowntree Village Trust* (1954).

Pearson, L.F. *The Architectural and Social History of Co-operative Living* (1988).

Powell, C.G. *An Economic History of the British Building Industry, 1815–1979* (1982; rev. edn, 1996).

Purdom, C.B. *The Letchworth Achievement* (1963).

Reiss, R. *The Home I Want* (1919).

Rookledge, G. and Skelton, A. *Architectural Identifier of Conservation Areas: Sutton Edition* (Carshalton and Reading, 1999).

Rothermel Thomas, *Sutton Garden Suburb Conservation Report* (1990).

Saul, S.B. 'House building in England, 1890–1914', *Economic History Review*, 15 (1): 119–36 (August 1962).

Service, A, *Edwardian Interiors: Inside the Houses of the Wealthy, the Average and the Poor* (1982).

Stamp, G. and Goulancourt, A. *The English House, 1860–1914* (1986).

*The Story of Port Sunlight: A Souvenir for Visitors in Golden Jubilee Year 1938* (Port Sunlight, 1938).

Sutcliffe, A. *British Town Planning: The Formative Years* (Leicester, 1981).

— *History of Urban and Regional Planning: An Annotated Bibliography* (1981).

— ed. *The Rise of Modern Urban Planning* (1980).

Swenarton, M. *Homes Fit for Heroes: The Politics and Architecture of Early State Housing in Britain* (1981).

Tarn, J.N. *Five Per Cent Philanthropy: An Account of Housing in Urban Areas Between 1840 and 1914* (Cambridge, 1973).

Thompson, F.M.L., ed, *The Rise of Suburbia* (Leicester, 1982).

Ward, S.V. 'The garden city tradition re-examined', *Planning Perspectives*, 5: 257–69 (1990).

— ed. *The Garden City: Past, Present and Future* (1992).

**May Day and Merrie England**

The subject of May Day, its history and customs has been rescued virtually single-handedly from the realms of fantasy by Roy Judge, and his books and articles are essential reading in the understanding of May Day and its interpretation in the nineteenth and twentieth centuries; he has recently (1999) updated his *Introductory Bibliography* on May Day. Strutt, Brand, Knight and Chambers provided ideas and imagery for the Merrie England attitude to May Day in the nineteenth and twentieth centuries. Shuel provides a basic introduction to folk customs in general, and Hutton a more scholarly yet readable survey of the whole range of calendar customs. The new *Dictionary of English Folklore* is an invaluable, comprehensive and historically reliable source for all aspects of the subject.

PUBLISHED BEFORE 1914

Brand, J. *Observations on Popular Antiquities, etc.* (1813).

Chambers, R. *The Book of Days*, 2 vols. (1863).

Ditchfield, P.H. *Old English Customs Extant at the Present Time* (1896).

Frazer, J.G. *The Golden Bough: A Study in Magic and Religion* (abr. edn, 1922; repr. Ware, Herts, 1993) [fanciful, but essential reading because of its great influence on twentieth-century thinking about May Day etc.].

Hampton, E. 'Pageantry and the workshop', *Co-partnership*, 17:72 (May 1911).

Knight, C., ed. *Old England: A Pictorial Museum, etc.*, 2 vols. (1845–6).

Lomas, S.C. *Book of the Pageant of the Festival of Empire* (1911).

Murray, K. *Merrier England: A Pageant of Progress* (n.d. [1912]).

— *Scenes from History . . . Book of Words of the Pageant Played at the Empire Fair, Hampstead Garden Suburb, 1911* (1911) [this was the pageant repeated at the Co-partnership Festival in Hampstead in August 1911; copy in Hampstead Garden Suburb Archive].

Neal, M. *The Espérance Morris Book* (n.d. [1910]).

Parker, L. 'Historical Pageants', *Journal of the Society of Arts*, 54: 142–7 (1905).

Sharp, C.J. and MacIlwaine, H.C. *The Morris Book* (1907).

Strutt, J. *Gig-Gamena Angel Dead, or, The Sports and Pastimes of the People of England* (1801).

PUBLISHED IN OR AFTER 1914

Basford, K. *The Green Man* (Ipswich, 1978).

Boyes, G. *The Imagined Village: Culture, Ideology and the English Folk Revival* Manchester, 1993).

Campbell-Dixon, A. 'Ruskin's romantic fancies', *Country Life*, 183 (17): 130–3 (27 April 1989) [on Whitelands College May Day].

Cooper, Q. and Sullivan, P. *Maypoles, Martyrs and Mayhem* (1994).

Dean-Smith, M. 'The pre-disposition to folkery', *Folklore*, 79: 161–75 (1968).

Gregory, C. *Masques, Monsters and Mushrooms: the Hampstead Garden Suburb Pageants, 1910–14* (n.d.) [copy in Hampstead Garden Suburb Archive].

Hutton, R. *The Stations of the Sun: A History of the Ritual Year in Britain* (Oxford, 1996).

Judge, R. *Changing Attitudes to May Day, 1844–1914* (PhD thesis, Univ. of Leeds, 1987) [copy in Vaughan Williams Library, English Folk Dance and Song Society, Cecil Sharp House, London NW1].

— 'Fact and fancy in Tennyson's *May Queen* and in Flora Thompson's *May Day*', in Buckland, T. and Wood, J., eds, *Aspects of British Calendar Customs* (Sheffield, 1993), 167–83.

— *Jack-in-the-Green: A May Day Custom* (1979; new edition forthcoming).

— 'Mary Neal and the Espérance morris', *Folk Music Journal*, 5: 545–91 (1989).

— 'May Day and Merrie England', *Folklore*, 102: 131–48 (1991).

— *May Day in England: An Introductory Bibliography* (3rd edn, 1999).

— 'Merrie England and the morris, 1881–1910', *Folklore*, 104: 124–43 (1993).

Karpeles, M. *Cecil Sharp: His Life and Work* (1967).

Shuel, B. *Guide to Traditional Customs in Britain* (1985).

Simpson, J. and Roud, S. *A Dictionary of English Folklore* (Oxford, 2000)

Withington, R. *English Pageants: An Historical Outline*, vol. 2 (Cambridge, Mass, 1920).

**Miscellaneous: background history, conservation, etc.**

The literature on Britain in the nineteenth and twentieth centuries is vast, and the following is just a selection of books and articles that have proved especially useful during the research for this book. Ealing Borough Council has produced a number of conservation reports and design guidelines in the 30 years that Brentham has been a conservation area. The most practical current booklet is the 'Policy and Design Guide' (1988), although an expanded and updated guide is currently being prepared. Information on all aspects of Brentham's conservation and planning may be had from the Planning Division of Ealing Borough Council at Perceval House.

### Published before 1914

Bellamy, E. *Looking Backwards* (New York, 1888).

Blatchford, R. *Merrie England* (1894).

Carpenter, E, *The Art of Creation: Essays on the Self and Its Powers* (1904).

— *Towards Democracy*, (1883).

Llewelyn Davies, J. *The Working Men's College, 1854–1904* (1904).

Mazzini, G. *The Duties of Man, and Other Essays* (1907).

Mill, J.S. *Utilitarianism* (1863).

Morris, W. *A Dream of John Ball* (1888).

— *The Earthly Paradise: A Poem*, 3 vols. (1868–70).

— *News From Nowhere: or, an Epoch of Rest* (1890).

Ruskin, J. *The Works of John Ruskin*, ed. Cook, E.T. and Wedderburn, A. (1903–12).

### Published in or after 1914

Brennan, J. *History of the Bradford Property Trust Ltd: 1928–1978* (Bradford, 1978).

Brereton, C. *The Repair of Historic Buildings* (English Heritage, 1991).

Briggs, A. *Victorian Cities* (1963).

Brown, K.D. *John Burns* (1977).

Calder, A. *The People's War: Britain 1939–1945* (1969).

Clifford, S. and King, A. *Local Distinctiveness: Place, Particularity and Identity* (1993).

Colls, R. and Dodd, P., eds. *Englishness: Politics and Culture, 1880–1920* (1986).

Cook, C. *A Short History of the Liberal Party, 1900–1976* (1976).

— *Sources in British Political History, 1900–51*, 6 vols. (1975–94).

Crawford, A. and Cunnningham, C., eds. *William Morris and Architecture* (Society of Architectural Historians of Great Britain, 1997).

Dixon, R. and Muthesius, S. *Victorian Architecture* (1978).

Gresswell, F. *Bright Boots* (1956) [autobiography of founder of the Bradford Property Trust].

Hardy, D. *Alternative Communities in Nineteenth Century England* (1979).

Harris, J. *Private Lives, Public Spirit: Britain 1870–1914* (Oxford, 1993).

Hobsbawm, E. *Uncommon People: Resistance, Rebellion and Jazz* (1998) [see first section on 'The radical tradition'].

— and Ranger, T., eds. *The Invention of Tradition* (Cambridge, 1983).

Holroyd, M. 'The political philosophy of Bernard Shaw and the St Pancras vestry', *Camden History Review*, 21: 2–6 (1997).

Johnson, P., ed. *Twentieth-century Britain* (Harlow, 1994).

Kingsford, P.W. *Builders and Building Workers* (1973).

Lees, A. *Cities Perceived: Urban Society in European and American Thought, 1820–1940* (Manchester, 1985).

McCarthy, F. *William Morris: A Life for Our Time* (1994).

Marsh, J. *Back to the Land: The Pastoral Impulse in England, from 1880 to 1914* (1982).

Miele, C., ed. *William Morris on Architecture* (Sheffield, 1996).

Nash, D.S. 'F.J. Gould and the Leicester Secular Society: a positivist commonwealth in Edwardian politics', *Midland History*, 16: 126–40 (1991).

— *Secularism, Art and Freedom* (Leicester, 1992) [for F.J. Gould and G.J. Holyoake].

Orwell, G. *Coming Up For Air* (1939).

Richardson, M., *Architects of the Arts and Crafts Movement* (1983).

Thomas, K. *The Perception of the Past in Early Modern England* (1983).

Thompson, E.P. *William Morris: Romantic to Revolutionary* (New York, 1961).

Thompson, P. *The Edwardians: The Remaking of British Society* (2nd edn, 1992).

Tressell, R. *The Ragged Trousered Philanthropists* (1914; repr. 1993) [this classic autobiographical novel is especially relevant to Brentham and the pioneers as it concerns a group of building workers in the early years of the twentieth century].

Swenarton, M. *Artisans and Architects: The Ruskinian Tradition in Architectural Thought* (1989).

Wiener, M.J. *English Culture and the Decline of the Industrial Spirit, 1850–1980* (Cambridge, 1981).

Williams, R. *The Country and the City* (1973).

Zweiniger-Bargielowska, I. *Austerity in Britain: Rationing, Control, and Consumption, 1939–1955* (Oxford, 2000).

# INDEX